Talking
Figure
Skating

OTHER BOOKS BY BEVERLEY SMITH

Figure Skating: A Celebration (1994)
A Year in Figure Skating (1996)

Talking Figure Skating

Behind the Scenes in the World's Most Glamorous Sport

B E V E R L E Y   S M I T H

M&S

Canadian Cataloguing in Publication Data

Smith, Beverley, date.
 Talking figure skating : behind the scenes in the world's most glamorous sport

ISBN 0-7710-8107-3

1. Skating.   I. Title.

FV850.4.S65 1997   796.91'2   C97-931494-1

The publishers acknowledge the support of the Canada Council for the Arts and the Ontario Arts Council for their publishing program.

Set in Janson by M&S, Toronto
Printed and bound in Canada

McClelland & Stewart Inc.
The Canadian Publishers
481 University Avenue
Toronto, Ontario
M5G 2E9

1 2 3 4 5   01 00 99 98 97

For Walter Farley,
my kind mentor, whom I will never forget.

CONTENTS

ACKNOWLEDGEMENTS

A special thanks to all who gave of their time to be interviewed, including Barbara Fitzgerald, Dr. Robert Lee, and Suzie Francis. And the Kneblis, who graciously and happily shared stories and photos only two months before the cobbler's death.

To Carol Rossignol, who, in the midst of a heavy workload, aiming to get coaches certified in time for the Nagano Olympics, took the time to educate an inquiring author.

To Ann Shaw, always at the ready to sift through rules and set the photocopy machines to humming.

To Susan Ward, without whose help this book would not have been possible.

To Renata Roman, for her generous help at every turn.

To Gay Abbate, for moral support.

To Joan Breckenridge, for her persuasive talents.

To the madcap trio, Joyce Foster, Grace Elliott, and Oz Colson, whose help in all matters of skating over the years has been invaluable.

To Arie and Joanne and Bob and Sharon, my neighbours, who kept the snow at bay while I was engulfed in committing prose.

To Dan Wilson, whose computer wizardry in moments of desperation set me on the right path.

To Barb Strain, for just being Barb, crazy about skating and ready to help at the drop of a sequin.

To my McClelland & Stewart family, Pat Kennedy, Heather Sangster, and my artistic geniuses, Kong Njo and Sari Ginsberg, all of them so diligent and happy about it, too.

Introduction

Sleepless in Vancouver, Susan Humphreys had finally done it. After five years of effort, she had become Canadian champion, dodging doubts that arose from coaching troubles, back troubles, confidence troubles. Her delicate, porcelain-skinned face crumpled into tears at the instant of her victory, in front of nearly ten thousand people. Almost unable to breathe, incredulous, crying without tears, crying with tears, Humphreys, nevertheless, was not alone. Even though skaters face the glare at centre ice like a solitary beetle in a floodlit garden, they never really do it all alone.

"That win was not just about me," Humphreys said later. "It was about so many people who have been involved and who have touched my life in so many ways."

Humphreys reached the pinnacle of her performance through the support of several others: her tiny, bright-faced coach, Cynthia Ullmark, who was able to establish a relationship that spelled belief for a troubled skater; her sports-psychologist friend John Hogg, who guided her through the pitfalls of her doubts; the doctors who worked on painful injuries to her fourth and fifth lumbar vertebrae and sacral joint that had hobbled her career for several years; her choreographer; her parents; her family.

The moment of victory sums up all that has gone before in a heart-felt emotional rush: the discouragements, the helping hands, the terror, the tears, the lessons learned. Life lived on a steely edge has its risks as well as its rewards.

Talking Figure Skating is about this life, as seen through the eyes of the sport's varied participants, the ones who make the skating world go 'round; the ones who aren't always at centre stage but who develop the Susan Humphreyses and the Scott Hamiltons, and the pre-novice dreamers; the ones that don't always find themselves in the focus of a photographer's camera.

Yet their views shed important light on lives lived behind the curtain. With that premise, this book takes a wide-striding look at a small cross-section of skating's bootmakers, psychologists, parents, judges, music makers, makeup artists, doctors, coaches, choreographers, tour skaters, and even its fans, who play such a major part without stepping onto the ice. All of them devise their own methods on how to make dreams happen.

The curious part of it all is that, no matter how a writer tries to define categories, people in the skating world always manage to elude them. Unless you are talking about judges, there are no rules on roles. A coach can be a choreographer and a music researcher and a psychologist and a parent-figure and a skate sharpener, perhaps even a makeup adviser. A choreographer is often a music specialist. A parent can work as a coach, sometimes with disastrous results. The categories get even fuzzier when a coach is the sibling of a skater he teaches, like Canadian Paul Wirtz. A music specialist – and there aren't many of them yet – can also help out with choreography, costume, hairstyle and makeup, such as Marijane Stong. A doctor may end up being a parent-chaperone while on an overseas competition assignment. Doctors and psychologists often look at different sides of the same health concern, such as an eating disorder; what one knows gives the other a more complete picture of the problem.

Sometimes doctors find themselves analysing the techniques of making boots, the skater's most important tool. This is often a must, because skaters and all of their coterie have been thrust into an exceedingly and increasingly complex world in which they are expected to do more athletically difficult and aesthetically mature performances at younger and younger ages. Bootmakers strive to make stiffer boots to support young ankles taking the constant pounding of landing triple – even quadruple – jumps. In turn, the stiffer boots cause injury. That sends sports-medicine specialists scurrying for answers.

Bootmakers are in a category of their own, and an increasingly rare one. For decades, Transylvanian-born cobbler John Knebli toiled at his craft in a creaky-floored factory that seemed to be from another era. And yet he always dreamed of the latest machinery – as long as it wasn't automated – and he often spoke of recording the tricks of his trade on videotape, bequeathing his skills to another generation of bootmakers. But he never got the chance. At age ninety-three, still musing about the videos, Knebli died after a day spent working in his shop. His last task was to fasten a pair of skate blades to the soles of a customer's new boots. The day after he died, the skates were delivered to the customer, as promised. They just don't make them like Knebli any more.

Knebli was interviewed and posed for the photos in this book only a few months before he died. They were the final interviews of his life. A couple of afternoons with the tale-spinning Knebli turned into an unexpected gift, a precious opportunity to take a last, lingering look back at a world where working raptly with hands and heart meant more than production quotas and profit margins. For a while yet, skaters will be jumping and spinning in Knebli-made boots, earthbound echoes of his passing.

One of Knebli's clients was Gary Beacom, who brings the curtain down on the book. Beacom cannot be fit into a category, but he is a curious counterpoint to any skating idea that goes before him here. Strangely enough, Beacom has made it all work, producing a quaint series of programs and methods that seem to quietly guffaw at routine music choices, rigid choreographic steps, judging systems, coaching methods, and even the practice of wearing skates only on the feet. Unlike most other skaters, Beacom does it all alone, a solitary beetle preening himself in the floodlights – and loving it. He is a one-man team: a coach, a music specialist, a nutritionist, a choreographer, a skate sharpener, a boot lover, and an educator. Heaven help us if he ever becomes a psychologist or a skating judge.

But Beacom's thoughts and those of his peers are all part of a unique world, colourful in character, rich in strife, dazzling in impact. *Talking Figure Skating* aims to open a window into this world and zoom in on a few hearts. Now it is their turn to talk.

And God Created Parents

A few have deep pockets. Most have shredded pockets, although sacrifice is not a word they commonly use.

Some parents, unselfishly, have made tremendous sacrifices for their skating offspring. And some have made sacrificial lambs of their children.

It goes without saying that the unselfish parents go to the ends of the earth to make dreams possible for their children, giving them the wings with which they can soar and grow and learn. They give up their own financial comforts and their time. They mortgage and remortgage their homes, drive patched-up jalopies, and forfeit sunshiny southern vacations for a weekend in some frigid, little backwoods town, shivering on hard benches for hours at one figure-skating competition or another. They become chauffeurs, cheerleaders, maids, and keepers of the scrapbook.

Sacrifice? Say what? Lucinda Ruh's mother wrinkles her brow at the thought. Sacrifice is not a concept she seems to recognize, and it isn't because English is not her first language. The Swiss Family Ruh has been split up for more than a year, with Mr. Ruh living in his native Switzerland and Mrs. Ruh living in North America, an ocean and several sets of mountain ranges away from hearth and husband. But

Mrs. Ruh says she feels no sacrifice, even as she signs the rental cheque for a California apartment, and refuses to worry about the lack of furniture within echoing walls. It's all in the name of finding the right coach for Lucinda, finding her child a dream.

But a sacrifice is a sacrifice, whether you call it that or not, and the Ruhs are not unlike many other skating parents around the world, undaunted by the pressures of their position: scraping together the money for expensive lessons that last more than a decade, for pricey boots and blades, for trips around the world to watch and support their children, for knowledgeable coaches, choreographers, and music specialists, and even for tutors, for those years when it is not possible for their children to attend school.

Despite the fact that only a precious few of these children will be distilled out of a pool of thousands and reach an Olympic podium, skating parents also tackle myriad other pressures. Every morning, rudely awakened by the annoying jangle of an alarm clock, these parents rise in the pre-dawn chill and drive darkened roads to rinks in far-flung areas. It is a lonely, cheerless time, before the world stirs. Their families learn quickly about separations: parents from children, spouses from spouses, siblings from siblings.

And parents are thrust unwillingly, sometimes even unwittingly, into further chaos when non-skating children may feel neglected over the rapt attention paid a skating sibling. Aside from their own jobs, worries, and dreams, skating parents must juggle the stresses and emotions of the family, and try to ensure that everything comes out all right in the long run. There are skating injuries to worry about, and priorities to set – is winning more important than self-esteem? – and building strength and character in their children, all of which will put them on a life path beyond the inward-looking world of skating and its ephemeral promises.

They all make sacrifices, the good parents and the bad. But the bad parents lose perspective along the way, stepping into an alluring world that is more quicksand than rock. They build their houses on this sand, using their own dreams and desires as the foundations, unmindful of the consequences. They seize on every slight to their children; they blanch at every failure. Building character in their children is an incidental, unimportant concept. They tie up the phone lines of coaches and officials with their concerns and needs. They are called Skating Parents.

The sport is rife with horror stories, and these are the tales most often heard. Such as the one about a top European skater whose parents slapped her if she did not skate well. Or obtrusive parents. Or parents who know more than the coach. Or parents who take offence when another skater emerges victorious. Or parents who put their children's wants before reason and common sense.

One of the most indulgent set of parents were those of Sonja Henie, who lived only for their daughter and her skating successes. Their once thriving fur business suffered at the height of Sonja's career because of their total devotion to her. In their eyes, Sonja could do no wrong. They spoiled her outrageously.

Selma Henie "would allow her own dinner to get cold rather than eat before Sonja came to the table," Sonja's brother, Leif, wrote in his book, *Queen of Ice, Queen of Shadows.* When Sonja became a professional skater, her mother became the troupe spy, informing her about skaters who might be trying to steal her spotlight.

Their indulgences did little to turn Sonja into a well-rounded human who had compassion and grace. "Stars are entitled to temperament," Wilhelm Henie once said after his daughter flew into a violent rage that lasted for several days. The precipitating factor? Rumours that she was turning professional.

The Henies had plenty of money at their disposal to spin dreams for themselves and their daughter. They rolled into corporatelike action when Sonja was only eight years old, a year before she was to contest the senior Norway championship. Already, Sonja was her own serious taskmaster, a child perfectionist. And already, the Henies dreamed of Olympic gold and European tours.

The Henies hired the best teacher in Norway, put Sonja on a strict diet, and closely supervised her daily training. They became expert critics who could spot her every skating flaw. Their lives revolved around Sonja, who, according to her brother, Leif, grew into a woman always wishing to be at centre stage and rarely feeling others' pain. It was all she knew.

After their father died, Leif noted, Sonja could be selfish and completely lacking in compassion and loyalty. Before his funeral, according to Leif, Sonja talked her way past an adoring bank clerk and seized $150,000 out of her father's safe-deposit box – money that should rightfully have gone to her mother. "She ran that family like somebody with a whip," said one of Sonja's movie producers, quoted in Leif's book. Her brother was not immune to his sister's greed either. During the 1950s, Sonja developed a kind of mania for taking over her brother's properties, starting with an apartment building he owned in Chicago and a ranch in California. Even though a bank appraised the building at $275,000, Sonja, in an explosive rage, told her brother: "You no-good sonofabitch, you'll take $50,000 for it and like it." Eventually, he did.

With that accomplished, Sonja began to muscle in on the ownership of her brother's 1,600-acre ranch, at first pestering him with her constant visits while in an inebriated state and accompanied by a troupe of like-minded friends. To silence her, Leif built her a house on the property, as a gift, but that only served to give his sister squatting rights on the land. After issuing drunken threats to kill her brother, his wife, and child, Henie sued him and, with her barrage of expensive lawyers, won. She also had legal papers drawn up that, in effect, stripped her mother of everything she owned, including properties in Norway. The Henie story is the ultimate tale of greed and family destruction, born out of the fact that Henie was raised living at the centre of her parents' dreams.

Sonja Henie's ambitions were the same as her parents'. But in today's skating world, there are some parents who push their own unfulfilled dreams and desires onto their children, crushing them with their passion. They direct their careers, refuse to listen to the experts, and demand complete control over their children's lives.

Suzanne Bonaly may be one of those parents. Slender as a bullrush reed, with a hard, drawn face, Madame Bonaly is a skeletonlike figure, drifting out of shadows to inspect the interest shown her daughter. At home in France, she calls herself a physical-education teacher. French national team leader Didier Gailhaguet, who once coached Surya, says she is not; she is a teacher of children with a special interest in physical education. And since her daughter has been on the international scene, Suzanne has not plied her trade. Her husband, Georges, by all reports a rather likeable fellow, has given up his job as an army draftsman to act as Surya's agent. "They are not poor," says Gailhaguet, who was impressed when he first saw Surya landing a single jump at a skating clinic in France. "But they are something different. . . . They want to succeed. And once they decide, they go all the way."

They were so dedicated as parents that they trundled from Nice, where they lived, to Paris, so that Surya could train under Gailhaguet. "For a year they lived in a truck," he says. "With three dogs." (Two poodles and a Doberman.)

Skating was not the only sport on which the Bonalys turned their attention in an enthusiastic way. The parents were very involved, too, when Surya took part in gymnastics as a youngster. Surya was more than promising; she was a world-novice champion in tumbling during the late 1980s. Then, "they [the gymnastics officials] kicked the mother out," Gailhaguet says.

The irony is that, at the time, Suzanne was doing good things with her adopted daughter, Gailhaguet points out. "Sometimes she was right. At the moment she got kicked out, she was really working well with Surya. She helped very well her career in figure skating. She tried to push her, to give her more variety of activities so that she would not just do figure skating. She was a complete athlete. She did a great job there." The gymnastics federation ran afoul of Suzanne because it tried to push her to make Surya give up figure skating in favour of gymnastics. The skating association played its cards a little differently. It encouraged Surya to continue with her tumbling.

Still, it was not easy to deal with Suzanne. While Gailhaguet instructed from ice side, Suzanne hovered several rows up in the arena, delivering signals. Frequently, during a training session, Surya's eyes travelled upward, past her coach to her mother's face. Coaches hate this kind of interference, because it divides the skater's focus. And, in

Surya's case, it was even worse, because the mother had no background in skating. "She never skated," Gailhaguet says of Suzanne. "But she gets up on the [coaches'] stand."

Gailhaguet's strategy of giving Suzanne some input into her daughter's activities off the ice didn't work forever, though. His association with the Bonalys ended in 1992 after a loud shouting match between him and Suzanne in a room directly adjacent to the media area at the Albertville Olympics.

Afterwards, although a series of coaches worked with Surya, it was Suzanne Bonaly who directed her training. At the 1994 world championship in Chiba, Japan, Alain Giletti, the 1960 world men's champion for France, was listed as Surya's coach. He was a quiet, almost meek, member of the group in Japan, however, and Suzanne did most of the talking. In truth, claims Gailhaguet, Giletti was a coach only for the sake of status. "I do this since she was small," Suzanne said of her coaching pursuits early the next season. She reasoned that she had had to develop her own theories on skating, after years of effort, because coaches weren't terribly forthcoming or helpful.

At the 1995 world championship in Birmingham, England, American Frank Carroll was listed as coach, although Suzanne had said the previous autumn that her daughter took lessons from him, but that he could not take her on as a student because he was also teaching Michelle Kwan.

At the 1996 world championship in Edmonton, Alberta, there was no doubt: Suzanne Bonaly was acting as coach – but for good measure, she placed American coach Christy Ness's name on the coaching list. Ness, who coached Kristi Yamaguchi of the United States to an Olympic gold medal, was startled to find out that she was listed as Surya's coach in the event's media guide, and figured the family, misguided, had included the information so that judges might be swayed to give Surya higher marks.

Although Ness, who works at a training centre in Oakland, California, says she has given Surya about ten hours of instruction, she denies ever having been Surya's coach. Ness says Suzanne would never receive accreditation as a coach from the United States Figure Skating Association, as she has in France. Is the French federation concerned about an untrained parent, such as Suzanne, coaching a daughter? French national trainer Allen Schramm shrugged when asked. "It's a weird situation," he said.

Weird, indeed. In recent years, the French federation has become frustrated at the direction Surya's career has taken under her mother's guidance. French law dictates that any sport coach must be licensed in order to work. But Suzanne receives no money for giving her advice, and therefore does not need a licence. "We don't pay her," Gailhaguet says. "You can't prove she is a coach. She's just there."

When one prospective Surya coach pointedly told Suzanne that mothers were not allowed to act as coaches in that rink, Suzanne replied, "But I am not really her mother." It was clear that she was prepared to resort to any loophole in a rule or argument to stay at the side of her adopted daughter.

Somehow Suzanne manoeuvres her way through all the cracks in the system. One international coach close to the French situation says, "She's successful at getting what she wants because she makes such a fuss. People don't want to make a scene, so they let it go. She got coaches' certification at Skate Canada [in 1989] and when they tried to remove her, I saw the mother go nuts. She was flailing around at people." She was also tossed, kicking and screaming, out of the coaches' area at rinkside at Skate America that year.

Even though Gailhaguet says Suzanne is not a certified coach, she is listed in the French federation's media guide in a section on coaches. In its brief description of her, it calls her "a model of rigour and determination." In the English language, the word "rigour" carries a connotation of harsh, stiff attitudes, "an exactness without allowance or indulgence," according to the Funk & Wagnalls dictionary. A person who practices rigourism, exercises austerity or severity in style or living.

And indeed, the lifestyle of the Bonalys is cast with an austere idealism. Surya, whose name means "sun" in Hindi, was not allowed to have her hair cut until she was in her late teens. The family beliefs also affected the kind of food they ate and even the medical treatment they received. They practised macrobiotics, the art of prolonging life through a special diet consisting of seeds, fruits, cereals, and vegetables. "They lived like birds," says Gailhaguet, with some incredulity.

"They ate birdseed. They drank no milk. They ate nothing from animal cells."

Despite her unconventional diet, Surya was a strong, young skater, Gailhaguet recalls. "She was never sick. It was unbelievable," he says. However, during her second international season, Surya developed pain in her right foot, the foot on which she lands her jumps. "You could see it in her face," he recalls. Fearing a stress fracture, he recommended that the foot be X-rayed. But, based on their beliefs, the parents wouldn't allow the procedure. Their adopted daughter soldiered on. Rarely does she miss practice.

Gailhaguet says he first saw the intrusive side of the Bonalys when Surya won the French national championship in 1989. "It was a really big surprise," he admits. "She was not supposed to win. She was only the fourth selection to junior worlds." The effort was impressive enough that the French skating federation decided to send her to the 1989 world junior championship. Surya surprised the skating world again by winning the bronze medal at that event.

"Then the parents started to go wild," says Gailhaguet, indicating that Suzanne began to see fame, fortune, and a place in sport history for her family as soon as Surya showed élite potential. Since then, no skater has competed in international events more often than Surya, even in the days before amateur events offered prize money. Surya danced every dance and trained full-out at every practice. While other élite skaters did two, maybe three, international events within a season during the early 1990s, Surya would do almost all of the major ones. Suzanne, as the director of these strenuous efforts, was indeed a model of rigour.

The strategy seemed reasonable: Surya, new to the skating scene, needed experience and exposure. But the push was apparent. The family machinery went into overdrive. Because of her tumbling/jumping ability, Surya developed a goal to become the first female to land a quadruple jump. The goal has always eluded her. Although she is known as a strong jumper, she has also never landed a triple Axel in competition. Only two women have: Midori Ito of Japan and Tonya Harding of the United States.

But the goal became as important to Suzanne as to Surya – perhaps more so – as the accomplishment would place Surya in the record books once and for all. The name Bonaly would be remembered along-side those of Ulrich Salchow, Kurt Browning, Dick Button, and Sonja Henie, all skaters who achieved firsts. It became clear how important the goal was to Suzanne at the 1994 world championship in Japan. When Surya was asked how she wanted to skate in the long program, her mother answered the question for her: "World championship is to show technique nobody has ever shown."

Giletti hinted that Surya might try a quadruple jump. Surya made no comment. During the long program, she landed no quadruples, and many of her landings of other jumps were shaky.

Still, Surya won the silver medal. It was a memorable podium cere-mony: the frustrated French skater at first refused to mount the steps, balking until Olaf Paulsen, a former president of the International Skating Union, gently urged her to reconsider. Immediately after he placed the medal around her neck, Surya, in tears, peevishly ripped it off. It hung at her side, dangling loosely from her fingers. It was Surya's worst moment, a time she no longer discusses. The crowd of normally silent Japanese spectators booed. Suzanne said afterwards, publicly, that she did not advise her daughter to behave that way. In the interna-tional uproar that followed, Surya offered an apology.

If Surya has had troubles in meeting the family goals, Suzanne's excuses are legion. The talk quickly swings to Surya's boots, which Suzanne maintains are not strong enough or adequate enough for her to complete her athletic feats. Surya has been said to have gone through as many as seven pairs in a year; perhaps they break down under the stress of trying so many jumps and unusual acrobatic moves, such as back flips. In practice, she tackles amazing tumbling feats on the ice, even moves that male skaters rarely attempt: one-footed back flips, double back flips, and back flips that immediately erupt into triple toe loops. (She does not incorporate these manoeuvres in competition, because back flips are illegal in amateur or Olympic-eligible events. But they are major features in her exhibitions.)

Still, Suzanne sees that Surya's greatest handicap is not so much her basic ability to skate and push and move over the ice (which is poor), the quality of her edges (which is poor), her body positions (her arms flap, one coach said), or her disregard for music. "She has big problems with the shoes," Suzanne has said. Many times. "At this level, they must be perfect. They must be like year 2000. But they are only 1000. . . . You must have best technical for shoes. Very slowly, we find solution."

One of Suzanne's solutions has been to mount the blades at unusual angles (not the normal 90 degrees) to Surya's skating boot. She shows off the boot to anybody who she thinks might be interested. Suzanne says the unconventional positioning gives her daughter a better grip on the ice. Other coaches say it wreaks havoc with her ability to execute edges or jumps with any consistency.

Gailhaguet groans at the subject of Suzanne and her preoccupation with mounting blades. "[Suzanne] changes the blade every day in order to make the jumps better," he says. "If [Surya] cannot do one jump, [Suzanne] will push the blade one way, so her body leans more this way. But suddenly the jump where you have to lean the other way doesn't work. So she puts the blade the other way. She spends all day doing this. I don't know how Surya can still skate. She cannot build memories of the motion."

Gailhaguet worries that the constant changing of the blades may have contributed, at least in a small way, to an injury Surya suffered during the summer of 1996. During the Tom Collins tour of world champions in the United States, Surya severely ruptured an Achilles' tendon while attempting a back flip. She endured the painful injury for one and a half days – flying back to France with the loose tendon riding up to below the knee – before she underwent surgery to repair it.

Gailhaguet advised the Bonalys to keep Surya away from any serious skating for a year, and to bring her back slowly. That didn't happen. There was always an exhibition the family wanted to do. At the last minute, Surya withdrew from the NHK Trophy in Japan, citing medical reasons, and then won her national championship, emerging triumphant after her competitors skated worse than she did. However, her victory resulted in a struggle with the French federation, which was not convinced that Bonaly was ready to live up to the international expectations she had set by winning five European titles and earning three silver medals at the world championship.

"I was glad for her, but [the victory] didn't show much," Gailhaguet says of her win in the French championships. In spite of her win,

Gailhaguet says the French federation saw that she could still not walk without great pain. "Her foot hurts really bad."

However, under pressure from certain circles, including Suzanne Bonaly, the French federation decided to change the selection criteria for the European championship, to allow Surya to be an alternate. When she made a late-in-the-game, last-minute appeal to the French federation to actually be on the team as a competitor, she was successful.

Still, at the European championship, Bonaly finished only ninth overall, landing only the easiest of triples. "It showed that she didn't have the level," Gailhaguet says. After that poor performance, the French federation was loath to put her on the world team, but gave her one more chance: a tryout in front of officials. At first, Surya did not want to submit to a test; after all, she had won the national championship, and that normally was enough to make the world team, she said.

But when she failed the test, the appeals and the excuses started anew. Surya said she hadn't been ready for the test on February 20, 1997, because she had been in Boston to train with Russian coach Tatiana Tarasova, a session she said she couldn't cancel. When she returned, she didn't have time to recover from the jet lag, she said. And she broke her blades two days before the test.

Surya requested another test. The French federation refused. "We've had a test," said federation president Bernard Goy. "It's over. Let's go on to something else."

Gailhaguet says the federation did not want Surya to continue on to the world championship, in order to "protect" her and allow her injury to heal properly. "If she finished fifteenth [after being five-time European champion and three-time world silver medallist], what would you say?" Gailhaguet says. "You'd say she was finished, a has-been. We didn't want that to be said. We wanted to give her a chance in the future. The mother does not understand that."

Gailhaguet believes Suzanne has reached the end of her system, a collection of beliefs about what she wants to do for her daughter that has not worked in her best interests. It is a system in which the mother wants to do everything, control everything, hear no suggestions, brook no interference from anyone. "Surya had the potential to be Olympic champion," Gailhaguet says. "But too many mistakes have been made. There was no strategy. It was just an emotional way of working. [If Surya is not successful], it's the skate, it's the judges, it's the sharpening."

Gailhaguet says Surya has huge potential, even in those artistic and basic skating areas for which she has long been criticized. The world could have been her pearl, except for her mother's desire for control and her staunch refusal to accept that she has no skating knowledge. "When you know everything, when you are certain of being right every time you talk to a person, and you explain to everybody how it's done, and then you don't do it, you find excuses. In three weeks, she broke one or two blades." But female skaters, who usually weigh little, Gailhaguet says, are unlikely to break blades.

Gailhaguet admits he was an "enthusiastic" supporter of Suzanne in the early days when her "system" worked efficiently. "I supported her in some ways I shouldn't have," he says. "But that was a long time ago when Surya was young. I slowly changed my mind.

"It is like you do your copy again and again, and you always have a problem, and you missed one word and you have to redo it all. Surya is this. We never got Surya to be the fine, well-written piece she should have been."

Gailhaguet says he prays every day that Surya recovers the flexibility in her ankle that she has lost because of her injury. If she does, he still hopes that she will become a champion, as long as her future does not lie in her mother's hands. But Suzanne has completely lost control in her coaching pursuits. And she is very proud and will not accept her mistakes. "It is a shame," Gailhaguet says.

With the heat on and the disappointments piling up, Suzanne has become more reluctant to speak with the media – or to let her daughter speak. When Surya skates poorly, she quickly vanishes without a comment. In February 1996, as soon as a small huddle of reporters struck up a conversation with Surya at rinkside in Paris, Suzanne instantly appeared, at first just listening to the queries about Surya's difficult season. Surya answered amiably, willingly. But when she was asked if she had figured out why judges seemed to dislike her skating, Suzanne quickly interrupted. "This is not an interesting question for you, sorry," she told reporters and dragged her daughter away.

It seems that where Surya goes, Suzanne will follow, instructing, pushing, drilling, worrying more about skating boots than about skating quality, about skating for joy. Even Chinese coach Li Mingzhu, who witnessed Suzanne's training methods, says, "Her mother pushes her too much. She needs a rest."

Suzanne has led Surya by the hand from the start, and kept her by her side at every step. "I wanted to keep her with me," Suzanne said. "When she was just walking, in each sport, I was doing it. So she do many sport, not to be a champion, but it was life. I was from Nice, a place where you can do everything." But freedom doesn't seem to be part of the plan.

During Surya's failed test to make the world team, Gailhaguet told Suzanne she was banging her head against the wall. "She goes in the wall and she doesn't even notice," Gailhaguet says, remembering the conversation. "She thinks she's right. She thinks the wall should not be there.

"But when you hit a wall, you drove badly the car."

On the other hand, there are scores of well-meaning, thoughtful parents who fumble their way into the expensive, all-involving world of figure skating, unaware of the commitment they will be making and the financial and psychological potholes along the way. "It comes on you gradual, like being choked with smoke," Dewey Browning, the father of four-time world champion Kurt Browning, said in Browning's autobiography, *Forcing the Edge*.

The Brownings, like many other parents, started out innocently enough, with a happy-go-lucky hockey-playing kid who turned his attention to figure skating. They were luckier than some: because Kurt was the youngest in the family, they had more finances and time to devote to his engrossing sport, and older siblings did not suffer from neglect.

They were more fortunate than many who are locked into an escalating series of expenses, family separations, sibling rivalries, injuries, and the psychological land mines that go with it all. The Brownings, experienced parents by the time Kurt came along, took great pains to ensure that their skating son did not develop what his mother, Neva, often referred to as "an arena head – big and empty."

Indeed, if parents aren't worrying about the money, they are stewing about the inner growth of their children. At least the good ones do. Add all the factors up and it spells enormous stress for a parent. One Canadian skating mother attributes her husband's heart condition and subsequent death to the pressures that come from raising a skating child to the élite level.

Henri and Liliane Duchesnay, parents of 1991 world ice-dancing champions Isabelle and Paul Duchesnay, guided the steps of their skating children with great care. But nothing prepared them for the commitment the sport demands. The Duchesnays look back at their harried lives and say they wish somebody had given them a parents' guide to prepare them for the financial responsibilities. Henri says he stopped calculating the financial drain when costs reached $250,000, just before Isabelle and Paul left Canada to skate for France during the 1985-86 season.

The Duchesnays aren't alone. John Eldredge, father of 1996 world champion Todd Eldredge of the United States, agrees that a warning would have been useful. "If you knew what was coming, you could make some plans," he says.

The Eldredges mortgaged their modest home in Chatham, Massachusetts – twice – in order to support their son's skating career. It was a tiny home, with two bedrooms, one bathroom, and "an upstairs that never got finished," according to Ruth Eldredge, Todd's mother.

"We started a child in skating, not ever knowing that it would turn out to be like this," Ruth says. "We thought it would be a fun thing once a week. Then it slowly creeps up on you. They need outfits, skates, better skates. It just escalated: bigger, better, and more. Then you're in a position where you can't say no."

Other parents started with just as much preparation. "I didn't know anything about skating in the beginning," says Danny Kwan, the father of 1996 world champion Michelle Kwan. Michelle had barely started school when she and her older sister, Karen, discovered public-skating sessions at a rink in a nearby mall in Torrance, California. In 1987, the year that Jill Trenary, Debi Thomas, and Caryn Kadavy were battling each other for the U.S. title, Michelle began to take lessons. She was seven years old, and Danny Kwan was just as new to the sport. "I didn't have any idea," he admits. "But if you want the best, it costs. You want best music, best programs, and a lot of little things that you just don't realize.

"I didn't know it would cost that much," he says. Kwan closes his eyes to the expense. "To be honest, I never think about it. I'm not anyone special. I'm like any other parent in the world. Most parents work for their kids, and they're never thinking about how much it costs. It was definitely difficult for a while, but I never think about it."

But, in reality, the financial costs to the family were steep. About a half-dozen years ago, the Kwans sold their home in Torrance for $375,000 to pay off mounting skating bills. After they had paid off all their debtors, they had $600 left to play with, and none for any more skating lessons, which stopped for a time. Both of Kwan's skating daughters, Michelle and Karen – also an élite skater who has finished as high as fifth at the national senior level – were able to train at the Lake Arrowhead centre with the help of scholarships.

Danny Kwan is a latter-day pioneer who forged a successful life in a new country. He came from humble beginnings, born in Canton in mainland China. When he emigrated to the United States in 1970, he had little understanding of the English language, but he offered job credentials from his work at Hong Kong Telephone and Telegram. Four years later, he returned to Hong Kong to marry Estella, whom he had met in Grade 5, then brought her back to California.

Currently, Estella lives with Michelle in a one-room cottage in Lake Arrowhead, while Danny lives with his aging parents near the family restaurant, the Golden Pheasant, in Torrance. Aside from giving his children important lessons on life, Danny has other responsibilities, too: a job and caring for his parents. "I'm pretty busy," Danny says. "My parents are getting old and I have to take care of them and the restaurant. Last year [1995-96], it was just too much."

But help came with Michelle's quick rise to skating prominence when she won the 1996 world title. During the summer of 1996, with his youngest child, Michelle, at age sixteen well on her way to becoming financially independent with income in the seven-figures, father

Kwan retired after twenty-five years working with Pacific Bell. He was forty-seven.

"I'm pretty well set," says Danny. "I am comfortable, but not rich. But it doesn't really cost a lot for me, just a plane ticket now." One or both Kwan parents accompanies Michelle to international competitions several times a year.

Danny Kwan is not the only parent to be staggered by skating bills. When the Eldredges' expenses reached $15,000 a year, they came within two weeks of pulling Todd out of skating altogether – until the small town of Chatham began a fund-raising campaign. The Duchesnays became expert penny-pinchers to finance the skating careers of their two children. Liliane helped with expenses by expanding a pre-kindergarten class she operates out of their home in Aylmer, Quebec.

"A lot of parents split up because of this sport," Henri Duchesnay says. "It's because of money, separations, arguments, the tension it creates." Liliane adds, "How many times have I heard, 'God, we only speak about skating in this house.'"

The first time that Liliane realized that skating could be expensive occurred at a local spring skating school in Canada, where she had to pay $12.50 so that Isabelle could get twenty minutes of one-on-one instruction during a group session with thirty to forty other children. Liliane had been amazed that the group session included no instruction. "It was just socializing on the ice," she recalls. "When I asked a coach if he could do something with my little girl, he said, 'I've got fifteen minutes left.' That was $12.50. That's when I really woke up. . . . I figured, my God, that's a lot of money. We didn't know what we were getting into." Liliane did not dare tell her husband that she had spent so much money for so short a lesson. "She hid a lot of things from me," Henri says.

The Duchesnays were not wealthy people. Henri, whose ancestors had emigrated to what is now Canada from France in 1634, had lived in France for four years while working for the Canadian Armed Forces. There, he met Liliane and married her. Paul was born in France, Isabelle after they returned to Canada. "When I came back to Canada,

I was making a reasonable salary," Henri says. "But it was no hell, really, a little less than a colonel."

After thirty years with the air force, Henri then worked as deputy vice-president in charge of the technological branch of the Canadian International Development Agency. Liliane wanted to work, too, and she was asked to try out as a hostess at the posh Château Laurier Hotel on the other side of the Ottawa River, in the city of Ottawa. But she refused to leave her children. "I've got to work," she said. "But I'm not going to work in an office or away from home."

The Duchesnays found the answer in their own home. Liliane would teach French to English-speaking children at the pre-kindergarten age. And while she was at it, she could ensure that Paul and Isabelle would learn to speak English.

She had worried about her oldest son, Gaston, who was twelve years old when the family moved to Canada. He could already speak French and German, but he wrestled with English. "I didn't want that to happen to my other kids," she says. "My idea was to have four or five children [in the school], just English-speaking children. . . . But out of the four or five, it became fifteen, twenty, twenty-five."

But when the Duchesnays decided to expand the school because they needed skating money, the number of children swelled to as many as fifty. Half of them would come in the morning, the other half in the afternoon. For a couple of years, Liliane attracted so many clients that she had to divide the day into three sessions. It became a full-time job.

Still, money was tight. The Duchesnays made a personal family rule: they decided they would not go into debt because of figure skating. They calculated how much money they had, and then decided how many lessons they could afford. Whatever money they could spare, they saved for their children's skating. "We saved *avec intelligence*," Liliane says. They did not eat out at restaurants. They did not go to movies. They drove an old Peugot for ten to twelve years. "It was an old rat-trap," Henri says. "But we kept it going."

At home, the family ate wholesome food, "but we were not going for filet mignon," Liliane says. She took a course and learned to sew, out of necessity. A slender, elegant woman with a soft voice and a sense of style, Liliane made clothes for the family and costumes for her skaters, too.

Whenever Isabelle and Paul had to leave Aylmer for summer skating schools in Kitchener, Ontario, Wilmington, Delaware, or Lake Placid, New York, Liliane accompanied them. They would rent a modest hotel room with a kitchenette and Liliane would do all the cooking. She would make sandwiches and take them to the rink. They would fill up their little car with pots and pans and pillows and drive to these destinations, during summer months, when Liliane's school was out.

While there, Liliane spent a lot of her time in chilly arenas, huddled over a pair of knitting needles while her children practised. Knitting served two purposes: to while away the time and to make winter sweaters for the family. It wasn't an easy hobby for her to adopt, since all the knitting patterns she could find were in English, which was not her first language. Ironically, to this day, Liliane cannot read knitting patterns written in French.

The Duchesnays also had to pay the freight for two summer sessions in Obertsdorf, Germany, where Isabelle and Paul trained while still skating under the Canadian flag. Obertsdorf was a national training centre in Germany, with top-quality facilities that attracted international skaters such as British Olympic champions Jayne Torvill and Christopher Dean, as well as their esteemed coach Betty Callaway. Skating every day side by side with the world's best was bound to push the Duchesnays to a higher level. But it was expensive. "The [Canadian Figure Skating Association (CFSA)] allowed them to go the first year, but they did not pay for it," Henri recalls. "The only thing we got was free travel.

"I remember when they came home, Isabelle said if [they] really wanted to do something good, [they had] to keep going the way [they were]. So they went back." But the second year, the CFSA was not willing to send them to Obertsdorf, Henri says. The Duchesnays paid 100 per cent of the costs: lessons, ice time, coaches, equipment, food, travel.

It was only after the French skating federation adopted the Duchesnays and paid their expenses that their parents were able to cobble together enough money to buy the home in Aylmer, Quebec, where they still live. It is tucked in a pretty clearing of trees near the Ontario–Quebec border, and is alive with flowers. "Liliane has been gardening ever since," Henri says.

Isabelle and Paul were not blind to the sacrifices their parents made, and hid their financial difficulties from them while in Europe. In Obertsdorf, they dined for weeks on a less-than-delectable dish they call "white spaghetti" – cooked spaghetti noodles with no flavourful sauce, no butter, no cheese.

"We had no idea sometimes what they were going through," Liliane says. "We would send money, sometimes $3,000, sometimes $5,000. But coaches and ice were very expensive. They kept the biggest part from us. They never asked for a penny."

The Eldredges got their first taste of the shelling-out syndrome shortly after they gave their sons, Scott and Todd, some hockey skates for Christmas. Todd, only five and a half years old and sixteen months younger than his brother, skated for two weeks in the hockey skates until he spotted other skaters jumping and spinning. The sight left a lasting impression on the small boy, and he asked his parents to buy him some new skates. Figure skates. "We changed him over from hockey to figure skating," Ruth recalls. "That was the beginning of the end."

Todd was in the afternoon session of kindergarten at the time, but, first thing in the morning, his mother would find him standing on her bed, asking if he could go skating.

"I thought, 'This is crazy,'" she admits. "This is going to die down." It didn't.

In the early years of Todd's skating career, the expenses added up to $4,000 to $5,000 a year, a considerable sum for a father who was a commercial fisherman in Chatham, Massachusetts, a town of four thousand people – at least until the summer, when the population quadruples with tourists and visitors to the Cape Cod area. John had bought a forty-two-foot trawler in 1973, when Todd was only two years old. But, because of skating, the Eldredges could never pour the money they made from the boat back into the business. It paid for Todd's skating.

The boat became a vital part of the family. The Eldredges christened it *The Scrod*, which is the name for a young codfish. But the moniker, John explains, actually came from an amalgamation of the names of the people in his family: Scott, Ruth, and Todd. When

John finally sold the boat in 1995, it didn't bring much. "I just about gave it away," he says. "I didn't get much for it. It wasn't worth a whole lot."

"But thank God for the boat," Ruth adds. "It really put Todd through skating." Ironically, little Todd did not care for the boat, or for fishing. He hated to lose sight of the shoreline. He disliked the rolling motion of the waves. He much preferred frozen water, on which he could glide and turn and jump, his blades scribing wavy lines on the slick surface.

In addition to the income from fishing, Ruth went back to work as a licensed practical nurse, to help out with the mounting bills. The family went through several cars, all used ones, because they were constantly on the road, taking Todd to lessons. For a couple of years, they were driving regularly back and forth to Boston for lessons. A trip to Lake Placid, New York, for a competition was a two-hour drive, one way.

The expenses increased when Todd was ten and decided to move in with a family in Philadelphia to take lessons from noted coach Richard Callaghan. When the costs reached $15,000 a year, the Eldredges gasped for air, like fish thrown up on shore.

"At that point, we couldn't keep going," John admits. "We either had to find a way to fund this, or he was coming home from Philadelphia." The Eldredges had not yet told Todd how bad things were; they agonized about how to break the cold, hard facts to him. But a circle of Ruth's friends went to bat for the family. Hair stylist Claire Leblanc heard about their plight and rallied the forces in the town. Another friend, Norman Howes, knew a former benefactor of Dorothy Hamill – Peter Hoyt – who had once been on the U.S. ski team. Judy and Peter Hoyt had a summer home in Chatham.

Judy Hoyt, intrigued by the situation, decided to support Todd's skating "to some degree," Ruth says. Howes started a committee in Chatham to raise finances through clambakes, dinner dances, cocktail parties, door-to-door solicitations, anything to enable Todd to continue skating. They sent out five-year pledge cards and, in all, raised $20,000 to $30,000 a year.

"Todd kept getting better and better and then went to the national championship," John recalls. "They couldn't stop either, and went another five years." The town sponsorship ended in 1993. By then, a handful of international skating events were offering small sums of prize money to athletes.

The surprising part of it all was that Todd's supporters really didn't know him. He was rarely home. "It was amazing," John exclaims. "But Chatham is a small town and they are real supportive." The timely town rally kept Todd from having to face the end of a dream; it kept him on the road to becoming a world champion. "He never knew that we were going to go down [to Philadelphia] and I was going to tell him, 'This is it.'" Ruth says. "I was in turmoil for two weeks.

"It was always tough for us. It was always a struggle. We just never had that kind of money. Todd is very appreciative, but I don't think he fully understands what we went through. . . . We never let Todd know how difficult it was, or the financial hassles of it all."

Money wasn't the only hurdle that the Eldredges, the Duchesnays, and the Kwans had to overcome. There were plenty of psychological and social ones, too. Skating splits up families, often when skaters are very young, learning the fundamentals of life. To gain the ability necessary to make it to the élite level, more and more skaters are moving to training centres, where they will be taught the top skills and where they will find more highly ranked skaters to inspire them. When a skater leaves home, it is not easy for child or parent.

When Kurt Browning left home in small-town Alberta at age sixteen to train in Edmonton, he found it traumatic and was "terribly homesick" the first few months, before he adapted to living with a young cousin.

"It wasn't until we started heading up the road that I realized I'd just left home," Browning wrote in *Forcing the Edge*. "No one told me it was going to feel like that. I didn't know that was part of the deal."

Jeffrey Langdon, ranked fourth in Canada in 1996, moved away from his childhood home when he was even younger – thirteen – to train with Elvis Stojko's coach, Doug Leigh, in Barrie, Ontario. But Langdon's move was not distressing, because of a sacrifice his parents made for him. They sold their home and gave up their jobs in Smiths Falls, Ontario, and moved with him.

"They didn't want another family to raise me," Langdon says. His father, an elementary-school teacher, was able to find a job in Barrie, while his mother got a job as recreation co-ordinator at a seniors' home.

"I was not going to have my children just to send them away," says Al Langdon. He had watched the parents of junior hockey players send their sons away to live with other families at an early age – with results that were "sometimes successful, sometimes not." Many other parents would have figured Langdon and his wife, Karen, were rather rash to sell the home he had spent six months building, with the help of his father-in-law. "For us, it was just a tool that allowed us to do what we did for Jeff," he says. "We are not millionaires. We're ordinary folk. It gave us the means to move. I drove away very easily."

Jennifer Robinson, the 1996 Canadian champion, also moved to Leigh's school at age thirteen, but without her parents. It was tearfully traumatic, but Robinson was determined to go.

"It was difficult," admits her mother, Louise, who had at first been relieved when her daughter had been taking lessons in Detroit, Michigan, which was just across the border from their home in Windsor, Ontario. It had meant that Jennifer could train while living at home. But after Louise found herself in a forty-five-car pile-up while driving in the United States, she was less willing to take Jennifer across the border. Jennifer went away during the summer to train at Leigh's school, while Louise regained her driving confidence. But Leigh was so impressed with Jennifer's eagerness to learn that he asked her parents if she could stay during the winter, too.

"She was really excited about going," Louise recalls. "I remember the trip up there. It was terrible. She was crying all the way. When we got there, we said to her, 'Jen, if you want to, we can turn the car around and you can go to school [in Windsor].'" But, with big tears running down her cheeks, Jennifer kept repeating, "I really want to do this."

Louise says that Jennifer's move was very hard on the whole family, which included her husband, Cliff, a vegetable wholesaler, and a hockey-playing son, Jason. Jennifer was young and energetic, and her sunshiny nature sent out bright rays in the Robinson household. Her absence left a hole in their hearts. The tight family unit had been broken. They worried about her loneliness, too, in a town far away from home and family. And, because the family had spent all of its spare change on skating, Louise and Cliff drove an old car, too clunky and bawky to make the long trip to Barrie very often.

But Leigh understood. Many of his students have left their homes in smaller skating centres. Many of them are very young, and board with families in Barrie. The fact that young skaters travel to larger centres or clubs to improve their skills is almost a given now in the skating world, but Leigh's Mariposa Skating Club is very unusual: it is located next to a public school, so that skaters can polish up their Salchows, then a few minutes later dive into science. He has a policy that very young skaters spend only one school semester in Barrie and one at home with their parents. In the first couple of seasons, that is what Jennifer did. "That's what kind of kept you going, knowing she was coming back again," Louise remembers.

Jennifer boarded with a family in Barrie, but she also had a family of skaters at the rink. During the first summer Jennifer was in Barrie, her parents came to see her only occasionally. The second year, Louise took a three-week vacation from her job working as a switchboard operator for a CBC station to spend time with Jennifer.

"I realized she was okay," Louise says. "She doesn't need me. But for myself, I had to go. I realized that the kids are so close to one another, and they're like a big family. They're so supportive of one another because they're all in the same situation. All of them are away from home, and they really develop some long-lasting relationships."

For parents, the concerns and worries accumulate and work to split families up. Like Jennifer Robinson and Kurt Browning and countless other young skaters, Todd Eldredge left home early to pursue his dream. He was a small boy of only ten with an unusually long attention span for tedious work when he moved away. His diligence at the rink amazed his parents. "It was an unusual attitude for a young child," Ruth says.

But Todd was always unusual: analytical, a perfectionist. Even when he was starting out in the sport, Todd showed an unerring dedication. His mother would take him to early-morning public sessions, and as she drove him to school, he would change his clothes in the car. Coaches thought he was too young to take figure-skating lessons, even compulsory figures, but Todd really wanted to, Ruth recalls.

By the time Todd was six years old, he was enrolled in fifteen-minute lessons, three times a week. Ruth thought it was a "ridiculous" idea. But it was clear that Todd had found his passion.

When he was seven, Todd went to Lake Placid, New York, for a pre-liminary-level competition. He was in a field of twenty-one boys, one of which was twenty years old. On top of that, Todd was small for his age, the tiniest kid on the ice. "You couldn't see him through the other boys," Ruth remembers. "He was always the little guy, for years and years."

Even as he stepped onto the ice, Ruth again thought how ridiculous it all was. But Todd seemed to be having fun. When one practice was scheduled at midnight, Ruth quizzed him: "Todd, you aren't going to do that." He replied, "Yes, I am."

Todd was persistent, a trait his father says he learned from his mother, an attractive lady who smiles easily. Only two of the twenty-one boys showed up at the practice. Todd was one of them. He finished second in the competition.

"I will never forget it," Ruth says. "I couldn't believe it."

For two or three years, the Eldredges burned up the highways, taking Todd to Boston for lessons with a Harvard undergraduate. When the teacher graduated, the family was left nonplussed about Todd's skating future. "He was in the public-school system, and we had been taking Todd out of school two days a week," Ruth says. "It was a hassle for

Todd, because he was trying to keep up with everyone and do his homework in the car. It just got to be a real problem."

Finally, Todd himself came up with a solution. "He's the one that said to me that he wanted to move and be as 'normal' a kid as he could be," Ruth recalls. "Normal" meant moving closer to a rink that was near a school.

That summer, Todd attended summer skating school in Rochester, New York, where he met coach Richard Callaghan. "We let him go," Ruth says. "When I went down to pick him up, he wanted to stay there. He said he wasn't coming home. We finally gave in to it. He's been so driven and motivated that we figured he must know what he wants, obviously. So we let him do it."

If Todd missed his family and felt lonely, he didn't tell them. "He wouldn't let us know," Ruth says. "It was a big adjustment. He wanted this so badly, he never complained."

By the time he was ten, as mentioned earlier, Todd moved out to follow Callaghan, who was teaching in Philadelphia. Todd lived in a house with five or six other skaters under the care of the stepmother of Callaghan's wife, Mandy. "We were sure that would wear off," John says, but Todd spent four years in the house. "We were so close as a family that we just really didn't think it would last," Ruth adds. "But he proved us wrong."

Ruth went to Philadelphia frequently to visit her young son. When she couldn't go, the family would call him. "His schoolwork was going well and his skating was going well," she recalls. "He did it all. He knew that if the schoolwork failed, he was coming home."

But the Eldredge family was put to the ultimate test when Todd's mentor, Callaghan, became assistant director of skating at the Broadmoor Arena in Colorado Springs. When Callaghan moved, so did Todd.

This was the most difficult decision of all. The move split up the family, geographically. Ruth moved to Colorado Springs to live with Todd.

"This was a major decision for the four of us," remembers Ruth. "I have always said we were never going to split the family up, and we already had." But husband John and Todd's brother, Scott, persuaded Ruth that this was a decision they had to make to support Todd's dream. "How can you say at this point, Todd, you can't do it?" she says. She lived with Todd for at least three years.

Todd later moved to San Diego, along with Callaghan. He kept on moving farther away from the family. "Almost as far away as you can get," John adds. Overall, the Eldredges put their marriage on hold for six years. Ruth and John would see each other during competitions.

"You need a real strong family unit to make this work," Ruth explains. "It just doesn't work unless it's supportive and very, very strong. My other son was the key to this."

"He was behind this and he never felt that he was neglected," John adds. "He was really good about it. That's why it worked."

As they had done with the decisions about money, the family never told Todd how hard the separations were for them. "He really didn't know what was going on back home," Ruth admits. "We didn't want him to think about that."

"It wasn't his problem," John adds.

The family got together as often as it could. They'd meet at Christmas, or at major skating competitions, like the world junior championship. When Todd won the world junior title in 1988 in Brisbane, Australia, his parents and brother were there.

Scott was the other brother in many ways, with a different outlook on life. He had distinct life goals, separate fires burning. Scott stuck with his hockey skates, and later went to a tennis camp. He was good at it, and although his parents asked him if he wanted private lessons to get more involved, he declined. Having fun was more important. Scott is now a gemologist, working at an art museum in Denver.

"He saw Todd and the intense training that it took," Ruth says. "He loved sports, but he didn't want it to the extent that he wanted to commit his whole life to one sport the way Todd did.

"But he admired him for that."

Not all skating children are separated from their families, at least not at an early age. But that doesn't mean that the parents aren't in for a rough ride of emotions along the way. As if tossed by a tornado, they are swept up in the politics and stresses of the sport. If parents are worth their salt, they steer their offspring carefully through the maze, setting values that will last longer than skating boots, emphasizing the importance of education and experiences outside of skating, and giving them the tools to eventually leave the nest, whole and prepared for life's journey.

At first, the Duchesnays bucked skating's trend of creating prematurely empty nests. Apart from summer excursions to other cities for training, the couple lived at home with their parents and did not leave home until they were in their twenties. There was a major reason for this. Aside from the financial advantages of having skaters stay at home, their parents were adamant about the value of education.

"You can do any sport you want, but education comes first," says Henri, a man with quietly twinkling eyes, but a firm hand. "After a certain age, you have to use your head."

"Who can tell you how far you will go [in skating]?" Liliane asks. "You can't [concentrate solely] on skating; it is just like a horse with blinkers, and suddenly there are no more roads for them and they have nothing else."

Paul did not leave home to skate for France until he had graduated from university with a bachelor of science degree in molecular biology in 1985. When they left, Isabelle had been in her second year of university, taking psychology courses.

Both are talented musicians, too, continuing the family legacy handed down by their grandmother, Alise Duchesnay, who co-founded the Quebec Conservatory of Music. Paul spent ten years taking lessons through the conservatory, becoming an accomplished pianist. Isabelle also played the piano and has the gift of perfect pitch.

School, music, and skating (in that order of importance) combined to keep his children out of mischief, Henri says.

The Duchesnays say they never pushed their children into skating, or music, or anything. "I just mentioned about the study and they understood from the beginning," Liliane explains. "They did it voluntarily." She shudders at the thought of other parents who did push. "I've seen so many parents slapping, screaming, pestering their children."

The Duchesnays did not want to wander down that unpleasant road. "We told them that, if you want to stop this skating, it's fine with us." Paul was such a skilled pianist that the conservatory wanted him to focus on music. In other words, skating would have to go, a sacrifice to Beethoven and Mozart.

The parents left the decision to Paul and Isabelle, and it was a hard one. "It broke your heart," Liliane recalls. But they chose skating. "If you are able to do what you like in life, then do," Liliane adds.

Skating became such an all-consuming passion that the Duchesnays did not grow up like other teens. "A lot of things they missed," Henri remembers. "High school dances, they had very little of that."

"But they visited the world," Liliane adds.

Michelle Kwan had barely begun school when she started to skate. But right from the beginning, her parents set their priorities: winning a skating competition is not life's most important achievement. With their careful attention to Michelle's inner psyche, they have developed a daughter who cherished – and was not disappointed by – the silver medal she earned at the 1997 world championship, when a tiny, perfect fourteen-year-old Tara Lipinski unseated her from her throne. Through her parent's guidance, Michelle has learned to see a world beyond medals.

"My only object was to make sure that school or education go first," Danny Kwan says. "There is no guarantee in sport. This is a short career in skating, and there are too many milestones in life. Maybe you have fifteen years in the sport. Maybe you go in a show after that for a few years. Education can wait, but it really cannot wait too long."

His eldest daughter, Karen, continued her skating career even as she attended her first year at Boston University in the fall of 1996. Concerned, Danny asked the United States Figure Skating Association (USFSA) to assign Karen to international competitions that took place before the start of her college season. With a good measure of understanding, the USFSA did just that. Karen competed at an event in

Obertsdorf, Germany, late in the summer, and missed only four days of school when she went to a subsequent event in Vienna.

With Michelle, however, the family had fewer choices. During the 1996-97 season, Michelle was a world champion who was just starting her first year in junior high school. A tiny skating prodigy, she had already been competing at the senior level at the U.S. championship by the time she was twelve. She had been only thirteen when she made her first appearance at a world championship in 1994. With such early successes came assignments to compete in international events. And with the boom of skating since the 1994 Olympics have come other skating opportunities. Michelle's seat at school sat empty too long. Michelle's school would allow absences of only ten to fourteen days. If she were away more than that, she would forfeit a year of schooling. The Kwans did not want their daughter to miss out on her education, so they hired a tutor for her instead.

Currently, Michelle studies for three to four hours a day with her full-time tutor. She still must set aside time to go to school and write her tests and examinations. And her home studies are no breeze. Of the five subjects she studies, half of them she cannot do on her own at home. For her biology class, for example, she has to go to school to do lab work. Michelle takes her homework with her to competitions. She studies on planes and in hotel rooms, though it's difficult during an important competition, when her mind is very much taken up by the details of the event. "There are really a lot of things she has to think about," Danny says.

As mentioned earlier, Michelle lives with her mother, Estella, at Lake Arrowhead, where she trains, while her father divides his time between the mountain town and Torrance. The first year Michelle trained at Lake Arrowhead, the Kwans would drive up every night after work and spend the night in her cabin. Estella moved up the second year. Even now, for a time, the family is separated by a three- to four-hour drive.

With the Duchesnays, there was never any contest when it came to education. It was still number one. Nothing could derail that aim. Even the Canadian Figure Skating Association (CFSA) found that out.

The Duchesnays staunchly refused when the CFSA advised Isabelle and Paul to leave the Ottawa–Hull area where they lived and move about five hundred kilometres away to Toronto to take advantage of a national ice-dancing centre that existed there at the time. "This was before Paul had finished his studies," Henri says. "[The CFSA] said they could leave all their studies behind. You could get a job in Toronto, they said, and do some studies at night."

"But that was exactly the reverse of what we believed. And we would have to pay room and board for them. And we had two of them."

That was the end of that.

It was also the beginning of what Henri calls "the Great Divide," when Isabelle and Paul, it seemed, began to lose favour with the CFSA and eventually decided to skate for France. The Olympics were coming to Canada, specifically to the western city of Calgary, in 1988, and the Duchesnays felt that the CFSA was more interested in pushing ice dancers Karyn and Rod Garossino, who were born in Calgary.

At the time, Quebec had yet to produce any élite skaters who competed successfully at the world level, and, if the Duchesnays were going to make any headway at all, Canadian officials felt they could do it best in Toronto.

But the Duchesnays felt the Garossinos' Calgary connection served to push their prospects at being assigned to top international events in the years leading up to the Calgary Olympics. After the Duchesnays finished third at the national championship behind the Garossinos during the winter of 1984-85, they were set aside as spares for important international competitions the next season, Henri recalls.

While the Garossinos were assigned to compete at Skate Canada in London, Ontario, that fall, the Duchesnays were sent to a competition for developing skaters at St-Gervais in France. They already had finished second in that event in a previous year, and it was a blow to them to be sent back to the same event. They were only alternates for Skate

Canada, and early in the previous season – even before they had a chance to show their goods – they had been asked to fill out forms to compete in the World University Games, not exactly an important stepping stone into the big leagues of figure skating.

"It was quite clear that they were going to be sacrificed," Henri says. The choice to skate for France did not come easily, however. "They had to make a very hard decision. They felt, 'We're leaving our country, and our country doesn't want us.' It was the worst choice they ever had to make," Liliane adds.

The Duchesnays had already been pursued by other countries that had seen them skate in Europe since 1982, three years before. Their parents watched in amazement as three countries made offers to their children over the years – in effect suggesting a breakup of the family – but even then Henri and Liliane let their children make the decision themselves. Both the German and Swiss federations expressed an interest in adopting the Duchesnays, as well as France. (Liliane was of French and German heritage.) The German federation promised to pay all expenses, but at the time Isabelle and Paul would have had to renounce their Canadian citizenship and become German citizens in order to have competed for them. There was no such thing as dual citizenship in what was then West Germany. Paul was adamant that he was a Canadian, and he wanted to remain a Canadian.

France offered the best option for the Duchesnays, who held dual citizenship in Canada and France. Still, it was "unbearable" in the house while the decision was being made, Liliane remembers. "Henri started to become very silent. He didn't want to make the decision."

British coach Betty Callaway, who had been working with Olympic champions Jayne Torvill and Christopher Dean in Obertsdorf at the time, gave the best advice. "If you stay in Canada another year, you will just be too old," she told them. "One day you're going to wake up and you're going to be too old."

Isabelle was almost twenty-two, Paul was twenty-four, and they hadn't yet been to a senior international competition. Time was indeed not on their side. Isabelle was the first to sign up to make the switch.

Afterwards, some CFSA officials tried to entreat the couple not to leave. According to the Duchesnays, one promised them a spot on the world team if they would stay in Canada, even though athletes were told publicly that they had to earn a spot on the team with their placements at Canadian championships.

"If that's the way things go with the CFSA, no thank you," Isabelle told them.

"We would just like to have what we deserve," Paul said.

"We knew it wasn't going to happen anyway," Isabelle said later.

The Duchesnays did not immediately leave home after they applied to skate for France. On the one hand, it was a relief for Henri and Liliane, keeping their children near them as they were going through major changes in their career. On the other hand, it was difficult financially, partly because of the switch, partly because of their stress on the importance of education. Paul hadn't quite completed his university degree. He had to finish it before he left.

For a year, the family lived in financial limbo. The French federation offered no support to the couple until Isabelle and Paul had accomplished three things: winning the French championship, finishing in the top eight at the European championship, and finishing in the top twelve at the world championship the first season. Of course, that meant there would be no French subsidies for training expenses until the end of the season.

And because Isabelle and Paul had left the haven of the CFSA, they no longer had either federal support or association backing – which included university tuition. They lost both their coaches and their free ice time at their home club, Minto Skating Club in Ottawa. The city of Ottawa provided free ice time to skaters at the national level, but the Duchesnays no longer qualified for that. Because their coaches worked at Minto, the couple was no longer able to use them. Lacking funds, the Duchesnays had to find a rink that would donate ice time – and those times would never jibe with the Minto coaches' schedule. For five months of the 1985-86 season, the Duchesnays trained without a coach. The risks the Duchesnays took when they ceased to skate for Canada were immense. So were the pressures on the entire family.

Had they failed to meet the requirements of the French federation, the Duchesnays' careers would have been over. As it was, they won the

French championship, finished eighth at the European championship, and twelfth at the world championship during that season, exactly what they needed to continue.

However, they had a scare at the French championship when they finished only second in the compulsory dances, the first segment of the competition. Everything seemed to go wrong. They arrived in France, suffering from jet lag, having trained without coaches, and having to adjust to the larger ice surfaces in Europe. A change in ice size affects ice dancers, with their large sweeping patterns on ice, more than skaters in other disciplines.

On top of that, the ice-cleaning machine at the event broke down, the rink suffered a power failure, and the ice began to melt. The ice conditions changed again when maintenance crew scraped the ice, affecting the slide of the blade on the surface. The Duchesnay family fretted together, concerned that their expensive gamble might not pay off. The entire season was a nerve-racking experience for all of them.

When Paul and Isabelle finally left home, they had suffered from another of skating's syndromes: they had little experience with everyday life. So that they could concentrate on their schoolwork and their skating, their parents had taken care of all of life's other details. "We took care of absolutely everything," Liliane says. "We had the time, and theirs was really precious. We did all the washing, cooking, and ironing, and they just had to skate and study and practise the piano. We wanted to maximize their time."

In Obertsdorf, a tiny, isolated mountain town in the German Alps, thousands of miles from Aylmer, Paul and Isabelle had to learn about all of life's little hassles and had to deal with them on their own. They had to fend for themselves, manage their own time, and cope with some new experiences as well. They skated and cooked and washed and ironed. "They learned more about street sense," Henri says. "They had to step down into the everyday world."

But at least, from a parent's point of view, Obertsdorf was an ideal place. It was not New York or Los Angeles or Paris, all exciting cities with plenty of distractions and temptations for young skaters. For the Duchesnay parents, Obertsdorf meant a relief from those worries. In Obertsdorf, Isabelle and Paul certainly didn't get into bad company, Liliane admits. "And they were so busy, skating six hours a day." Ballet classes and off-ice training took up most of their time.

Still, it was a lonely place for Isabelle and Paul. But, with the traditional Duchesnay emphasis on full lives, they looked for ways to expand their horizons beyond skating while they were there. They considered certain options: get a computer and learn how to use it; or perhaps Paul could take up playing the saxophone. But in Obertsdorf, there was no opportunity to take computer lessons. And Paul's dormitory mates would have been less than pleased, perhaps, when the Canadian set out to practise a musical instrument such as the saxophone.

"There were a lot of pluses and minuses," Henri says. "Being so isolated, they lost a lot of social contact. They found themselves a little lost when they came back to [Canada]. It requires a re-adjustment."

Instead, while in Obertsdorf, the Duchesnays picked up a third language, German. And they gradually adapted to life on their own. These were facts that gratified their parents.

Like Todd Eldredge, the Duchesnays were fortunate in having a sibling who understood the rigorous world of figure skating and the demands it made on their parents' finances and time. The Duchesnays' brother, Gaston, was a confidant, a mentor, a non-athletic intellectual who was not affected by the attention paid to his two skating siblings. For one thing, he was ten years older than Paul. "If Paul had been the oldest – or Isabelle – and Gaston the little one, it would have been more difficult for us," Liliane admits.

When Isabelle and Paul skated at a pairs summer school in Preston, Ontario, Paul was sixteen, Gaston, twenty-six, and old enough to live on his own. Gaston was already taking a bar exam. He had his own friends. It was Gaston who gently gave Isabelle and Paul advice when they contemplated leaving Canada to skate for France.

"He was a class-one big brother," Henri says. "He was highly intellectual. Gaston read stacks and stacks of books. He liked to travel."

"The summers we spent in Toronto, Gaston was overseas visiting our relatives," Liliane says. "Once he went to Greece. Or he'd just zip off down the road, cruising on his moped."

Gaston died of lung cancer at age thirty-nine in the fall of 1991, just as the Duchesnays were going through a stressful stretch in their skating careers. The Duchesnays had won their world title earlier that year, Isabelle had married ice dancer Christopher Dean, and the Duchesnays found themselves swept wildly into the Olympic fever that engulfed France. The Games in 1992 were held in Albertville, and the nation hung its gold-medal hopes on the Canadian-born Duchesnays. The number of media requests for interviews and features became so overwhelming that the Duchesnays had to unplug their telephones.

Gaston's death was a dark time for a family that had already been through so much. His skating siblings had little time to mourn; they returned home from Europe only long enough to attend the funeral. And afterwards, the parents grieved alone at home, their only other children living on another continent.

Not all siblings are as understanding as Gaston Duchesnay or Scott Eldredge of the attention and finances heaped on skating brothers and sisters. Most skating families deal with a scenario in which non-skating children watch wistfully as the family car heads to the rink, toting expensive skates and garb, and wonder when their turn will come, when their parents will pay attention to their needs and fears. "It has to be a real contentious issue in families, about what child is getting x and y and z," said Susan Heffernan, who organized a parents' seminar at a Canadian national training camp one year. Karen and Al Langdon – parents of Canadian Jeffrey Langdon, ranked ninth in the world – lived to talk about it.

Al will never forget the sight of his daughter, Christi, eleven, sitting cross-legged on the floor in an empty dining room and weeping sorrowfully the day the family moved from their home in Smiths Falls to Barrie, solely to allow Jeff to pursue skating. Jeff was eager to go, and both parents made the move without regret. But Christi did not.

"She really struggled with the move," Al recalls. "She didn't understand it. She knew we were doing this for Jeff, but how could we?"

Christi never fought with her parents over the issue and was never obstinate about it, but she "struggled with who she was the first year" in their new environment, Al says. When her mother took a job to help pay the skating bills, Christi became a latchkey kid, and fell in with the wrong crowd at her school. After teachers warned her parents about the direction in which she was headed, Al and Karen pulled her out of the school. Christi understood.

But the change in schools did not end Christi's push to let people know she was not just the sister of Jeff Langdon, a skater who was moving up in the world. She could not tolerate the phrase "Jeff Langdon's sister." Rather, she preferred people to recognize that Jeff Langdon was her brother, a narrow distinction that allowed her to feel she was a person in her own right. It was not easy to make that distinction for several years, because she skated as well, but Christi was never really a part of her brother's rarefied world. In fact, Jeff pushed her out of figure skating. "She was not welcome," Al says. "He resented her being there." When his parents suggested Christi would be an ideal ice-dancing or pairs partner for him, Jeff would have no part of it. His parents were angry with Jeff for rejecting an opportunity.

A couple of years later, Christi gave up skating altogether, but discovered her own strengths. Skating would never have been her forte anyway. She was completely unlike her brother. While Jeff was a thin wisp of a teen, quiet and shy, Christi was boisterous, big, outgoing, and rugged. She excelled in many other sports – such as hockey, basketball, tennis, and fastball – at the regional and provincial levels, but her favourite sport was rugby, a rough-and-tumble game that is about as far removed from figure skating as you can get. She even played quarterback for a flag-football team.

In order to maintain her identity, Christi also refused to attend Jeff's school, next to the skating rink in Barrie. Cleverly, she found a way out. She took up playing the euphonium, a band instrument affectionately referred to as a baby tuba, and was accepted into another school that welcomed students with musical interests. While her brother was setting his sights on getting to a Canadian or a world championship,

Christi found her own passion and goal – to go to university, another expensive project for a parent. But it was her way of saying she deserved to have a turn.

"She saw these exorbitant funds and resources going to Jeff," Al says. "He couldn't do it without that. That's the nature of the beast." Acknowledging that, the Langdons devised a five-year plan in order to cater to both children: the finances would have to turn to Christi when she was ready to attend university [the fall of 1997]. After that, Jeff would be on his own.

All the while, Christi and her skating brother "tolerated" each other, according to her parents. They had nothing in common. They lived in different worlds. "Jeff didn't care to get along with her," Al recalls. However, now that both Langdon children have survived the tumultuous teen years, they are closer than they have ever been. Christi admires what her brother has done. She cheers for him at skating competitions. Jeff goes out of his way to say hello to his sister at big events, even when the pressure is on.

And despite all their differences, in a pinch, Christi was ready to help her brother and her parents with finances. One year, she saw her parents struggle with having to pay a $4,000 skating bill during a season in which Jeff suffered such debilitating injuries that he missed most of the season and lost government backing. "Where in God's name would you ever find that kind of money, just to pay a skating bill?" Al ponders. "That one year really hurt." But Christi offered to help, with her own money that she earned in part-time jobs.

The Langdons didn't take her money – they cashed in some registered retirement savings – but the gesture was telling. It meant that the Langdons were, indeed, a family.

"I feel good with what we have been able to do for both children with our meagre means," Al says. "I feel very proud of both of my children. I walk like I'm a king. I've been blessed and fortunate."

If parents sprout white hairs during the skating lives of their children, they try not to show them. But inside, they suffer, too, at accidents and incidents surrounding rink life. They watch, helpless, as injuries threaten to derail their children's goals: back problems, skull fractures, rounds of surgery on knees, feet, and shoulders. They see, too, the double-edged sword of fame. On the one hand, it might bring a needed sponsor or an invitation to a rich skating event. On the other hand, parents such as the Kwans have looked on as their young daughter has become an international star in her early teens, thrusting a quiet family into the spotlight and leaving them to deal with the unreal glare – and even a fan threat – that fame brings.

Todd Eldredge's career seemed to be on the upswing after he won a bronze medal at the 1991 world championship in Munich at the age of nineteen. But John and Ruth Eldredge watched quietly, knots growing in their stomachs, as Todd endured two years of skating hell, felled by injury and self-doubt.

First, Todd developed a back problem so severe he had to pull out of the 1992 U.S. championship. The USFSA gave him a medical bye to both the Olympics and the world championship that year, but, because of that, U.S. bronze medallist Mark Mitchell missed out on his only possible Olympic experience. Todd was well aware of Mitchell's sacrifice, and it bothered him even more after he finished only tenth at the Albertville Olympics.

"There were so many things going around about 1992 and whether I should have actually competed at the Olympics or not," Todd said later. "I was feeling a little bit of pressure about that for almost the whole year of 1993. All that pressure kind of caught up with me. It was a real difficult time."

Its effect? At the 1993 U.S. championship, Todd skated as if he had given up. He finished only sixth. He had worked hard to fix his back problem, doing stretching and strengthening exercises and wearing a heel lift in his right boot to offset a discrepancy in leg length that probably contributed to his wonky back. But his inner turmoil was not solved at all. He failed to make a world team for the next two years. He almost quit.

"He took off at least two months," says his coach, Frank Callaghan. "I told him to quit unless he learned to love the sport again. I didn't know if he would come back. He lost his focus because of his age [he was the youngest U.S. senior champion when he won in 1990 at age eighteen]. He got caught up with what people were seeing. When you get to the top, people want more and more and it turned negative."

In the third month, Todd decided to come back. And he returned with a vengeance, winning three major international competitions. But he missed the world team again when he caught a flu virus that manifested itself at the 1994 U.S. championship in Detroit, developed a fever of 104 degrees, and fainted in his bathroom, hitting his head on the sink. Still, he finished fourth, but it was another roadblock in his comeback.

His parents persevered. "It was a difficult time for all of us, but you hide it," John says. "We didn't push him into it." Ruth agrees it was not a time for pushing, but a time for supporting. "You let them know you still believe in them," she says. "Even though he had the back problem, we knew, once he got better – and we knew he would get better – that he had so much to give the sport. We fully believed in him. His goal the whole time was to be a world champion and an Olympic champion, and it was just a matter of him knowing we believed in that."

When Todd was injured, many of his fans jumped off the bandwagon faster than they jumped on. But his parents and a few very close friends wouldn't budge. "A lot of people had a lot of doubts," John says. "A lot thought he was all done."

His parents' only doubt was about whether Todd would pursue his goal, not whether he could if he wanted to. "When he makes his mind up," says John, remembering Todd's boyhood, "he puts everything into it."

"It makes you angry," Ruth says. "People that support you when you're great aren't there for you when you're not. It's discouraging. He really grew up a lot over that."

The Duchesnays know their way around hospitals. They have spent far too much time in them. Over the years, Isabelle has undergone four rounds of surgery on a knee, another on a foot. Along the way, surgeons have become family friends. The visits started in July 1978.

Isabelle and Paul began their skating career not in ice dancing, but in pairs skating, a discipline in which Canada has historically been prominent. It is also one of the most dangerous of disciplines, with its lifts and throws and twists and speed. Isabelle was only fourteen and a half and Paul seventeen when they were honing their skills that summer in Kitchener, Ontario, at a school run by top pairs coach Kerry Leitch. The Duchesnays had just started their second season of skating pairs.

The work was tough, the hours brutal, for the French-Canadian teens. "They were overtired and overworked," Liliane recalls. "But I had not had enough experience to see that. I was just concerned."

Isabelle was in tears, Liliane says, after some strenuous off-ice outdoor training in 30°C temperatures at a football field. Their ice time was from 11 P.M. until 3 or 4 A.M. "I remember she woke up in the morning and she was crying," Liliane says. "She never did this, before or after. She said she must have been really tired."

Liliane told Isabelle to stay at home from the rink that night, but the pair refused. Although Liliane usually drove them to the arena, then stayed until they finished, Isabelle and Paul told her to go home, since it was so late. Leitch told her someone else would bring them home. Liliane agreed, the first time she had ever made such an arrangement.

But about midnight, Liliane woke up, startled, as if from a nightmare, her heart uneasy. With a mother's instinct, she quickly got dressed and drove to the arena, just in time to see her children step onto the ice. Two minutes later, Isabelle collapsed from a lift, directly in front of her mother. Slender, quiet Liliane leaped over the rink boards.

Isabelle had suffered a compound fracture of her skull, a circum-cranial break that ringed her head. She also broke her collarbone, so severely that the bone pushed up against her skin. Because there were no stretchers at the rink, somebody found a billboard and carried her out.

The news at the hospital was horrific. A doctor warned Liliane that Isabelle might become epileptic from the accident. Worse still, while Isabelle was being X-rayed, Liliane overheard a doctor use the word "paraplegic." Although she knew that doctors were also examining an injured motorcyclist, who had arrived at the hospital directly after Isabelle, she did not know that they were not talking about her daughter. She did know that Isabelle complained about a lack of feeling in her foot. "I was crying," Liliane says. "I was out of my mind."

It took doctors half an hour to read a second set of X-rays, but to Liliane, the minutes seemed like days. "It was hell," she said. "It was the longest day. It seemed an eternity."

For four to five days, until after Isabelle had undergone a test of her nerve impulses, Liliane kept the accident from Henri, who was working at home seven hundred kilometres away. She feared the news would aggravate his weak heart. But when Henri did learn about Isabelle's condition, he was furious. "I drove all night," he remembers.

For ten days, Isabelle drifted in and out of a coma. When she recovered, her father put an end to the pairs career of his children. Although they had always felt that ice dancing was a boring sport for skaters that couldn't succeed in the other disciplines, the Duchesnays decided to take it up. It was safer. Thirteen years later, they won a world title in the discipline they once scorned, and they made ice dancing very interesting, indeed.

"I still cannot watch pairs," Henri admits.

The pain and the hospitals didn't stop after Isabelle and Paul retired to become widely heralded professional skaters after the 1992 Olympics in Albertville. One summer, three years after the Duchesnays won an Olympic silver medal, their careers screeched to a halt. During a stop on the Tom Collins tour of world champions, on June 23, 1995, Paul felt something click in his back as he lifted his sister off the ice. He finished the program, but the next day, when he tried to skate, he doubled over in pain.

The flight home, through Seattle, was interminable. Paul travelled on his knees, with his head in the airplane seat. When he got off the plane at home, he could not walk.

X-rays showed that he had shattered a disk in his back. Surgeons removed it immediately, because it was pressing dangerously on a nerve, causing him to lose feeling and mobility in his left leg. The disk had damaged the nerve, and the incident left his leg weak for almost a year.

Paul was just getting his legs back under him when he had another accident in June 1996. He was in-line skating in the Gatineau Hills with a family friend, David Hoffman, a reconstructive surgeon, travel-ling downhill at about fifty kilometres an hour, when he hit a reflector that was embedded in the pavement. He had not been wearing a helmet, and it was almost dusk.

Paul tumbled for about sixty metres, landing on his face on a paved roadway. Hoffman raced to halt traffic: one car stopped five feet from Paul's head. He was unconscious for six hours.

The next day Hoffman reconstructed Paul's face, and he had plenty of work to do; he inserted a series of plates and screws to rebuild a cheekbone that had crumpled like cornflakes. In all, there were seven fractures in his face. Hoffman put thirty stitches to close a deep wound on Paul's eyebrow and forty more on the inside of his cheek.

Isabelle was frantic. So were his parents, who had bleak flashbacks to Isabelle's accident eighteen years before.

"It was a close call," Isabelle remembers. "We almost didn't bring him home at all. He was the luckiest man on earth, the doctors said, because he didn't break anything else, neck, arm."

If skating families are lucky, all the traumas and sacrifices that parents and skaters face can sometimes have happy results. The travails can serve not to tear the family apart, but to knit it into a strong, cohesive unit. So often the shoulder-to-shoulder closeness can set family members against each other like squalling cats. But all the togetherness can become a blessing. Families build strong bonds after having fought the good, long fight together.

Isabelle and Paul Duchesnay have had their squabbles, too, but they share an indefinable bond, linked by hopes and fears, cares and needs, blood and passion. They protect and watch over each other. "Out of skating came a lot of nice things," says Liliane, who watched the rela-tionship develop. "They would get nervous about things," she recalls. "But when they got off the ice, all was back to normal." All of those life experiences bred a certain lasting complicity between the two of them.

During a lull in their professional career, Isabelle decided to take a week-long holiday in St. Lucia. After the first day, Paul began to talk about Isabelle. "I think he asked about ten to twenty times if she had phoned," Henri says. Finally he broke down and called her.

During their amateur career, when Isabelle required knee surgery in Switzerland, Paul became concerned. There was no money for him to accompany her from Obertsdorf, and he did not dare ask his parents for more. "Paul sold his bicycle so that he could go with her," Henri says, with quiet pride. "He wouldn't let her go alone."

In one thing, Danny Kwan feels he is particularly blessed. "My kids get along well," he says. "They very seldom argue. They love each other a lot, and they all support each other. That's something I am very pleased about."

Kwan's oldest son, Ronald, is a twenty-one-year-old biology student at the University of California at Irvine. For the first time, his other two siblings, Karen and Michelle, have been separated, since Karen has moved to the other side of the United States to go to university. "I call her," Michelle says. "I miss her a lot. When she was in a competition in Vienna, I faxed her a little thing and called her and wished her luck.

"We're like two peas in a pod. We were always together. Our bedrooms were right next to each other. She skated with me all the time. She's like my best friend. She's gone now. It's so sad, but it's also good for her to go to college in Boston."

Skating has obviously brought the two sisters even closer together, sharing the same passions and pastimes. But the bond they have will survive beyond the skating world. In two years, Michelle said, she intends to follow her sister to Boston University and study with her there. "I don't think I'll be skating forever," she said. "I want to do something else besides skate my whole life." Danny Kwan has taught his children well.

The Kwans have done such a careful, thoughtful job of instilling values in their children in the face of fame, stress, and pressure that the USFSA points to them as model parents. The Kwans have taken their responsibilities seriously, balancing on the fine line between guidance and overprotection, teaching their children to expect no favours, and figuring out how to relinquish their control over their children when they grow up.

Ever since Michelle Kwan became a skating road warrior, dashing around the world from Paris to Tokyo, her parents have accompanied her as chaperones. "You have to," Danny says. "I don't know if you are going to change anything, but with a twelve-year-old kid, you have to. The federation provides a team leader to take care of the skaters, but they are not babysitters."

As parents, Estella and Danny say their task is not necessarily to direct their children, but to give them the tools for their lives. "You give them your experiences, what you have gone through," Danny explains. "People always talk about pressure from the parents, but it depends on where you draw the line. There is a very thin line between discipline and pressure. If you overdo it, it is pressure. You are pushing and abusing your children. But if you don't discipline them, then they don't have any guidelines."

Michelle, however, is growing up, and her father is well aware of it. "At some time you have to be able to trust your children," Danny says. "But with freedom, you have to earn it. You cannot have freedom just to do what you want. You cannot just let go. That is part of the responsibility of the parent. But from eighteen to twenty-one, what can you do about it?"

At sixteen, and a millionaire, Michelle does not have her own credit card, evidence of her parents' belief in guidance.

"There will be two more years [before Michelle is eighteen] and I have to figure out what I will do with my life," Danny says. "I have just let go of my boy and my daughter [Karen], and Michelle is the last. I will have to learn how to adjust."

Because Michelle has been making international headlines since she was twelve years old, the Kwans have had to deal with unusual pressures: ensuring their famous daughter is, underneath, just plain folk, with all of the normal struggles that life brings. It's not hard for a child to lose her way in the crucial years of finding her feet in the world while growing up in the public spotlight. Danny Kwan constantly brings his daughter back to earth. So do her siblings.

Shortly after Michelle Kwan became one of the youngest world figure-skating champions in history, she took her driver's licence test in San Bernadino, California. She flunked the first time.

It was a nerve-racking moment for Michelle, even though she was a veteran of the cloying pressure that comes with skating at the top levels in a do-or-die sport where careers can soar or crash during a four-and-a-half-minute program. "I've never been so nervous in my life," Michelle says of her driver's test. "I don't know why. Worlds was easier than taking my test." The test was merely one stop on a long train ride of life, says her father, in his allegorical way of speaking. But it was an important one that delivered a valuable lesson on perspective. It was a tool her parents used to keep their famous daughter tied safely to the everyday world.

"We went and saw all the people lined up [at the vehicle test station]," Danny recalls. "I said to her, 'You are no one special in that group. The difference between you and the rest is that, for you, it's tougher. You have to learn how to get used to being a normal person. You still have to take the test. You don't get special treatment. You cannot sleep or walk by anything. Anything you do, you have to earn it.'"

Her examiner did not know who she was, Michelle says. After she failed the first test, Danny urged Michelle to write the instructor a note thanking him for reminding her of the importance of safety.

Michelle's siblings ensured that she continued to live in the normal world, too. While sister Karen felt sorry for Michelle's initial failure in getting a driver's licence, brother Ron howled. "My brother gave me a hard time," Michelle says. "My brother was laughing so hard. Everybody was. It's so embarrassing to tell you."

The difference between Michelle and the string of unheralded folk who, for instance, line up for their driver's tests, is that the young skater has additional responsibilities, whether she likes it or not. Perhaps, because of her notoriety, someone may give Danny's daughter a better seat at a restaurant or good tickets to a Broadway show – complimentary, of course. "For you to get it, gives you a bad image on the news," Danny says. "People expect a little bit more from you. People want to treat you like a role model."

Danny's answer to that life riddle is to tell his daughter to be herself, always. "You don't worry about what they think," he says. "Michelle is pretty normal, and that's the way I really want her to be. . . . If you try to act something different, you will bring pressure on yourself."

It's difficult sometimes to avoid the stardust. By all accounts, 1994 Olympic champion Oksana Baiul has lost her way in it. Baiul rose from starved orphan to wealthy U.S. megastar in a few short years. Fêted at every turn, admired by thousands of young American girls and networks and fans and skaters, young and old, subject of a made-for-TV movie, Baiul was inevitably locked in a frail tower of false images. With no parents to guide her through the booby-traps of fame, Baiul took to rebelling against her coach and surrogate mother, Galina Zmievskaia, and throwing tantrums on tours. Things only got worse during the winter of 1997, when Baiul destroyed her expensive automobile, crashing it in a Connecticut ditch with an alcohol level that was higher than the legal limit.

Only two years after her Olympic triumph, Baiul floated into a room, packaged in immaculate makeup, with coiffed hair, and swathed in luxurious fur, smiling with glamour, seeing no one. The media blitz, like a distorted mirror, has cast an unreal glow about her, a reflected glory.

"The media make skaters believe they are someone special," Danny Kwan says. "This starts the trouble, because [the skaters] try to act like they are someone special. But if they could only think of skating as a sport, something they like to do, it would be better. It is the same in any sport." But the media – whether it includes news, advertisements, commercials, or promotions – is an unavoidable part of an information age. Danny spends a long time thinking about its effect, and how to steer his daughter through this aspect of fame. "If you want to be known, you must deal with the media," he says. "You have to be recognized. If you want to catch a big fish, you have to go out in the boat, in deep water. The waves, you can't control it. You have to go with the flow.

"Maybe Michelle wants it. Some people enjoy these things."

Michelle Kwan has rarely lost her way in the stardust. In the year following her world championship win, Michelle faltered, losing three major competitions, including her world title, for various reasons: she had started to think too much about winning and living up to her public image of perfection, because she had forgotten why she had started to skate in the first place, because she was growing up and learning how to deal with situations she had not encountered before. But, in spite of it all, Michelle has not been cowed by the experience, thanks to her parents. A tiny bit of dynamite with a single-minded focus on her tasks, she has learned how to be unflappable in the face of storms because of the example of her father, who says his whole life has been like a pond, smooth, unworried, unruffled on the surface, calm at all times. "There is nothing shining about it," he says. "There is no shining moment. This way, you never get hurt."

As a person, his daughter is very strong, in her way, he says. "Normally, you don't see it. Sometimes when you watch her practise, you know. Sometimes when she has to struggle, she fights for it. That's what Toller Cranston said to us [at the world championship in Edmonton.] But every day is a different story. He saw her at that moment. She may seem strong one day, and maybe he would never see her weak side." It is a parent speaking, who recognizes the tossing of a young personality on a stormy journey.

With this kind of support, Michelle will find her way. Her parents, as well as her grandparents, are proud of her. Around her neck, she wears a special charm, a gift from her grandparents. For Michelle Kwan, family is strength.

After Todd Eldredge finally won his world title in Edmonton in 1996, there was one thing on his mind. He skated across the ice and slipped his gold medal around the neck of his mother, Ruth.

Even today, Ruth's eyes get misty when she is reminded of it. "I didn't expect it," she admits. "It was like twenty years being flashed in front of your face. The appreciation of that – I don't think it's ever been done."

"It's definitely the culmination of a lot of hard work," John says. "That's just the kind of kid he is."

Ruth barely pauses for a moment, her eyes bright, even as she thinks of the hardships. "I think I know we'd do it all over again in a minute."

A Master at Work: Bootmaker for the Stars

John Knebli was one of a kind.

A vanishing breed.

In early 1997, Knebli was ninety-three years old, stooped and full of reminiscences, and he still had plans. In his workshop, there were shelves stacked toe to toe with the finest and best-fitting skating boots in the world, ready for his customers to pick up. And there was a lush roll of rose-blush leather on his workbench for a female customer who wanted him to craft skates of an unusual hue. He was happy to oblige. Knebli was always very obliging. He had been making skating boots for fifty-four years. All by hand.

Knebli was one of the last crafters of handmade custom skating boots in the world, who oversaw production from beginning to end, who laid his hands on the leather himself. When he was at his prime, his little company – tucked onto a sidestreet in Toronto's fashion district – churned out a hundred pairs of boots a week for skaters in Australia, the United States, Czechoslovakia and other parts of Europe, Hong Kong, Japan, even Africa.

Knebli and his wife, Elizabeth, and their apprentices and workers would toil through fifteen- to twenty-hour days to make skates for people such as Peggy Fleming, the 1968 Olympic champion from the

United States. Even then, about thirty years ago, he was one of the most highly respected custom bootmakers in North America. Skaters knew his stitches were sound and consistent, fashioned under his meticulous eye.

Bootmaking in the Knebli way is a dying art. Knebli called himself "a hand man," because, although he used some machinery to make the boots, he never resorted to using automated machines or methods that use robotics or computers. There are only about fifteen "hand" bootmakers remaining in the world today, and that is a generous estimate, according to Phil Kuhn, president of Harlick and Company, Inc., based in San Carlos, California. Harlick, founded in 1935, is one of only two or three hand bootmakers in the United States today. Klingbeil Shoe Labs, Inc., in Jamaica, New York, is another. In Canada, Rose Custom Boots, Ltd., in Cambridge, Ontario, has been making handmade boots since 1974.

Perhaps one of the most famous hand bootmakers of all was Gustave Stanzione, who emigrated from Italy to New York at the turn of the century. Trained as a shoemaker, Stanzione produced high-quality hand work that was revered by the top skaters in the world – Olympic champions such as Barbara Ann Scott, Carol Heiss, and Dorothy Hamill. A short man with a walrus moustache and a penchant for eating raw fish, Stanzione was meticulous about his work. His fittings and the stitching on the boots were so precise and tidy, there wasn't a need for the leather strip at the back of the boot that normally covers seams. After Stanzione died, his three sons carried on his work. Many years ago, without the master himself at the helm, the company went out of business.

Although there are several well-known boot manufacturers such as Riedell and SP-Teri (both in the United States), Austria-based Wifa (catering mostly to European skaters), and Risport, in Italy, Harlick is rare in its desire to stick to handwork with its custom boots. About 65 to 70 per cent of its business lies in making handmade boots, the rest being less-expensive and less-labour-intensive stock boots, made to standard specifications. When they are working on custom boots, Harlick workers cut out each piece of leather, stitch all the pieces together on special sewing machines, and mould the boot uppers into the shape of skating boots by stretching the leather around lasts (or moulds of the feet), all by hand.

Some companies have turned to more automated lasting machines, which stretch and pull the leather uppers over the moulds. But hand-work is best, Knebli maintained. And Kuhn agrees. "That's what gives you a really good fit on a boot," he says. "When it's done by an auto-mated lasting machine, you can't get the upper pulled on as tight. And you can't get it pulled on as straight as you can by hand, because [with hand methods] you can visually check with every pull to make sure that it's done right."

A critical and time-consuming skill in hand bootmaking is the alter-ing of wooden – or these days, plastic – lasts or moulds. In the making of custom boots, bootmakers take a series of measurements and trac-ings of skaters' feet. (Harlick takes two sets of measurements, when a skater is both standing and sitting, in order to account for the move-ment of a flexing foot.) They send design models of the boot they wish to make off to a manufacturer of lasts, who produces a wooden model for both feet.

But the fastidious bootmaker's job is not yet done. The real trick in bootmaking is in knowing how to modify the last so that it is an exact replica of a skater's foot, complete with bumps and swellings. To cus-tomize the last, a skilled worker cuts, sands, and shapes pieces of leather to duplicate the bumps and gnarls on a foot. They then glue them to the last. This step is so important that, at Harlick, only the three owners of the company build up the lasts, not its seventeen production workers. "It's a real skill in itself to know where the corrections go," Kuhn explains.

In more automated methods, bootmakers will use die cutters, a cookie-cutter-like machine that chops out dozens of layers of leather pieces at one time. Because there are eight or nine different pieces of leather needed to make up a boot, the automation definitely saves time in production. With die cutters, workers can cut out several hundred pieces of leather in an hour. When making custom boots, Harlick cuts out ten pieces an hour by hand. The company uses a die cutter when it makes stock boots – although even its stock boots are sewn and stretched over the lasts by hand.

A handmade boot can take a couple of weeks to make – that is, if the bootmaker were to concentrate on making only one boot at a time. Skaters may find that it can take up to six weeks to get their custom boots from a hand manufacturer. But a bootmaker like Risport, which has turned with great enthusiasm to assembly-line production and robotics, can produce a complete pair of boots every forty-five minutes. At this rate, Risport can churn out a thousand pairs a day. By contrast, Harlick makes about twenty to twenty-five pairs of custom boots a day, with the help of their specially trained employees, all former cobblers from Mexico and South America who have spent from six months to a year learning how to transfer their skills to making skating boots.

At the very low end, skates are mass-produced as cheaply as possible through automation, and arrive in the stores with the blades permanently fastened. Skaters in search of high-end custom or stock boots buy the blades separately and have a retailer, or even a knowledgeable coach, attach them. Knebli had been known to attach blades to boots for a client. Mounting blades, too, is an important skill. A skater will be thrown off-balance if the blades are simply mounted along the centre line of the boot sole. Because each skater balances over the foot in slightly different ways, the blade is attached temporarily at first and shifted slightly until the skater is satisfied.

Most blades tend to be made by British manufacturers; a pair can cost about $500. And not all blades are the same. Free-skating blades have more prominent ice picks than ice-dancing blades; singles and pairs skaters need the picks to do jumps, even to set up spins. And dancing blades are shorter than free-skating blades to prevent a dancer from stepping on the heel while doing quick and intricate turns.

But a blade is only as effective as the person who sharpens it. "People live and die by their skate sharpeners," says skating official Louis Stong, former coach of Kurt Browning. Once skaters find one they like, they stick with them, and travel miles to have them sharpen their skates. Audi Racz, who has been sharpening skates for twenty-four years, says he is still learning. "It's all handwork," he explains. "Some aspects of sharpening you can't measure. It's entirely by touch. With some people, it seems no matter how long they do it, they will not acquire the necessary light-handed touch. And everybody's got their own little method. You will rarely find two sharpeners that will do it the same."

The difference between their results is often immeasurable – but the skater can sense it. Racz, who sharpened Browning's skates from the time he was a junior, said his clients can tell if another experienced sharpener in his skate shop has done the work instead of him. The task is so precise that Racz has had special sharpening equipment constructed by a tool-and-die maker. With it, his sharpenings are accurate to within five one-ten-thousands of an inch. It takes Racz about fifteen minutes to sharpen one pair.

Talented skate sharpeners are everywhere: they may operate specialized businesses or they may be coaches or skaters who do double duty on the side. There is no shortage of this kind of handwork. But there is a dearth of bootmakers who work by hand.

These days, many skaters are wearing manufactured boots, according to Stong. These are boots that are "made to fit," as opposed to boots made by Knebli or Harlick that are "made to measure." Today, it is a common practice for many skaters to buy boots that are approximately the right size, and then depend on a skilled retailer to stretch the boot out in all the right places to fit, using special tools. The trend is catching on, because skaters can get boots more quickly – and more cheaply – this way, Stong says. And custom bootmakers who start from scratch and work by hand are getting harder to find.

Audi Racz, who, in addition to his skate sharpening, owns National Skate, Inc., a retail outlet in Edmonton that sells hockey and figure-skating boots, says the bulk of his sales are boots made to fit. Not all manufacturers offer the same designs: some offer high-end stock boots with wider toe boxes, or higher heels, or higher arches than others. "We try to sort through all the different makes and try to determine which boots are best-suited to certain foot types," he says.

The store does have the proper tools to stretch out the skate to fit a foot. And, if he must, Racz is equipped to do very extensive custom rebuilding of a boot. "We will literally take a skate apart and rebuild the entire inside of the skate to accommodate the skater's foot," he says.

To customize the skates, Racz says all he needs are specific measurements and tracings of the feet. With this information, he can alter a boot without ever having seen a skater's foot. He can even sell a custom-fitted boot to a customer in Toronto, thousands of miles away.

If a skater's foot has such unusual characteristics that a stock boot cannot be fitted to it, Racz will order custom boots. And sometimes a little advanced technology helps. The Riedell Skate Co., based in Red Wing, Minnesota, is probably one of the more technologically advanced bootmaking companies, Racz says. The company uses a computer CAD program to design custom skates. Its designers record the dimensions and measurements of a skater's foot into a computer, and a printer spits out custom patterns.

All of the advances in machinery automation and computer fittings failed to move Knebli, however, born of a different age and inspired, always, by the touch of leather. "There are some things computers can do," said Knebli of the modern trend in boot-fitting. "And there are some things computers cannot do. Everybody is different. No two people are the same. No two feet are the same. About 70 per cent of the boots out there are garbage. Today's shoes are made for everyone, but they fit no one."

For many years, skaters around the world have depended on the skill of Knebli's hands. As he continued to make skates into his nineties, his hands were freckled liberally with age spots. The underside of his fingers were flattened from years of pressing leather and steel, moulding and shaping. He was severely stooped, pitched forward from the waist, like a sprinter reaching for the tape. His body had been shaped gradually, too, by years of work, to fit the height of his workbench. He and his workbench were truly one, fitting together like the pieces of some wondrous jigsaw puzzle.

Knebli had moulded the sport of skating in his own way, too. Canadian Bob Paul, a native of Toronto, was already a customer when he approached Knebli in the late 1950s to make skates for his pairs partner, Barbara Wagner, who had very tiny feet. "She was a small girl," Knebli said. "So when I made the shoes, I cut them low."

Knebli's idea was as novel to skating at the time as was flying to Mars. Female skaters had been wearing white boots, cut high up on the calf. Wagner and Paul were well-known skaters, having won world titles and an Olympic gold medal in 1960, and when they won major competitions with Knebli's boots on their feet, they brought attention to his work. When other skaters saw Knebli's low-cut boots, they came to his door from all over the world.

The idea, Knebli said, was that the low-cut boots gave a better-proportioned look to the body of a tiny woman. "Women used to skate in long skirts," he said. "Then, people looked only at their face. But skirts are shorter now. You look at the whole body."

Knebli reinforced his idea in 1959 when the North American Figure Skating Championship was held at the Toronto Skating Club. He was quietly pleased when spectators applauded and commented on the perfect look of an American skater who was wearing his low-cut boots. High-cut boots soon disappeared from skating fashion. Even women who weren't so tiny started to wear them.

Knebli, the son of a Transylvanian farmer of Hungarian heritage, became a bootmaker for the stars. He made skates for 1973 world champion Karen Magnussen, for 1962 world champion Donald Jackson, for 1976 Olympic bronze medallist Toller Cranston, for 1988 Olympic silver medallists Elizabeth Manley and Brian Orser, for 1984 world champions Barbara Underhill and Paul Martini, and for entire groups of young Japanese skaters who used to spend summers in Toronto, honing the fine points of their craft.

Knebli took great pride and interest in the careers of skaters who wore his boots. Orser found something very special about a pair of boots that Knebli made for him after he lost the 1984 Olympic gold medal – even though he had won both the short and long programs. For a joke, Knebli decided to sew a couple of pieces of gold into his skate boots. He would tell Orser where he hid them, he promised, only if he became a world champion.

"I got the leather for those skates and sat down to drink some coffee," he said, remembering the time when he hatched the idea. "Then I said to myself, when I make that shoe, I'm going to make a joke. I went to the bank and asked if I could get some gold, the smallest plate they had, and I'd like to buy two."

At first a bank employee told Knebli it had no plates on hand, that they would have to order them from the main bank. But, somehow, two hours later, Knebli had them in his hands. They cost $35 each. He pulled aside the apprentice who had been working on Orser's boots on the pretext that he wanted to check them. When the boy looked away, Knebli slipped the gold plates between the two layers of the soles, one for each foot. No one knew where they were – no one but Knebli.

By the time Orser finally won his world title, in 1987, he was wearing a different pair of boots; skaters tend to break in a new pair every year. But Orser hadn't given his old skates away, and Knebli finally revealed the hiding place of the gold pieces. Knebli, who loved telling a good tale, said that Orser was jumping for three gold medals, not one, at the 1987 world championship. "You never saw such a high jump like he had [at the world championship]," Knebli said afterwards. "He had something up there with him that was pushing him up. He had two pieces of gold. It was the gold that pushed him up."

Knebli's trophies were these memories and the collection of mementoes on the bleak panelled walls of his office in a nondescript brick building. Everywhere, he and his wife, Elizabeth, had tacked up newspaper and magazine clippings, now yellowing and curling with age, about his feats, his clients, his sport. Young skaters who had worn his boots had even sent him their graduation photos. Posters of Underhill and Martini, and of Orser, brought bright dashes of colour to a drab interior. There were family photos of coaches, such as Doug Leigh, arm in arm with his wife, Michelle, and his five-year-old towheaded son, who was already experimenting on skates.

An eight-month-old newspaper, showing a Knebli client, Elvis Stojko, at the 1996 world championship, sat in a stack beside a collection of patched-up, re-covered chrome chairs. Dangling from above was a plastic model of a hip joint and thigh bone, for Knebli could – and surely would – tell you that the feet affect the rest of the body and vice versa. A long red cape that a member of Canada's skating team wore at the opening ceremonies of the 1994 Lillehammer Olympics, black fur hat and all, clad a mannequin that greeted visitors by the door. Outside, an enterprising graffiti artist had painted on one exterior wall: "Got bunions."

Knebli's clients don't tend to get bunions from his skates, but he saw plenty of them in his career of looking at skating from its netherside, the sweaty-feet side. Skaters have some of the ugliest, most gnarled, calloused feet on earth. "That's because their skates don't fit," he said.

When Knebli created, he was like a maestro, taking into account every foot note, every curvy arch.

Knebli claimed he knew more about feet than most doctors. He had plenty of training. He got into shoemaking by accident at home in what is now Hungary. He was "a farmer boy," he said, and was working for a family friend who decided to open a shoemaking school. "He had to have thirty-one persons to start the school," said Knebli in his heavy European accent. But he only had thirty.

"He came to me and said, 'Mr. Knebli, we need a signature.'

"I said, 'What kind of signature?'"

When the friend filled him in on his problem, Knebli, all of eighteen years old, agreed to give the man his signature. But the signature, at first, was all he got. The friend was nonplussed when Knebli did not show up for class. A couple of weeks later, he sought him out. "Mr. Knebli," he said. "I do not see you in school."

"You told me you only wanted my signature," Knebli said.

With a little persuasion, the teacher had his thirty-first student.

"To make long story short, I learned a lot," Knebli said.

Knebli studied under the friend, a Polish shoemaking professor, for two years. For another year, he left to learn how to prepare leather. Then he studied orthopedics in Bucharest, Romania, where a foot doctor taught him not just about feet, but about how the feet related to the entire body. "He was a very old man, but he was smart," Knebli said, pointing to his temple. "He could tell exactly what was wrong."

His teacher tended to concentrate on children's feet. "He had an idea that children are more important than the older people," Knebli said. His influence caused Knebli to make children's shoes when he eventually set up his own shoemaking business in Canada.

Knebli left Romania about the time the country wanted to enlist him in its army. He was less than thrilled about the prospect. In 1930, he caught what he says was the last boat to Canada, which allowed only farmers on it. Farming was not in his heart, but he had grown up with his father's profession and it saved him from a boot camp of another kind.

Knebli was in his twenties when he arrived in Canada at the height of the Great Depression and took whatever job he could find. He worked on a farm until the farmer told him he didn't need him any more. The harvest was over. He went to the city and found work as a milkman, a truck driver, anything to buy a meal. He struck gold when he got a job repairing shoes at a Simpson's store. He earned $18 a week and had money in his pocket.

It was an important first step. The repair shop had all the right equipment to actually make shoes, so Knebli started making them, too. He had two or three clients who liked his shoes, and they were businessmen.

After four years in Canada, Knebli looked into going home again, but he was told that, if he did, he'd immediately be drafted into the Romanian army. Its officers hadn't forgotten that Knebli had never reported for mandatory duty. Knebli decided to stay where he was, wait another year, and get Canadian citizenship instead.

Just before the Second World War, Knebli returned home to check on his parents, but they did not wish to move to Canada. And they did not want him to leave. But with political unrest looming, Knebli was urged by a friend to get out. He married Elizabeth, a young woman who had grown up in the same city, and they immediately set sail.

In 1938, Elizabeth, a dressmaker who could speak no English, suddenly found herself in Canada, and the trip became a long honeymoon. Knebli had left with return tickets in hand, promising his parents he would come back after the war. When the war ended, Knebli was busy with his new life in Canada. "I forgot about going back," he said.

But, while the Second World War was at its height, Knebli played a vital role in the army anyway – just not for the Romanian one. He made shoes for Canadian and American spies. If, for example, Allied intelligence officers were trying to infiltrate German areas, Knebli would expertly copy German-style boots, right down to the nails that German shoemakers used. The governments would hand him photos of the shoes they needed and all the materials to make them. "I was a bad boy," he said with a grin.

Otherwise, Knebli went on with more peaceable pursuits, making children's shoes and using his expertise in orthopedics to set up his own shop. In 1942, a tall man walked into his store on Bay Street and asked Knebli where he bought the shoes he was selling.

"I make them here," Knebli said.

The man's gaze swept around the store, with one happy result: he asked Knebli to make him a pair of shoes. The shoes were perfect. The man asked him to make him another pair exactly the same.

"No sir," Knebli said.

"What?" the man said, bewildered.

"No, I cannot promise they will be exactly the same," Knebli explained. "Every piece of leather is a little different."

"That's what I want to hear," said the man, impressed by Knebli's honesty. "You do the best that you are able to do."

Knebli charged him $25 for the first pair, but the man paid him $50. He also paid $50 for the second pair. "That's the kind of customer I want," Knebli said, with a smile.

About seven or eight months later, the man returned, asking him to make a pair of black shoes for his son. But Knebli protested, because the shoes would not match an elegant brown suit the boy was wearing. The man insisted. "They have to be black," he said. "They're going to be skating shoes."

"Thank you very much," Knebli told him. "But I don't think I'm going to make skating boots for you. I can't take the order. How can I make something when I don't know what it is?"

Pressed, Knebli finally consented. He told the man to bring a pair of skates with him, he would examine them and do his best to produce a new pair for his son. "But I'm not saying that they're going to be the same thing," he said.

The boy, named Gerry Blair, got his black skating boots and became a junior champion for the Toronto Skating Club. After that, everybody in the Toronto Skating Club wanted Knebli to make skating boots for them. Knebli obliged.

One day, Elizabeth, who also served as a receptionist, bookkeeper, file clerk, and all-round handyperson in her husband's business (daughter Elizabeth helped out, too), made an interesting point. "Skating people have good feet," she told Papa K., in coaxing him to take up skate bootmaking. "Why not make shoes for good feet, not for bad feet?"

But Elizabeth had a misconception about the status of skaters' feet. Her husband did, too. Later, Knebli discovered he had to make use of his orthopedic studies in bootmaking. "Skating is murder on the foot," he said. "And you have to find just the right balance."

In 1948, Knebli's bootmaking career was slowly building while Barbara Ann Scott was training to become Canada's first Olympic skating champion. Knebli never made skates for Scott, but, while she was a professional skater, he often repaired the ones she had. Clippings and photos of Scott adorned his office walls. When Scott helped make skating a national sport of prominence in Canada, she helped Knebli's new career, too.

In recent years, Knebli watched as skating went Hollywood. It is now a world of agents, spotlights, money – big money – glamour, television ratings, image-making, deals, pressure, strife, knee-banging, and beige skating boots. Knebli lived in it, but he was not of this world and never strove to be. He never spent a penny on advertising. His clients all discovered him by word of mouth. And he never told a little white lie to make a sale. Making money was not his prime aim. "We really never worked for the money," he said. "We worked for the smile. That's the way we went, day by day."

His career afforded him a gracious white stucco house in a stately area of Toronto, festooned all around with the floribunda roses he loved, a white Cadillac convertible, and a cottage in Northern Ontario. His shop surroundings were less spectacular. In his shop, Knebli sat on his tattered chrome chair as if it were a throne, welcoming customers in his scuffed black shoes, puffing on a chain of cigarettes. "You like the people who come," he said. "If someone comes in, but doesn't know something, and asks you if you know anything about it, you are going to tell him. It doesn't matter who comes in, you don't know them when they come in, but they go away like a friend. That is the whole story."

And Knebli tended to tell the story as he saw it. More than once, he met a parent who cringed at the cost of custom-made boots. (Knebli's boots cost between $375 and $500, depending on the work involved.) More than once, cost-conscious parents have asked him to make the boots a size or two larger. Let little Tommy grow into them, they say.

However, an ill-fitting boot throws a skater off-balance, and making young skaters train in such boots does them no real favours while they're learning skills, Knebli told them. "Do you want me to make what you want, or what you need?" he'd ask. Knebli feared an accident. He felt responsible. "You must love the people," Knebli said. "When you love the people, you do your best for them. If you don't love the people, you don't care."

Knebli's inquisitive eye took in a wider view, too; he looked beyond the wooden lasts and the boot soles of his trade. He didn't care just about feet. He cared about the skater. He and his wife were regular patrons of an annual bursary dinner that raised money for struggling skaters. He was once keen about starting a skating school. He secretly studied the training methods of skaters in Europe until coaches found him out. In other words, he was spying. They tossed him out of their European clubs.

As a young man with money in his pocket, Knebli had taken himself to ballets and shows and developed an artist's eye. Based on what he saw, he preferred to make white skates for female skaters. White skates "lift" a skater, making her look as if she floats on the ice, hardly touching it, moving with light, he said. A strip of white on the skirt area helps, too, for the same reason, he said.

In Knebli's opinion, the now-popular beige skates don't have the same effect. Knebli made no bones about it: he didn't like them for competitions. But a handful of finished beige skates sat on his shelf, ready for pickup. Knebli made them if he was asked.

Knebli always looked for ways to improve on boot design. There was evidence everywhere within his humble shop. Through an unremarkable doorway in his shop, an enormous room opened up. It was crowded, almost to bursting, with immense, ancient bootmaking machines, each with a specific purpose. Another room, at the back of the store, harboured a handful of powerful devices that looked like industrial sewing machines. Tucked into a lunchroom at the back, right beside a little stove, were two gigantic bootmaking machines that were older than Knebli. Every step through his boot factory revealed yet another layer of handwork history.

The fruits of his labours over the years were piled high in boxes in a dark room tucked into the corner of his factory. Wooden lasts of every size and description, all bearing the name of their owners, jumbled together in crates and spilled out along tables. Some of the lasts were tiny, neat as teacups. Some were enormous, larger than life, it seems, and lumberingly flat-footed.

Knebli's building was not only his workplace; it was a museum. The first bootmaking machine ever offered on the market was part of his collection of tools, still alive in his workroom. Knebli had been using some machines for thirty-five to forty years. He always had the most modern machinery for bootmaking in the world, he said. That is, unless they were automated or computerized.

"I taught the people who made the machines," Knebli said. "I would see something and I would tell [the manufacturer] that it is no good like that. I had one fellow from the United States who would send up machines and tell me, 'I make a new kind of machine that would do a job better than before.' But I explained to him that it is no good, that [a certain part] must be on the opposite side."

Ten years later, the machine showed up at an exhibition, but Knebli still wasn't satisfied with the design. The foreman and the factory owner seemed bewildered at what Knebli was trying to tell them, until a workman stepped forward and said he understood.

"The people who work on the machines know what I was talking about exactly," Knebli said. "So the boss told [his employees], 'Make the machine the way Johnny tells you.'"

Knebli passed on his skills to many apprentices, but with today's emphasis on production and profit, there is little call for their hand-crafting skills.

But more and more, the same refrain is heard around the world: skaters are having problems with their boots. At the beginning of the 1996-97 season, world champion Michelle Kwan struggled with boot problems that affected her success with edge jumps, like Salchows and loops. During the summer of 1996, Chen Lu struggled with boots that were either too soft, too small, or too large, before a foot injury took its toll. Kurt Browning has been hampered by boot problems many times as a professional. Boot problems plagued many skaters at the Canadian figure-skating championship in Vancouver in early 1997. Sebastien Britten had the inside of his boots torn out and rebuilt just weeks before the competition. Two-time pairs champion Jean-Michel Bombardier went through four pairs of skates before he found something to his liking. "It's like playing roulette," says skating coach Carol Heiss, speaking of the chase to find a boot that will fit well.

Knebli's handmade boots were enjoyed by generations of skaters, such as Louis Stong. "I wore his skates always," he recalls. "He was one of the last of his kind. There won't be more like him."

"Hand people are dying out altogether," Knebli said sadly. "Skaters are going to go crazy. People now are looking only for money, not anything else. The most important thing that anyone can do is to keep the hand people going in the world.

"If not, what happens later on, God only knows."

Knebli wanted to help, as long as he was able. He was very obliging. But Papa K. died in his pretty home on March 4, 1997, after a day spent toiling over leather and wooden lasts. And with him, an era of fine bootmaking died too.

Coaches: The Guiding Force

$\mathcal{P}$hilippe Pélissier is more expressive, more unusual, than most. Although he is a coach, he is sometimes the most interesting performer at a competition. He is a picture of intense emotion when his pupil, French skater Thierry Cerez, takes to the ice. As Cerez launches into a technical trick of his trade, Pélissier is right with him at rinkside, racing like a snuffing bull up and down the corridor behind the barrier. The camera lenses turn his way, forgetting all about Cerez. For these short minutes, rightly or wrongly, Pélissier is the star.

Whenever the frail-faced Cerez lands, Pélissier jumps, crow-hopping unsmilingly, with a complete absence of inhibition. Cerez lands a triple Axel; Pélissier leaps into the air like a sullen Jack-in-the-box. Cerez mistakenly stabs his mitt onto the ice after a triple toe loop; Pélissier stamps his feet angrily in frustration. He is serious about this. It is as if he were on the ice himself. But he is not. Physically, he cannot help Cerez now. He is powerless, but it is as if he were trying to push his will with his racing heart over the boards into Cerez's pocket. His dark eyes are riveted to Cerez's every move.

Pélissier does not look like a coach. His limp mouse-brown hair is pulled back into an unkempt ponytail. He wears jeans, while others wear leather and wool and furs. Yet he is one of the top coaches in

France, having worked with most of the best in his country: Didier Gailhaguet, Gilles Beyer, Jean-Christophe Simond, Anne-Sophie de Kristoffy. Some of his skating students are now themselves some of France's top coaches. As a skater, he finished fifth at the 1969 European championship. Now his opinions are sought. Apart from his coaching duties, Pélissier works as a skating consultant with Eurosport, the European sports broadcasting network. Pélissier is wonderfully wacky and French and emotional. It takes all kinds to make a coach.

Coaches can be many things: part-time psychologists, surrogate parents, choreographers, music specialists, motivators, confidants, trainers, political gamesters, unrelenting taskmasters. Some are generous-souled mentors who think less of their own victories than the well-being of their students. Some are controlling demons, exerting unquestionable power over their charges. Often skaters spend more time with their coaches than with their parents, peers, or schoolteachers. This gives coaches an extraordinary influence over their students and, with it, an extraordinary responsibility.

Highly esteemed coach Carlo Fassi, who died of a heart attack in March 1997 while working at the world figure-skating championship, always took his responsibilities seriously. In his colourful way, in broken English, he would say that there was a difference between a good coach and a good teacher: a teacher shows a skater how to do a skill correctly, but a coach teaches skills as well as dollops out advice on diet or training, keeps the skating parents away when they become bothersome, makes sure the skater has the right boots and blades for an event, and makes skaters believe in themselves. A coach takes on more responsibility and more personal care than a teacher, according to Fassi.

In the early days of skating, coaches served as chiefs-of-all-trades, picking the music for their skaters' programs, designing the choreography, acting as motivator, as well as teaching skating skills. Today, many coaches still carry out all of these functions. But as skating becomes more competitive and sophisticated, some coaches advise their students – particularly the élite ones – to seek specialized help. Therefore, skaters will often leave their clubs to work with other coaches during a summer-school session to improve their weaknesses before returning to their home club for the season.

Not all coaches are proficient in all areas of skating. In the past, there have been compulsory-figure specialists, such as Karol Divin, the 1962 world silver medallist from the former Czechoslovakia, who helped skaters such as Brian Orser with his tracings. American Kathy Casey is widely known for her knack of teaching jumps to skaters. "She could teach a camel to jump," one of her peers said.

Fassi seemed to have the magic in all the right places. He taught four Olympic champions: Peggy Fleming, Dorothy Hamill, John Curry, and Robin Cousins. Because Fassi was such a popular and busy coach, most people had to "grovel on their knees" to get him to teach them, according to Cousins. But he made each one of his skaters feel as if they were the best, he adds. He treated no two people the same, nor did he train them the same way, adjusting his approach to all of their temperaments and skill levels. He built up an enormous degree of trust with his students, and had all the knowledge of a sport psychologist. "He pumped up my confidence level by 200 per cent," says Romanian skater Cornel Gheorghe, who began to train with Fassi in 1994.

At one point, however, even Fassi felt burned out with the heavy responsibility that comes with coaching élite students. In the early 1990s, he went back to basics for a time, training young children. That is something that almost all coaches do anyway. Skaters with high potential do seek out top coaches, but, most of the time, coaches work with what they have. "There are very few coaches in North America that don't teach all levels of skaters," said Christy Ness, coach of 1992 Olympic champion Kristi Yamaguchi.

These days, even though she is the skating director of the Oakland–U.S. Ice Center in California, Ness, too, is teaching a beginners' class. And she is happy to do it, because she can spot emerging talent more easily and point young skaters in the appropriate directions before they get discouraged or are taught skills incorrectly. "If you get them too late, they have all this excess baggage," she explains.

Although Ness has a salaried position at the club where she works, most coaches are not rink employees. Rinks sell ice time to skating clubs, whose executives hammer out various contracts with a specific number of coaches who will teach there during a season. The contracts will specify if the coach is to work at the club full time or part time. The clubs may guarantee that a resident coach has the exclusive rights to teach students who belong to the club, but, in turn, the coach may have to agree to teach a certain number of group lessons, for which the club pays them. The clubs may also allow freelance coaches to use the facility, but these freelancers have none of the guarantees that come with contracts.

In the beginning, skaters may start with relatively inexpensive group lessons, which they buy from the club (usually ten lessons at a time), but they will not get individual attention. If skaters wish to improve their skills more quickly, they book private lessons with a coach at the club. Private lessons may last fifteen minutes or half an hour, depending on the agreement between skater and coach.

Although the clubs pay coaches for the group lessons they teach, the coach almost always bills the skater directly for private lessons. A very small number of clubs will bill coaches' students for them, but they charge a collection fee of, say, 5 per cent. Former Canadian coach Louis Stong, who used to be a resident coach at the posh Granite Club in Toronto, figured the fee was worth it. "If you get a few bad payers, it's a pretty inconsistent way of living," he says. And it's a daunting task for a coach to do the billing himself. "It's a lot of bookkeeping, if you have thirty-five students," Stong adds.

Some coaches can be very expensive, particularly if they teach in the United States. When Ness first began to ply her trade in the 1970s, as a university student, she earned $4 (U.S.) for a half-hour lesson. Now she, like most of the top coaches in the United States, such as Frank Carroll or Kathy Casey, charge at least $90 (U.S.) an hour. Famous Russian coach Natalia Dubova, who now works in Lake Placid, charges $39 (U.S.) for a twenty-minute lesson (an hourly rate of $107).

The rate for Canadian coaches lags far behind, mostly because a handful of Canada's top coaches refused to increase their prices during an era of galloping inflation during the early 1980s, according to Stong. Apparently, they feared price increases that matched inflation would discourage skaters from taking lessons. Their stand had the effect of depressing the rates all coaches would charge. A lesser-known coach wouldn't dare to charge more than a top coach who was holding the line on prices; they'd lose business quicker than they could say Philippe Candeloro.

While a small handful of Canada's top coaches, like Doug Leigh, trainer of three-time world champion Elvis Stojko, can currently command $60 an hour, most Canadian coaches charge about $40 an hour. "The U.S. coaches laugh at us," Stong says.

Most Canadian coaches do not become wealthy from their work, says Stong, remembering the heady days in the early 1960s when the amount he and his coaching wife, Marijane Stong, earned was enough to put them in the low end of the high-income bracket. In recent years, because coaches' pay has not kept pace with inflation, Stong says their income would now put them in the middle of the middle-income bracket. "We are very conservative shoppers now," he admits. "We don't buy expensive things any more."

At the best of times, coaches did not earn as much as doctors, Stong says. But now plumbers' wages have left the earnings of skating coaches far behind. On top of it, because coaches are not employees – and this holds true in the United States as well – they have no company benefits or pensions. If they fall ill and miss a day of teaching, they earn no money for the lessons lost. Many coaches purchase expensive disability insurance, and buy registered retirement plans as hedges against misfortune and old age – if they are able, Stong says.

To the outsider, their lives seem glamorous as they hustle about during important competitions. At an event, coaches watch over their charges like nervous hens, directing their twice-daily practices, handling all their queries, consulting with doctors if necessary, and hovering over them at pre-practice warm-ups. The days are long; it seems that the coaches are earning their pay.

Yet all the while, they are forfeiting their income, because they are not at home teaching lessons. In other words, they don't get paid for lessons while they are away at competitions. This creates an unfortunate irony for many who dream of coaching a world champion someday: the more successful they are, and the more competitions they attend, the less money they earn. Canadian coach Sheldon Galbraith, who trained a handful of Canadian Olympic and world champions from the 1940s to the 1960s, said his family could not eat the gold medals won by his skaters.

Years later, after Stong had coached world champions such as Barbara Underhill and Paul Martini and Kurt Browning, he understood what Galbraith meant. "Coaching is not an attractive field," Stong says. "It's not a great job." He no longer works as a coach.

Coaches deliver their teachings and exert their influence in a chill, still atmosphere. They spend stupefying amounts of their lives huddling, shuddering for hours in a dank arena, their feet turning to blocks of ice, their minds spinning to keep up with a deluge of rule changes. As the sport evolves, the coaches must adapt to it. Coaching is an important role. But it is not an easy life.

Unlike Philippe Pélissier, Frank Carroll is not an emotional coach.

He stands erect at rinkside, composed, certain of his role, neat and polished. "Maybe I'm emotional at home when I'm alone, when I'm disappointed or devastated about something," he admits. "But never to the outside world and never to my students.

"I'm not emotional in my teaching at all. I keep my teaching as strictly a business. I try to be very professional with my clients. I demand that they treat me professionally and with respect."

Carroll does not tell his students he loves them. He does not put his arms around them and hug them. He does not try to be a parent to the skater. "I think they have a mother and a father," he says. "They would resent my usurping their position. It would be unfair of me to ever drive a wedge between a parent and a skater."

Carroll knows it is unwise to become personally attached to his skaters. "They have been given to me for a very short time and then they're taken away. It would become devastating to me if I became involved emotionally and they moved on."

Setting limits on emotional bonds with students is a lesson he learned while coaching Christopher Bowman, a California-born skater with a high, wild spirit, who failed to reach his ultimate potential because of drug abuse, a problem he eventually admitted. Although the worst problem many coaches face in their relationship with their students is a simple lack of communication or a dislike of each other, the Bowman–Carroll partnership disintegrated into chaos. Carroll found himself in the midst of a horror story, a coach's worst nightmare. Bowman took Carroll through a roller-coaster ride of unpleasant emotions, particularly through the last three years of their relationship. "I think drugs were a dreadful part of his life," Carroll says.

"It was a situation where I was helpless. I would never again work with kids that I knew did drugs. I would never try to help them. They need better than me for help. My being a skating teacher and having some [knowledge of] child psychology and having a teacher's credentials is not enough to deal with drugs. It doesn't work. I don't know how to do it."

But it was difficult not to become attached to Bowman, an engaging scamp with a quick wit and a nose for devilry. To know him was to laugh at him, to want to shake him, all at once. He was a hyperactive child of Hollywood, who grew up too quickly, knowing all of the dark nooks and the roundabouts and the whim-whams of a show-business lifestyle. And Carroll watched Bowman ride the merry-go-round for eighteen years, from the time he was a tiny four-and-a-half-year-old bundle of energy who didn't know his left foot from his right.

"He was adorable," Carroll admits, remembering Bowman in more carefree days. "He was really a baby. He didn't know his outside edge from his inside edge, but he could skate over the ice like a little bat out of hell."

Young Bowman was a natural, Carroll found. It wasn't hard to teach somebody with that much talent. He could imitate anything. Carroll would show Bowman a jump, and he wouldn't know what it was, but he could do it. Bowman would jump up in the air and touch down on command, just as easily as flipping flapjacks. When Carroll got fed up with his antics, he would dump the smirking boy into a trash can.

"He was a delight when he was a baby, very impish and full of fun," Carroll recalls. "It was constant hysterics, with somebody who was that funny and full of life, and that young and mischievous. Well, he was very cute. It was charming."

But as Bowman grew up and his behaviour didn't grow up with him, it was not so charming any more for Carroll, an intelligent coach who guided the careers of world champions Linda Fratianne and, more recently, Michelle Kwan. "It ended up being a very ugly scenario and very painful for me," Carroll admits. "I don't think you can spend eighteen years with somebody, start them out as a baby, spend more time with them than their parents, and not be attached. Christopher skated a lot. I was very attached to him."

The last three years Carroll spent with Bowman were a torment. It was agony for him, seeing the pain in the eyes of Bowman's parents, feeling his own pain when Bowman was totally unreachable – because of drug abuse, Carroll says. "To try to plead and explain, and reach him and help him, and go to the counsellors and psychiatrists and psychologists at the Betty Ford Center, trying to do what you can to help someone. And you see it going nowhere."

Later, Carroll compared notes with Canadian coach Ellen Burka, who, along with Toller Cranston, also dealt with Bowman's excesses: failing to show up for a skating show at a Toronto club, capriciously turning up instead to watch it in a darkened second-storey gallery, a beer in his hand; arriving for work out of shape and overweight; disappearing from the home where he boarded and limping back a day or two later, so badly beaten he ended up in hospital; partying at competitions; locking himself in his hotel room and emptying the mini-bar; undermining his coaches. They all realized that Bowman had a way of chipping away at their self esteem.

At the end of their relationship, Bowman craftily played mind games with his coach, trying to make him feel he was no longer in control. "He would whittle away at my self-esteem," Carroll explains. "It was also beginning to make me sick."

Carroll became alarmed at the anger welling up inside of him, knotting his stomach, furrowing his brow as soon as Bowman would walk into the rink. Sometimes it was because Bowman hadn't bothered to show up for two or three days. Carroll's face would turn red as a bonfire poker. "I'd get angry before I ever said a word to him," he says. "It was immediate anger, resentment. How do you deal with somebody when you're starting out a lesson like that?"

Carroll was so angry that another teacher had to put Bowman through his programs. Carroll couldn't stand to watch the rebellious teen act out for his benefit: stopping deliberately during a routine when he knew his coach did not want him to; missing a jump, pausing, sort of picking up the routine again, all tests to see how far he could push him. "Belittling things," Carroll fumes. "Anything to get my goat, like, 'How far can I go before you pull the plug, Frank? How much am I going to get away with, here, until you start to blow your stack? Let's see you get red in the face.'"

Finally, Carroll could not take the battle of wills any more, particularly since he had left no stone unturned in an effort to help Bowman through his difficulties. "If I feel this way about myself, I'm not going to be any good for anybody. So I thought, 'No, I'm sorry. You're not going to do this to me. If you think you're going to develop the upper hand, and that I'm going to be supplemental in the relationship, you're nuts, kid. I'm bowing out.' I've got to be happy when I go home. I've got to be happy in what I'm doing. I'm not going to be in turmoil because someone else has an illness."

Six months after Carroll ceased coaching Bowman, friends, even some skating judges, remarked to him that he looked ten years younger. "You look fabulous," they said. "Why is this? It must be because of Christopher," they joked. But he knew, in all truth, that letting go of the Bowman tragedies had allowed him to feel better about himself and his career. A great psychological weight had been lifted off his shoulders. Frank Carroll was back in business, free.

"It sounds like I'm painting a terrible picture of Christopher," Carroll said. "And I really don't mean to do that, because Christopher is very funny, very amusing. He can be just darling. He charmed the pants off everybody. He oozes charm. . . . But I was helpless."

Bowman ended his amateur career by being carried off the ice at the 1992 world championship in Oakland, California, having suffered an injury near the end of his long program. Although he was seen as a brilliant heir apparent to 1988 Olympic champion Brian Boitano, Bowman finished fourth at the 1992 Olympics in Albertville. "He was so good, it bored him," four-time world champion Kurt Browning said once. Although as an amateur Bowman denied reports that he had been beaten in Toronto and later in a seedy section of Pittsburgh while out on the prowl for drugs, he eventually recanted his stories and admitted his problems publicly. "I was a human garbage pail," he told "*Sports Illustrated* Television," as he listed the drugs he had tried: LSD, ecstasy, cocaine, heroin.

"Things had turned so bad that they had to admit me to the Betty Ford Center before the 1988 Olympics and get me squared away and all cleaned up," Bowman confessed on the show. He said he spent an "astronomical" amount of money on drugs, and had many serious close calls with overdosing. He never tested positive for the banned substances, because he did not use them during competitions. The United States Figure Skating Association did not conduct random doping tests between events.

Bowman, who says he is now sober and clean, has since married. He's a grinning, enormous bulk of a man, and was last seen charming the pants off viewers as a host for the Rock 'n' Roll Skating Championships on the Fox Network. And Carroll has maintained his sanity.

Even after the relationship between coach and student had been severed, Carroll would watch Bowman in interviews and read his quotes in newspapers with a pang. What he saw in Bowman's words was his own humour, his own wit, his own sharp Irish tongue. It was as if he were listening to himself on a recording. "All those years together, he had picked up so much," Carroll says. "It's like being able to answer a direct attack by somebody and being able to come back with a verbal answer that would devastate people. I have that knack."

Irish people, says Carroll, are masters of sarcasm. Carroll was brought up in an Irish family that used sarcasm to great advantage, as humour. He sees the same wit in Bowman. "There's part of me that is in him that will probably always be there," he says sadly.

Not all coaches use the same teaching techniques or relate the same way to their pupils. The differences are as varied as human emotion. Aside from Christopher Bowman, Frank Carroll has found a technique that appears to work. After all, his methods have produced world champions Linda Fratianne and Michelle Kwan. The relationship between Kwan and Carroll is ideal: Kwan looks to him for strength and direction; Carroll knows how to impart just the right measure of psychology at the opportune moment. Even though China's Chen Lu had skated before Kwan at the 1996 world championship and drawn two perfect marks of 6.0, Carroll knew how to influence Kwan's mindset so that she could step out on the ice and fight for the win without fear. One of Carroll's favourite teaching tools is that very Irish humour.

Although Bowman often scuttled his coach's sense of humour, Carroll generally brings humour into the mix if he has a bad day with a skater. "I try to lighten it up, because sometimes they are too hard on themselves," he says. "If we don't have a sense of humour, what's the point?"

Carroll prefers to use humour over anger and threats. "I'm best at my work when everything is going smoothly and everybody is happy and we're having a good time together," he says. "I hate the gloom-and-doom part of teaching, the threatening, the nastiness, and raising your voice, the negative side of telling people this is wrong." He prefers to be more positive: "You're getting better. You're improving. Tomorrow is another day."

Humour or not, Carroll imposes an iron-clad discipline – "my royal command" he calls it – that skaters must not mess with. "I feel, if I can't train people, then we have no business working together," he says. "If they won't discipline themselves the way I want, then I can't do anything for them at all." Carroll is known for his well-structured sessions; to destroy the structure is to damage his scheme for a skater's progress.

If a skater strays across the line into dawdling territory, Carroll has a personal rule: he tells the skater to take off their skates and leave. He brooks no impertinent remarks, no chatting with others, no stopping in the middle of a routine to do as one pleases. He will hold no hands, spoon no Pablum, he says. There is little room in Carroll's day for skaters with no nerve.

But Carroll always leaves plenty of room for a skater to find redemption. The next day is a new day, and Carroll holds no grudges. "The next day, when they come in, I don't even mention it," he says. "It's the start of another day. The record is clear, *tabula rasa*. Get on with life. Let's see what you're going to do today."

Usually the next day (unless their name is Bowman), skaters apologize to Carroll. And life goes on at the Ice Castle International Training Center in Lake Arrowhead, California.

Other coaches have no sense of humour at all. Sometimes they are psychologically abusive, misusing their power over their students. For several years, Stanislav Zhuk, one of the most heralded coaches in the former Soviet Union, made the life of 1985 world champion Alexander Fadeev a bleak, foreboding experience, with his demands and his black-balling efforts. Olympic pairs champion Irina Rodnina and partner Alexander Zaitsev dumped Zhuk, their long-time coach, after the feisty Rodnina had an argument with him. For the last two years of their amateur career, they skated with Tatiana Tarasova.

Zhuk, a former pairs skater who was the first Russian to compete at the world level, was a powerful figure in the Soviet skating world. All of the major coaches in the Soviet Union divvied up the top students, who had little say about who their instructors would be. That is precisely how Fadeev ended up in Zhuk's stable. "I was drafted," Fadeev says. But the quiet, sandy-haired Fadeev was as unlike Zhuk as rain is from draught. Zhuk was a dark, imposing man. It seemed as if he came straight from Hollywood's central casting department: square jaw, boring eyes peering out from under shaggy eyebrows, stern mien.

"Nobody could get along with him," Fadeev says. "He was very powerful. You had to do exactly what he said, not one step on either side. It's like the army system." He also drank copiously. Zhuk was not keen on allowing his skaters to seek help from another choreographer or coach. Talented program designers like Marina Zoueva, working in the same rink, were off limits. Instead, Zhuk sometimes insisted on designing the choreography himself, though his work was without imagination or creativity. Finally, frustrated, an entire group of skaters left Zhuk *en masse*, an unusual rebellion in a country where, according to Olympic Russian gymnast Olga Korbut, "everyone is supposed to be just like everyone else, like a country full of little broiler chickens." Fadeev eventually left, too. Ekaterina Gordeeva and Sergei Grinkov, who had been trained by Zhuk when they won their first world pairs title in 1986, also found his rule oppressive, and left to skate with another coach.

They all trained in Moscow's Central Red Army Club. Because it was an army club, Fadeev could do his military service while skating there. He would be a captain by the time he left Zhuk. But the set-up of the army club only gave Zhuk more opportunity to wield power. At the end of every season, the club committee held a meeting to tally up the sport results. While Fadeev was still under Zhuk's command, the committee queried Zhuk about why Fadeev had finished only fourth at the 1989 world championship in Paris. "Why did he not finish first or second or third?" they asked Zhuk. Whenever Zhuk's position at the club was imperilled, he sought scapegoats. It didn't take him long to make one of Fadeev. Without hesitation, Zhuk told the meeting how bad Fadeev was, that he didn't train hard enough and partied too much. Because of Zhuk's remarks, the army club decided to punish Fadeev. It put a mark on his army record. He was essentially blacklisted.

Being on the army's blacklist meant that Fadeev could get no favours or privileges. It meant that he would have more difficulties in leaving the country. It meant that, if he wanted to buy a car, he would be placed far down on the waiting list, behind those who had no mark beside their names. "It was like he make a mark on my life," Fadeev says. "It tears me very much."

The system under which Fadeev suffered does not exist any more, although politics have not died. As the sport system and its bountiful government financing collapsed, coaches either left the country or found another way to survive. The system was changing, but Zhuk wasn't. "He tried to do his own thing, but it doesn't work any longer," Fadeev says. "Nobody believed [in] him. He tried to start his own private school, but he had no idea how it work. He had no idea how to organize these things. He's not a person who can easily get somebody else involved to help him organize it. He wants to be number one."

As a coach, Sergei Tchetveroukhin straddled two cultures, two systems, two ways of thinking about how to impart skills to skaters. He was one of the coaches who left the former Soviet Union after its borders opened up. He was unhappy with his life in his homeland. As soon as he had a chance, he accepted a coaching position in Ottawa and moved to Canada with his brother and his sister-in-law, Marina Zoueva. "My reason to leave this country was because I couldn't handle it any more," says Tchetveroukhin, who was the first Soviet male skater to win a world championship medal, back in the 1970s. "I don't trust these people. The same people are in power. [Boris] Yeltsin can't do anything. They're still driving him. The country is very dangerous."

When Tchetveroukhin arrived in Canada, in October 1990, he found the sports systems very different. In both Canada and the Soviet Union, coaches had to be certified. But in Canada, certification is tied to a number of courses that pertain to coaching, like nutrition, competition strategies, music, and choreography. In the Soviet Union, certification and salary levels were tied to results. And coaches were certified every year. One year could be golden. The next could be mud.

"If you don't have results, your salary gets less," Tchetveroukhin explains. "In Canada, if you've got [a certain level of certification], you keep it. Over there, it depends on how you're working. It was quite a bit of pressure." There was little pressure, however, for coaches who had friends in all the right places, connections in the political stratosphere, Tchetveroukhin says. During his coaching career, Tchetveroukhin did not attach himself to the system of favours, he adds.

Tchetveroukhin hadn't actually planned on becoming a figure-skating coach during the years that he skated for the Soviet Union. While he was competing, he was also studying to become an engineer at the Technology Institute in Moscow. Then reality sank in. The salary for engineers in the Soviet Union was very low. Tchetveroukhin had graduated from the university, but it would take many years before his salary would grow into anything respectable. So, when he looked at the opportunities open to him in the skating world, and compared the salaries, the decision was easy. He decided to become a coach. And for the last five years that he lived in the Soviet Union, he also worked as a figure-skating commentator for a television network.

In the western world, élite coaches are paid by the hour or half-hour by each student. But in the former Soviet Union, they were paid a salary. Although parents of skaters at preliminary levels had to pay for lessons, there were no charges for advanced skaters. The sports ministry's intent was that skaters were to be taught in groups, and it didn't matter how many pupils a coach had; the coach would still earn the same wage. A coach could not teach a group of less than eight, or more than sixteen.

But sometimes the Soviet rules didn't fit the task all that comfortably, or well. Coaches were expected to give individual attention to each member of the skating group. "None would have the same ability," Tchetveroukhin says. "They would all be different. Of course, you want to spend more time with the good ones, who want to learn more, do more. But you are not allowed to do it, because students will complain."

Giving individual lessons to a group of two or three, or perhaps even four, students worked very well, Tchetveroukhin recalls. But even in a small group of eight, it was difficult for a coach to apply himself to each of them. "It doesn't work properly like it is supposed to," Tchetveroukhin says. And always hanging over the coaches' heads was the threat of having their certification – and their salaries – cut if their skaters did not produce results.

When he moved to Canada, Tchetveroukhin began to teach in a country that expects a lot of its coaches, too, in ways that the Soviet Union didn't: certification. Even the United States does not have such a rigorous system, although Australia and New Zealand do. The Canadian Figure Skating Association requires its 4,600 coaches to become members. The United States Figure Skating Association does not.

Instead, American coaches have the option to join the Professional Skaters Association (PSA), an association of professional skaters and coaches. Membership is not closed to coaches from outside the United States. Executive director Carole Shulman says more than three thousand coaches from seventeen countries are members, although most are from the United States. Every year, a member can take advantage of the PSA's annual educational conferences. In the fall, coaches can attend free seminars dealing with concerns that face them in an increasingly complex sport world: dealing with agents and parents, choreography, eating disorders, sexual assault.

By contrast, Canada's system of certification is highly structured, and mandatory. Based on a general National Coaching Certification Program used by sixty-two amateur sports in Canada, skating coaches must take time away from their jobs to complete a complex series of courses that takes them from level one to the highest, level five. A coach cannot work at a local CFSA club unless he or she mounts the first level. Just before the Atlanta Summer Olympic Games, the Canadian sport system ruled that a coach could not accompany an athlete to an Olympic Games without level-four certification. At the time of the Winter Olympics in Lillehammer, Norway, in 1994, Canadian coaches needed only level three to accompany their athletes. But with the new rule, a year before the Nagano Olympics in Japan, only about half a dozen figure-skating coaches in Canada had passed the muster. About two hundred more were busy sitting through seminars and doing their homework.

Attaining these levels is no small matter. At each level, a coach has to prove his mettle in theory (sport safety, analysing skills), technical aspects, and practical work. Level one is the least involved. Just to reach the first level, a coach will spend about fourteen hours in seminars poring over skating theory, another thirty hours brushing up on the technical aspects of the sport, and an additional year showing an ability to put what he or she has learned into practice. Not everybody automatically passes the courses. CFSA coaching co-ordinator Carol Rossignol says that, if the work is unsatisfactory, the association will ask the coach to try again before granting certification.

A coach can take from two to three years to complete practical work to achieve level three alone. Attaining level four and even five is another story altogether. The system is so new that all of the eight tasks for level five have not yet been hammered out. To get level four, a coach must complete twelve "tasks," or courses, on different aspects of coaching, complete with theory, technical learning, and practical work.

Most tasks come in the form of an assignment, with a workbook the coach must complete. Some are more time-consuming than others. One task may take only two hours of classroom work. The longest task, an important one involving leadership and ethics, takes five days. Most take nine to ten hours, Rossignol says.

The tasks range from learning about energy systems, strength training, biomechanics, and nutrition to mental preparation for both
coaches and élite athletes. The workbook on music and choreography
asks the coach to submit a videotape, showing music choices and choreography composed for an athlete who is competing at least at a qualifying event for the Canadian championship. The coach is asked to
explain the theme behind the choreography and the various decisions
taken to arrive at the final package.

The task on mental preparation takes a year to complete: the coach
must write a diary of the skater's mental preparation throughout a competitive season. Another task entails getting an international assignment. It involves the least work – perhaps only two hours in a
classroom – but there is a catch. It can't be completed unless a coach has
an athlete who is good enough to get an assignment to an international
competition. "You actually have to take an athlete to get credit for it,"
Rossignol says. "Some people take a long time. People are complaining
about that particular task, because they think [their skaters will] never
get an international assignment."

To make the task more accessible, the CFSA is considering setting up
a system in which a coach could get a credit by attending an international competition as an apprentice, handling certain duties at a competition, and shadowing master coach and skater.

Coaches have widely varying opinions about Canada's strict
coaching-certification system. Coaches of élite skaters are so busy, they
find it difficult to set time aside to take the certification courses, says
Christy Ness, who has worked under both the Canadian and American
systems. Because younger coaches, with fewer responsibilities and
fewer élite students, do have the time, they are getting certification
while master coaches are not, Ness says.

But choreographer Lori Nichol, even though she no longer plans to
act as a coach, continues to take the coaching-certification courses,
finding time in her busy schedule. "I'm very grateful for having taken
those courses," she says. "They started my mind thinking that I had
to have a process and a philosophy. I think a lot of times you start
coaching – at least I had – without any rhyme or reason. . . . These

courses were just a way of giving you insight into developing your own philosophies, and understanding the process of teaching and child development and what they can handle at what stage."

Nichol has already completed more than half a dozen tasks at level four, one of which was a course on understanding the physiological demands on a skater's body. "It's very important for a choreographer to know what a skater's body is experiencing and how to pace a program around their physiological needs," she explains.

For example, some skaters can "sprint" for two minutes before their energy drops. At that point, it is wise for a choreographer or a coach to design a program where the skaters can calm down and catch their wind. Perhaps they need one minute of recovery time before they can pick up the pace again. Some skaters, both for emotional and physiological reasons, need to start their programs slowly and get the feel of the ice first.

In the United States, a coach may gain certification as a master coach by taking an exam and discussing teaching philosophies and technical know-how in front of accredited master coaches. But American coaches don't need to have the rating in order to coach skaters.

Ness leaves no doubt that she prefers the less-formal American system. An American-born coach best known as the guiding hand behind 1992 Olympic champion Kristi Yamaguchi, Ness worked at the Royal Glenora Club in Edmonton, Alberta, for six years. But Ness moved back to the United States in November 1995 to act as skating director at the new Oakland–U.S. Ice Center in California. "The control was the hardest thing for me," she says of the Canadian coaching system. "The biggest difference is that they [CFSA] try to control the coaches more. In the U.S., there isn't so much emphasis on control by the association. They pretty well leave us alone."

The American-based PSA does have a system of educating and even testing its member coaches that the United States Figure Skating Association is looking into adopting into its fold. The pressure to adopt a coaching-education system has come from the U.S. Olympic Committee. But Ness, for one, does not want the United States to follow Canada's strict example. "I'm trying to explain to them what is happening in Canada," says Ness, who took a level-four task course before she left Canada. "The course was fine. I went to the courses over a weekend . . . and I enjoyed it. But it took me probably twenty to twenty-five hours of work after the course to write it."

But it's forced learning that nettles Ness. At a PSA conference in Chicago during the summer of 1996, hundreds of delegates, many of them coaches, attended four or five days of sessions of their own free will, paying their own expenses, she says. Many coaches in Canada attended the sessions, too, she adds. "They wanted to see what was going on, to talk about the current trends, to hear other people speak. Why not let them do that rather than this forced type of learning?"

The Canadian system only promises to get tougher, perhaps for good reason. Carole Rossignol says the CFSA's coaching co-ordinating committee wants to start talking about licensing coaches, as well as certifying them in order to get a firm grip on ethical behaviour. "Ethics is something we will always have problems with," Rossignol says. "If we have licensing, if someone does act in an unethical manner, then you can suspend their licence. As it is now, there's nothing really that we can do if someone is unethical, except give him some kind of a reprimand. It's not like if somebody is speeding, you can give them a ticket."

Ethics involves many issues, but one of the darkest and most frightening is physical and sexual abuse by coaches. In early 1997, the coaching profession in Canada came under a social microscope after Graham James, a respected junior hockey coach, was found guilty of sexually assaulting two young male players under his care. When it turned out that one of them was National Hockey League player Sheldon Kennedy, who had suffered behavioural problems for years after the assaults, the scrutiny became intense. It seemed that sport, one of the biggest contributors to the physical and moral development of youth, had instead sacrificed its youth.

The abuse of trust was more than a rending of a moral code; it was a crime: James was sentenced to three and a half years in prison. Outrage was in the air, as a dirty, silent secret finally was laid bare. Until this, the coach had been untouchable; the young players had been cast adrift on a wave of isolation, frozen in a code of silence. Earlier complaints had a way of falling on deaf ears. Afterwards, everyone denied prior knowledge of James's activities.

But abuse is not hockey-specific. No sport is immune to the event of a coach straying over a line that should never be crossed. Some young athletes feel powerless to refuse a coach's advances or his physical abuse. The horror is that at times parents, swept up into an enchanting whirl, with bank accounts dwindling and visions of gold medals dancing in their heads, don't want to know about something that will derail dreams.

The most public case of sexual and physical abuse in figure skating surrounds German coach Karel Fajfr, former trainer of élite skaters Christina Riegel and Andreas Nischwitz, Heiko Fischer, Cornelia Tesch, and some international-level pairs skaters. A German court found Fajfr, fifty-two, guilty of sexually abusing one teenaged female skater and beating another, and handed him a two-year suspended sentence, banned him from coaching for three years, and ordered him to pay compensation of $5,566 and $6,957 to his two victims. The trial took place in the fall of 1995.

The court found that Fajfr had sexually molested one of his students, who was seventeen at the time, a total of eleven times in 1994. They also found that he kicked, pinched, and choked another skater who was only ten years old when she was entrusted to his care at the Stuttgart training centre in 1986. Once, he injured her so badly, she ended up in hospital. Fajfr denied the charges, but several people testified they had seen him beat skaters.

His main accuser was Nadine Pflaum, a pairs skater who once competed at a world junior championship. She said Fajfr fondled and kissed her breasts several times and regularly suggested they share a bed during their stay in a French alpine training camp. One psychologist told the court that Pflaum was believable.

A prosecutor said that Fajfr would try to push his students by shouting "fat pig" and "stupid cow" at them so loudly that the rink would echo with his cries.

According to news reports, the girl who said she was beaten did not come forward sooner because her father "taught me to mind my own business." The girl did not live with her parents; her father worked far away in the oil fields of the Middle East. The court heard that the father had told Fajfr that he might beat her "like a father" if she refused to obey him.

The court also fined the director of the Stuttgart training centre, Brigette Foell, and her son, Michael (treasurer of the German skating federation), 8,000 German marks each for having knowledge of Fajfr's abuse, but failing to stop him.

German skating officials have denied knowing anything about Fajfr's behaviour.

Although a couple of other skaters came forward to back up Pflaum's accusations, others in the skating world weren't so sure that he was the lion he was painted as. Women's singles skater Astrid Hochstetter, who worked with Fajfr for ten years, said publicly that he had never abused her. He had been her only coach, from age five to fifteen.

"I never saw Karel doing anything wrong," says French team leader Didier Gailhaguet, who uses the same alpine training camp at Orcières, where the abuses allegedly took place. Gailhaguet also considers Fajfr a friend and believes that many other coaches who opposed his behaviour were motivated by jealousy. "He's a strong coach, stronger in the voice than the reality of actions. He's a fighter. I never saw anything wrong with Karel's attitude."

Gailhaguet questions one girl's accusations of horrific beatings, because she had not come forward for almost ten years. "Suddenly she had many friends around her that had trouble with Karel," he says. "He got trapped in something. Probably he didn't handle the whole thing well. I don't know if [the accusations] were right or wrong. I have no idea. I know nothing of what this girl was saying and I know her very well."

No one knows how widespread the problem is of sexual abuse in skating. Carole Shulman of the Professional Skaters Association says that, in the twelve years she has served with the PSA, she knows of only three or four legitimate incidents of sexual misconduct by coaches among her three thousand members. The legitimate cases of abuse

Shulman prefers to keep quiet. When asked details, she bristled and refused to comment.

However, an additional charge against Barbara Fitzgerald, a coach from Cleveland, turned out to be a false accusation, Shulman says. The charges against Fitzgerald were dropped, but not before she lost her coaching job and her reputation. According to Shulman, her income "came to a screeching halt."

Frank Carroll, who heard the story at a PSA conference, says an accusation of sexual misconduct against a coach is one of the worst accusations a skater can make against a person. "Your life is ruined," Carroll says. "I think children can be very manipulative. They're very clever sometimes and very intelligent. If they're really angry at you and they really want to get back at you, and they feel like you've abandoned them or done some terrible things, what is the way that they can get back at you the best? I'm not stupid enough to think that they don't think of these things sometimes."

But, on the other side of a very serious issue, the PSA had also seen a small number of notorious cases with inappropriate behaviour when coaches have abused the trust of a young skater. "That has gone beyond the skating world. That ends up in the court system," Shulman says. These are the cases the skating world doesn't want to talk about. The code of silence continues.

In 1993, Stephen Savino, who won a silver medal at the 1976 world professional championship in Spain, was sentenced to four to twelve years in prison for raping and sexually abusing several of his teenaged skating students in northern New Jersey. Savino pleaded guilty to abusing five girls, four of them students, between the ages of fourteen and seventeen, from 1986 to 1991. The other victim was under the age of eleven. Savino skipped bail once charged, but was located after police received a tip about his whereabouts on a local television program called "Westchester's Most Wanted."

The charges involved rape, sodomy, and endangering the welfare of a child. One teenager said that, when she was fourteen, Savino earned her trust, took her to the movies, gave her some whisky, and raped her. Then he made her believe it was her fault, she told a court. Another victim said Savino was like a father to her.

Although Savino was found guilty on some charges, fifty-five others were dropped as part of a plea bargain.

In 1996, David Stone, fifty-four, a former skating coach at Palm Beach Gardens in Florida, was sentenced to three years in prison after pleading guilty to molesting a female student in 1995 and 1996.

As part of a plea deal, the court dismissed ten other counts of sexual activity with a child in custodial authority.

Prosecutors said Stone gained a psychological hold over the girl when she was twelve, while she was living with Stone and his family in Pompano Beach during her training. That's when they first had sexual relations, detectives said. Later she was molested at hotels and during skating competitions, when Stone would tell chaperones that she had to come to his room to meditate.

The girl's parents said it will take years for their family to recover from Stone's breach of trust. Stone had coached their daughter from the time she was nine years old. Before the girl disclosed the abuse, she had become anorexic.

Stone also must face one year of house arrest and fifteen years' probation. The judge ordered Stone to pay the girl's therapy expenses, and have no unsupervised contact with girls younger than eighteen.

Investigators were shocked at what they heard on a recorded telephone conversation between Stone and the victim, when he tried to persuade her to meet with him.

"His attempt at manipulation was amazing," Assistant State Attorney Scott Cupp told a reporter. "He's involved in transcendental meditation, he was speaking in metaphysical terms. Just going after the mind first, then the body follows."

During the early 1990s, a female figure-skating coach in Edmonton was charged with sexual assault and touching a skating student under the age of fourteen for sexual purposes. The alleged victim was a boy. Although the coach admitted at the trial that the boy stayed overnight with her several times and that they slept together, she was acquitted of two assault charges. The charges of touching resulted in a hung jury and a mistrial. The Crown later stayed the touching charges because of insufficient evidence.

Barbara Fitzgerald only wants peace. In 1990, the mother of one of her skating students, a ten-year-old girl, filed charges against her in every municipality in the Cleveland area in which she worked as a coach. The charges: gross sexual imposition, or improper touching. After Fitzgerald endured two gruelling, tension-filled years – "an absolute nightmare" she calls it – the court dropped the charges. But the false accusation devastated Fitzgerald's life and those of her children. Six years later, she is still picking up the pieces, trying to earn a living as a single mother, supporting three children on an income that has been halved by the unsavoury incident.

"What happened to me changed a lot of people's lives, and how they coach," Fitzgerald says, "Anybody can walk into a police station and make an accusation and file charges. It can ruin your life."

Fitzgerald had never known such horror. She had grown up in a loving home, the daughter of a figure-skating judge. She had a story book childhood, she says. "It really blew everybody out of the water how this could happen. And how could it happen to somebody like me? I thought that I represented everything that was good and wholesome. I prided myself on the fact that a lot of my students have grown up, have families of their own and careers, and I've launched them. To have something like this happen, it was devastating."

She found that she was judged guilty until she could prove herself innocent, she says. She felt that no matter what she tried to tell the police, it didn't matter: she was guilty in their eyes.

When the police arrived to arrest Fitzgerald in front of her skating students, she was mortified. They told her the arrest was necessary, because she had failed to show up at her arraignment on the charges. But Fitzgerald said she knew nothing about the arraignment. Afterwards, she found the court had sent the notices to the wrong address. "And the police won't tell you anything," she says. "I really did not know until after all this was over what allegedly I had been said to have done to this child. I could only go on guessing, from the [police] questioning."

Fitzgerald's world began to fall apart immediately. Two rinks expelled her as a coach before she was even indicted, without giving her a chance to explain. In a very short time, she had no income at all. She had lessons on life she never really wanted to know. She learned how to roll her fingers for printing records. She learned how to stand for a mug shot. In jail, dressed in a bright warm-up suit, she stood out like a forlorn star against a dark night. She ended up spending six hours in a holding cell with thirteen other women accused of anything from prostitution and drug possession to assault with a weapon. One was accused of shooting a woman in the pelvis because she had insisted on coming over to her apartment to sell drugs. The setting was far from the generally safe world of cupcakes and Disney cartoons.

In this cheerless setting, Fitzgerald decided to pass the time by interviewing the other prisoners, asking them what circumstances brought them to the dingy cell. As she was about to speak to a seventh woman, the group turned and said to her: "What you in here for?"

"You're not going to believe this, but . . ." Fitzgerald said, and related her story.

"Something is wrong with this picture," said some, a group made street smart by hard experiences and unfortunate environments. There was something about her manner and her personality, perhaps even her appearance, that made it difficult for them to believe she would have committed such a crime.

To Fitzgerald, the story was "so off the wall, so absurd." She had taught the girl for two years, while working as a part-time coach, preferring to stay at home with her two young children. The girl missed nine weeks of training after breaking her arm in an off-ice accident, but by the time she returned to the rink, Fitzgerald, out of economic necessity, had gone back to work full time and had taken on more students. The change meant that the girl received less attention. "She desperately needed attention," says Fitzgerald.

The last evening the girl spent at the coach's house, she begged and pleaded with her coach not to send her home, Fitzgerald says. "I have to," she told the girl. "I have dinner to prepare and you have homework." The girl had never made such an impassioned request. It was the last Fitzgerald saw of her until she met her again in court.

Fitzgerald said the girl never acted abnormally around her, but she did not realize that the child had apparently fastened onto her attentions in desperation. Fitzgerald feels she missed the signals that the girl was in a problem situation. "I knew nothing of this. I never thought along those lines. I could not figure what I ever could have done to this child."

The case was resolved not with a bang, but a whimper. The girl stuck to her story. Just as Fitzgerald was about to go to trial, lawyers attempted a plea bargain. Fitzgerald staunchly refused, saying she had done nothing wrong. Finally, the judge called her into his chambers and offered her a deal: he would dismiss the charges if she would promise not to sue the police for false arrest, and go for counselling. "I absolutely bristled," she says, pointing out that agreeing to counselling would imply to the public that she needed help for what she had been accused of doing. She protested.

"Just one session of counselling, after all you've been through," the judge told her. "That's all you have to do." Her lawyers talked her into the deal. The case was widely reported in local newspapers, which made much of her agreement to take counselling, she says.

The whole issue should never have gone as far as it did in the first place, because the accusations did not make sense, Fitzgerald says. The police investigated the girl's claims that Fitzgerald's husband had molested the skater as well, but did not pursue it. "It wasn't even possible, because he was with me and the children the whole time [during which she said the incident took place]," Fitzgerald says.

Police reports show that the girl also accused her coach of improperly touching her during a practice. "When you look at that stuff, I don't know how on earth anybody in their right mind could even think that I could do something like that," Fitzgerald says. "It just doesn't make logistical sense. Out on the ice, there's thirty-five people around.

. . . You're out on stage, basically. The police department doesn't understand the circumstances, because they don't skate."

Away from the courts, Fitzgerald's family had to deal with fall-out from the charges. When the girl made the accusations, Fitzgerald was already in the process of divorcing her husband. Lawyers told them to stick together because "it wouldn't look right" if they separated. That led to more stress. Fitzgerald says she lost her appetite for about a year, and dropped twenty pounds. Her children suffered as well. When the issue first flared up, they were four, six, ten, and twenty years old. During the hype of the trial, they dropped their extracurricular activities to duck intrepid reporters. Fitzgerald had to ask teachers in their school not to allow reporters to talk to them. Her ten-year-old son was in an uncomfortable quandary, too. He had been friends with the girl who had accused his mother. They were in the same class at school. But worst of all was the uncertainty. "They didn't know what was going to happen to me," Fitzgerald recalls. Although she initially did not tell her six-year-old son about the accusations, he cleverly figured out that something was wrong.

One night, he marched into her bedroom at 1 A.M. and blurted, "What's going on!" The next day, she gently told him, eliminating as many of the details as she could. "What's going to happen to us?" he asked.

"It has created terrific insecurities," she says. "It has taken me away from my children for a couple of years, paying attention to them, doing things with them. . . . The damage started to appear as time went on."

To Fitzgerald's great surprise, coaches rallied around her in support and even started up a fund to help her. Most of her students' parents stuck with her after the furore subsided. Some took their children elsewhere, but only because Fitzgerald could no longer work in the rinks they wanted to use, she says. Eventually, Fitzgerald filed lawsuits against a couple of municipalities and rinks that had turned her away. She dropped one lawsuit "in the best interests of the community," she says, and eventually settled the other out of court four or five years later.

Although her close friends did not abandon her, more remote acquaintances forbade their children to visit her home. "That hurt," she says. It also hurt her children. "It's a hard lesson to have to teach your children."

The girl continued to skate for several years after making the accusations, but found it difficult to find a coach willing to take her on. One young coach who was unfamiliar with the issue did accept her as a student. But when she discovered the girl's history, she asked that her parents sign an agreement stipulating that one of them must be present during the practice. Whenever the girl skated at a local competition, the rink went silent.

Fitzgerald's trauma has made other coaches ponder their positions with students. Now many of them are aware they should no longer drive their students to competitions or even to the rink. They should no longer share hotel rooms with skaters. They should no longer be alone with skaters. "All the little extras that we as coaches have done in the past that makes coaching special and rewarding, we really can't do any more," Fitzgerald says. "It's incredibly sad.

"There are kids out there that need that nurturing, and that enjoy the sport because of the relationships they establish with their coaches. We spend more time with the students than their parents do. I know my coaches had a marked influence on how I grew up. They were a very important part of how I conduct myself as an adult. The values that they instilled in me certainly have carried over."

Fitzgerald fears that her profession has been changed forever, that now people are on a "witchhunt" to find abusers. When she hears of any similar charges against coaches, her first thought is to remember how important it is that people be judged innocent until proven guilty. At the same time, however, she knows that sexual abuse does occur in figure skating. After Fitzgerald's case made headlines, one of her peers, a male coach in Cleveland, was found guilty of abusing a young male skater and was sent to jail.

Ironically, he was the first person Fitzgerald had called when she was accused by the ten-year-old girl. At the time, she had no idea that the man had been abusing children, she says. "I couldn't understand his silence on the other end [of the telephone line] when I was telling him the nightmare that I was experiencing."

Now she does.

"There are people out there who are abusive, but . . . there has to be some kind of way to differentiate between somebody that is and somebody that isn't without destroying their lives the way that they tried to destroy mine."

In the past year, Fitzgerald has been searching for peace. She is now a single mother trying to raise three children. She does not dwell on the incidents that marred her life. In 1993, the Professional Skaters Association gave its Betty Berens National Spirit Award to Fitzgerald. The award is given to someone who "has given selflessly through her time and talent both on the ice and off to overcome adversity with generosity and love."

But Fitzgerald hasn't quite overcome all the ramifications of the accusations, she says. "It's like a wave that hasn't come to shore yet."

A changing world has put coaches on edge. Now, just like schoolteachers and any other profession that deals with children, coaches are having to relearn appropriate modes of touching. Figure-skating coaches can no longer take for granted the methods they used, without regret or worry, only a short time ago. For them, it is a quandary: instruction has always gone hand in hand with touching.

In recent years, the CFSA has turned to dealing with the issue in its annual meetings. The PSA stages seminars where the problem is discussed. The PSA's Carole Shulman, a former coach, knows that it is an issue that cannot be ignored. "It's very easy for a coach to put their hand on the thigh of a skater and tell them to raise their hips, and to touch their rear end and tell them to tuck it in – only thinking of positioning the body, and not of personal touching," she explains.

"Today you can't do that. Years ago we didn't think about it. Back in my day, it wasn't unusual for a coach to slap a skater on the rear end and say, 'Go out there and skate hard.' Just a little pat. You can't do that today."

Yet the easiest way for a coach to teach students how to position their bodies for a well-pointed three turn or a well-extended spiral is not to explain verbally the parts of the anatomy and where to put them, but to physically put them in the proper position, Shulman says.

It may be easy, but it may not be wise in today's climate. If coach and skater build up a long-term relationship based on unsullied trust, the practice may be more acceptable. But, when in doubt, a coach should ask, says the PSA. Coaches are now being advised to ask the skater's permission to touch them in order to show a body position. "If the child or the parent is comfortable with it, then they know it up front," Shulman says.

The issues swirling around the heads of coaches these days strike at the heart of the teaching methods of a well-respected coach such as Frank Carroll. He describes himself as a hands-on coach. He learned his craft from coaching legend Mirabel Vinson Owen, who was also a hands-on coach. Carroll practises her teachings like a disciple. And he doesn't follow the lead of most other coaches, who hustle to the judges' dais at a competition practice. It is a handy spot, right at rink centre, with a perfect view of their skaters' work and a row of chairs, offering a nestling respite during an hour-long session.

But, because coaches sit at this dais, they are separated from their pupils by not only the rink board, but by the imposing depth of the dais, at least an arm's length away from the skaters. Carroll doesn't sit at the dais. He climbs down into the corner of the rink, away from the dais, so that he is able to lean directly over the rink boards and get closer to his students.

"Total hands-on, that's the way I teach," Carroll says. "That's the way I work with Michelle [Kwan]. . . . I want to grab her. I don't want to say, 'Get your hip in.' I want to put her hip in, and I want her to feel where her hip should be and how her posture should be."

But Carroll's method got him into trouble once – and only once in all of his years of teaching – with the parents of one of his students. It was many years ago, when he was only in his twenties, a young, inexperienced coach. "I had a father say to me once, 'I don't like the way you put your hands on my daughter's hips. Do you need to do that in your teaching? I just don't think that's necessary.'"

Carroll thought the father had a dirty mind, and that he was being accused of having one, too. "Hold it, mister," he told the father. "Don't intimidate me from teaching the way I think is best, the way my methods are. If you have a dirty mind, my relationship with your daughter is over. I don't want to go into a lesson with her again and have to think about what I can do and can't do as a coach. I know I'm a good person."

Carroll's sentiments, however, create a problem in the minds of athlete representatives, such as Ann Peel, chairperson of Athletes Can, a group that gives voice to Canada's amateur athletes. "[A coach's] comfort level isn't the issue," she says. "The issue should be entirely the comfort of the athlete.

"Too much in sport goes on in private behind closed doors. We seem to think there is something sacred behind this coach-athlete relationship – which there is. But there has to be a bond of trust. That trust has to be earned. It's so dangerous when the potential is there for it to be betrayed or violated. Coaches not only have to provide a safe environment, they have to be seen to be providing a safe environment for their athletes. Any action or behaviour that undermines this has got to be considered unacceptable."

From across a yawning canyon of fear, coach and student – and student's parents – peer nervously at each other. It can't be bad for a parent to question a child's safety. Yet, in the absence of malice, a coach feels his methods are compromised. Carroll maintains he just didn't want somebody sitting on the sidelines and analysing whether he is doing something with a dirty thought in his mind, when he's really touching a skater's body to improve their technique.

"I find it better to step out of the situation," Carroll says. "It's a no-win situation for a coach. Once you sense that it's going in that direction, and that there is suspicion, you had better step out of the picture completely. Move on and do the best you can. Those flames are hard to put out."

Coaches these days have to be very careful of their behaviour, Carroll warns. He is careful, too. Coaches are wise not to put themselves in situations where they are alone with their students. "If I have a skater over listening to music in my house, and I'm there alone," Carroll says, "I always make them bring another skater."

Sexual abuse is horror enough. But physical and verbal abuse leaves its mark on young skaters as well. Stories of this kind of abuse by coaches travel the informal skating chat lines like lightning from rod to rod.

One Canadian skater says it took him months to lose the sound of his former coach's yelling, angry, strident voice that rang and rang and rang in his ears. He had switched coaches, but the din from his past lived on in his heart.

Coaches live with stress, too. The talk has always been about the stress on skaters, on parents, on judges. But the coach is a silent monolith, hovering in the rink for extended stretches at a time. Coaches have their own set of hardships: lonely, long hours, cold feet, dank rinks. Coaches of élite skaters have additional worries, too: the responsibility that comes with turning out a top-notch competitor who has all the right programs, tricks, attitudes, nutrition, advice. It can burn out a coach.

Music specialist and former coach Leonore Kay is one of the lucky ones: she found work in skating that got her out of the rink, out of coaching. She couldn't take the life any more. "One of the biggest factors is the cold," she says. "When you get up in the morning, it's cold and it's dark. When you go to the rink, it's cold and it's dark. When you come home at night, it's cold and dark. You spend your whole life being cold and in the dark."

"In the middle of January, you'll be standing in the centre of the ice with a ski suit on and a fur coat and steel under your feet for hours on end. It's unbelievable to me that I didn't realize it until it stopped."

Talk to any coaches by January or February and Kay will guarantee most of them are sick with colds or flu. It's because, she says, the working conditions are so poor and the stress level is so high, as they worry about skaters' tests and competitions. "It's a combination of the teaching cycle and the cold and the teaching environment. These are not optimum working conditions," she says.

Kay says she hasn't been sick since she stopped coaching.

Skaters spend many hours on the ice every day, but coaches spend more. Skaters may be on the ice for one and a half hours at a time, then they move on. The coach stays on for the next group. And sometimes it's tough to keep the spirits up all this time. "It takes a special character to do it," Kay admits. "You have to motivate each skater every fifteen minutes or every half-hour. Most coaches like what they're doing. It's a good thing. It's a challenge, no doubt about that."

Frank Carroll hasn't quit. Wouldn't think of quitting. But it is a very lonely life, he says, his face pale, framed with just the slightest touch of Irish red still, long, thin fingers jammed into his dark coat. "It sounds corny, but there have actually been times in my life when I've cried going to the airport to go on a two-week trip," he admits, remembering countless, endless voyages to figure-skating competitions. Going to a country where he wouldn't understand the language on the television, where it is excessively expensive to do anything, where he wouldn't have time to do anything expensive anyway, where the schedule takes the coach from ice rink to hotel and back again. "After you've done it for thirty-five years, it's a segment out of your life," Carroll says. "This period of time is taken away from me."

There is companionship of sorts on these pilgrimages to competitions: other coaches of other competitors. But they have their own agendas and schedules as well. "It's difficult to get together sometimes with your friends, because you're all working at different hours," Carroll says. "It can be a very, very depressing thing, depending on where your life is at, or if something is bothering you, or if there has been emotional trauma in your family."

In Carroll's case, he may take these trips six or seven times a year. "Then when you return to the rink and you walk in the door, the parents come up to you and say, 'How was your vacation?' They don't really realize what it has taken out of you."

Because skaters' families foot the bill to send coaches to competitions, invariably some complain about the expense. But every time Carroll goes, he says he forfeits two-thirds of his income from lessons lost, eats food he doesn't like, and lives in an uncomfortable, inconvenient hotel room.

On the road, Carroll finds himself at the mercy of local organizing committees that determine his billeting arrangements. He landed in Lethbridge, Alberta, for a Skate Canada competition one year in the middle of a windstorm with gusts up to a hundred miles an hour. This memory has never left him. And his assigned accommodation was not the stuff of Sonja Henie movies, all sparkle and glitz and marble. The barren motor-hotel room had no closets, no dresser drawers for clothes. Instead, there were hooks on the wall to hang clothes and an uncovered rack to store sweaters. A tiny television set perched on a wall shelf. Carroll stared blankly upon entering the bathroom. The ceramic tiles were lined in black mildew. A cheap Formica countertop had yellowed with age. The mirror was cracked down the middle, an omen of bad luck. Someone had attempted repair by plastering thin adhesive tape to the crack. The life of a skating coach may be glamour on the outside, but cheerless in reality.

Once at a world championship in North America, Carroll was assigned to a hotel with a noble name but a salty history. He stepped into his room and immediately spied a bloodstain on the floor. The bed had been well used; the lining of the mattress hung down in shreds to the floor beneath it. The sheets were washed, but they were stained. "There was this great big chair with a hole in it, as if possibly a rat had gnawed it," Carroll recalls. Downstairs, prostitutes roamed the lobby. Carroll's skin crawled. He stayed in the hotel one night before Christopher Bowman's parents, who were paying him to be there, found out. Horrified, they booked another, more respectable, hotel room closer to the rink and gladly paid the price, Carroll says.

"They were wonderful people," recalls Carroll, speaking of Bowman's parents, Joyce and Nelson, an employee of the Los Angeles transportation department. "They never thought a thing about any expense. Anything I wanted was never questioned. Anything for my comfort." Not all parents are so willing to shell out more money for a coach. Some simply can't afford to.

In the hierarchy of room assignments at international competitions, coaches do not appear to rank very highly, Carroll muses. A coach's greatest frustration is in being placed in hotels far removed from where their skaters are staying. In Lethbridge, Carroll was told there was no room for coaches in the hotel where skaters and officials stayed.

"Coaches are usually shlepped off somewhere, like it's unimportant," he says. "Separating an athlete from a coach is a really bad environment, because a lot of times, there are no parents there. The skater and the coach spend a majority of their time together. The team leaders are too busy going to all the practices and taking care of the whole team to be concerned whether Suzie Q. is really going to bed at nine o'clock because she has a 7 A.M. practice the next day. They're not babysitters, yet some of the kids on these teams are very young. They really need to have their coaches in proximity to them at these events."

Carroll speaks from firsthand experience, as coach of Christopher Bowman, who needed twenty-four-hour supervision, he says. And even though Carroll was coach of a current world champion, Michelle Kwan, he was almost placed in a very remote hotel at the Austria Cup in Vienna in the fall of 1996. He thought he had a room at the main hotel, which was only a few minutes' walk from the rink, and the team leader had even checked on its status and pronounced it ready. But quicker than it takes to fall from a quadruple toe loop, the hotel gave the room away and Carroll found himself without a place to stay. Organizers decided to put him up in a hotel that was a forty-minute drive from the rink – and Carroll had no mode of transportation. "It was up to me to take a taxicab, back and forth," he says.

The situation was onerous. Carroll had three competitors at the Vienna event, with three different schedules. He had to be on the ice from 7 A.M. until 4:30 or 5 P.M. for practices. Competitions were in the evening. He was told that the hotel could not help him.

The American team leader set to work. As Carroll sat in the lobby for two hours, she arranged to double up some of the male skaters and free up one single room that the U.S. team had in its block. "If it wasn't for her efforts, I would have been stuck," Carroll says. "Austria is expensive. It would have meant a $25 cab fare – one way – back and forth all week long."

Carroll is not alone in this shuffle and jumble. Other coaches find themselves strung out in remote hotels, struggling to accomplish their tasks. Carroll says it is discouraging. "I spend my life in this sport, every day on the ice, ten to twelve hours a day. Trying to do this right, try-ing to teach people how to skate, or make them champions. Then you go to a competition and the organizing committee and the officials say,

'You're only a coach. It's not important that you're in the hotel with your skater.'

"You want to scream."

Every coach comes to his or her profession in different ways. Most of them are former skaters. At one time, when skaters retired as amateurs and they wished to remain part of the skating world, they had few choices: join a show such as Ice Follies or Ice Capades, or become a coach. A retired skater either took one of the choices or left the sport to pursue another career. At least a coaching job held the promise of future employment, unlike the shows. But these days, there are far more opportunities for skaters who leave the Olympic-eligible world. Ask most élite skaters about their plans following retirement, and they will quickly say they want to join one of the professional skating tours, perhaps even get into broadcasting. Few say they want to be coaches when they finish. In some ways, it's not exactly a great job. Even years ago, when the amateur world was different, neither Frank Carroll nor Christy Ness set their childhood sights on becoming a teacher of skating.

Carroll didn't become a coach on purpose. Instead, he aimed to become an actor or a lawyer. He came from a family of educators, but all he knew when he was a small boy growing up in Massachusetts was that he loved to skate. It was a passion that affected the rest of his life, although he didn't know it then. Skating was magic. He skated outdoors in the winter when the ponds froze over in his home town of Worcester. When the frost was in the air, Carroll was on the ice, at a place aptly called Crystal Park. He'd put his skates on in the morning and skate until nightfall in this dreamy place, until his father went looking for him and sent the fantasy reeling with his screams: "Frank! Where are you? It's time for your dinner!"

In Frank's boyhood, during the 1950s, there were no televised skating events. No Peggy Fleming specials, no Rock 'n' Roll Championships hosted by a Christopher Bowman, no Tonya Harding reruns. There were only newsreels in the movie houses. To the young Carroll's great delight, the cinemas in his town would run films showing skating champions such as Dick Button, Sonya Klopfer, and Barbara Ann Scott. "I used to break into a sweat," Carroll says. "I'd get so excited I could barely sit there. I wanted to do that sport so badly, and there were no opportunities to do it." He had not yet entered his teens.

But the lack of opportunities didn't stop Carroll from dreaming. "I just died to skate," he says. It all started when he bought a pair of figure skates in a local sporting-goods store. He was probably the first boy to own a pair of male figure skates in Worcester, but he didn't really know how to skate – not with any skill.

Fate was on his side, however. Out of the blue, town leaders announced they were building a new ice rink, a few strokes and a Salchow from Carroll's home. Carroll found that, if he crossed his neighbour's back yard and hopped their fence, he was there. He followed this adventurous path every day and hung out at the site, waiting for the rink to be built. He watched every pipe go into the building. He watched every piece of flooring from what was a former roller rink get hoisted out.

The owner-manager of the new rink, Lars Andersen, noticed the slight, redheaded boy and wondered, "Who is this weird little kid?" The kid was there every day, talking constantly about skating. Andersen developed a soft spot for him. "He was immensely kind to me," Carroll recalls. When the rink finally opened, Carroll was the first skater on ice. Andersen gave him a key to the rink and said, "Frank, any time there is nothing going on, and there's no hockey and there's no public skating, it's yours." It was a great gift for a kid with stars in his eyes. "I was a little kid, maybe thirteen years old, and I had my own key to a private ice rink," he says.

At the time, since there were few skaters in the town and Worcester had no hockey club, Carroll had unlimited time to practise his passion. "Instead of learning how to do the figures . . . I'd go out there on clean sheets of ice and skate all over it. I didn't know anything about school figures or how to go about being a competitive skater."

One day, a skating teacher arrived, with basic skills and a kind heart. Carroll was really on his way. He knew all the skating terms. He knew what flips and Salchows were – though he didn't know how to do any of them. Mind you, he had his own book-learned ideas. When the coach saw Carroll's fancy tricks, she was aghast. His methods were all totally wrong. Gradually, she made them right. A teacher had set Carroll on the right path.

The most memorable part of Carroll's skating career centred on his next teacher, Mirabel Vinson Owen, a nine-time U.S. women's champion, a six-time U.S. pairs champion, a world silver medallist behind Sonja Henie in 1928, and an Olympic bronze medallist in 1932. She later became the first female sportswriter for the *New York Times*. Vinson Owen died in the 1961 air disaster that killed the entire U.S. skating team over Belgium, en route to the world championship in Prague.

Vinson Owen became the most important influence on Carroll's life, a goddess of instruction, deportment, and bright intelligence. "I give her credit for [being] the coach I am," Carroll says. "Whatever I've developed in skating is really because of Mirabel. Without her, I would have been nothing.

"She was the smartest woman I ever met in my life," Carroll says. Vinson had graduated *magna cum laude* from Radcliffe, one of the most prestigious women's colleges in the United States.

"She was a genius. A total absolute genius," he says. "In fact, she's the only woman I've ever been afraid of in my entire life. She scared me to death. Not the principal in my high school. Not the nuns in the school I had. I would stand up and argue with them over religion, tell them what I believed about the Catholic faith and what I didn't. Whether they were horrified or hit me or screamed at me, they didn't scare me. But Mirabel scared the crap out of me. The reason for that was that I felt that her mind was better than my mind. And that frightened me."

Carroll thought he was bright and clever. (Choreographer Lori Nichol, who works extensively with him, classifies him as a genius.) But he had never met anybody like Vinson, who could look at him and see through him.

Carroll took lessons from Vinson Owen, and eventually lived in her house in Winchester, Massachusetts, on weekends. Her two daughters, Laurence, who was killed in the same plane crash as her mother, and "little Mirabel," became his close friends. Vinson Owen was more than a skating teacher to him. She was a mentor, an educator, an example. Her lessons went far beyond how to execute an Axel jump. On the way to the rink, they would talk about philosophers like Descartes and St. Thomas Aquinas and argue their merits. They would talk about the difference in pronunciation between ecclesiastical and classical Latin. None of it was the usual pre-practice ramble of skaters. "She knew about everything," Carroll says. "It wasn't just skating with her. She cared about your whole development as a human being."

Her most important lesson, Carroll says, went beyond spirals and spins. Vinson Owen taught him to take responsibility for his own life and not to blame others for his losses and shortcomings. It was a lesson he needed, Carroll admits. "I was brought up in a background where you were always looking for political or ethnic or religion issues as . . . the cause of prejudice or favouritism or discrimination."

"Get off that kick," Vinson would bluntly tell Carroll. "Accept the responsibility for your life yourself. Blame no one or nothing for what you become or what you do."

Now, Carroll tries to pass the same lesson on to his skaters. "Don't look at your parents," he tells them. "Don't come to me if you've had a bad performance. Don't blame the skates or the ice. Look to yourself to find what went wrong."

Every experience in a coach's life lays the groundwork for his or her skills and attitudes. Not all of the experiences come from skating. Perhaps some of them get a taste of the dance or music or acting worlds, aside from the technical lessons they learned as a skater. Skating is all these worlds rolled into one. Some coaches have strengths in certain areas, depending on their personalities or interests. Sometimes, without knowing it, a potential coach gets his teaching education from off-ice interests.

Even with Mirabel Vinson Owen's example, Frank Carroll did not turn to coaching – at least not immediately after his amateur career came to an end. For a time, he signed with Ice Follies, but that, too, came to an end in 1964. Carroll was at a turning point in his life. He was accepted into the University of San Francisco's law school, but he decided he didn't want to end up sitting behind a desk, flipping through legal documents. A stronger lure was Hollywood. He had friends who appeared in movies, and that, like skating, was magic, too. He went to Los Angeles, stayed with friends, and got a few bit parts in films.

The first piece of advice he got was to enhance the muscles of his upper body. His lower body was finely tuned from his work with Ice Follies. Carroll listened. He spent many hours every day working out in the gym. This work produced one happy result. "I was in every beach-blanket picture that was ever made by Universal," he says. There was Carroll, a moving statue in the background.

"I did some terrible movies," he admits. One of them, *The Loved One*, was not too bad, he ponders. But mostly, his acting career was a joke. "I would go to a cattle call auditioning for a part," he says. "I'd walk into this room and there'd be fifty other guys, every one of them fantastic-looking, every one of them trained in New York, every one of them gone through university drama schools. Everybody had experience. I thought, 'What am I doing? I don't have a chance in hell.'"

Carroll spent his days drifting from gymnasium in the morning to beach in the afternoon. During the afternoon, he started teaching skating lessons to pick up some extra income. His students started to do well at competitions. He was a very good teacher, right away, because of his past, with Vinson Owen as a mentor; teachers can actually teach others to become good teachers, too, because of their methods in making them understand what they are doing. "Every one of her students could have become a teacher because they had that training," Carroll says. "They could teach in a minute. If they didn't understand everything they were supposed to do and they had a bad lesson, she'd give them holy hell. You had to turn around and repeat everything and explain it to her in detail. And if you couldn't, you had to sit down that night and write it out like an essay."

Eventually, Carroll found that teaching gave him more fulfilment than being a performer or an actor. Once he thought about it, he found performing in a show disappointing. "In the days when I performed in Ice Follies, we did one number all year long with one costume," he says. "It was very monotonous to me. I felt like kind of a wind-up toy at Christmastime that you'd push through a curtain.

"To see development, to see the seeds you plant in people and to be able to get them to grow, or to teach them a technique that eventually developed and grew and they became very fine, gave me that intellectual satisfaction that was lacking when I was a performer."

Like Frank Carroll, Christy Ness admits she kind of fell into a career as a skating coach. It was not a career she had planned. She was not a high-ranking élite skater, although she skated with reasonable resolve. The coaching option perhaps came to the fore because her other career choices were only vaguely defined. She drifted into typing, when her mother enrolled her in a business school. She went to study at the University of California at Berkeley in 1970, starting out with a major in mathematics, floating into English, and eventually to sociology. Then, outside the university, she drifted into coaching. But "it wasn't something where I had sat down for years and thought, 'I want to be a coach,'" she says.

Ness did not have a mentor, as Carroll did. Her first coach was Gene Turner, the 1940 and 1941 U.S. men's champion, who never had a chance to compete at a world championship during the war years. As a professional, he had skated with Sonja Henie. But at the time that Ness – whose name then was Kjarsgaard – took lessons from Turner, he was not teaching many jumps at all.

"I was thirteen or fourteen before I learned how to do anything," Ness says. "I'd wandered up through juvenile as a young child just skating around, not knowing what I'd done. I didn't give it much thought. It certainly didn't worry me."

Suddenly, when she arrived at a level where she had to do some jumps, a coaching change was necessary. But even after she made it, she always found it difficult to learn jumps as an older child. She made it to the U.S. championships at the novice level, and just missed qualifying at the junior level. "But I always really loved to skate," she says.

As her life outside skating continued, Ness began to coach as a hobby. Her first class, when she was nineteen, was a horror. "It was probably the hardest one I ever taught," she admits. She was faced with a group of Girl Scouts, all friends, who really didn't want Ness as their coach. "To get respect and to get them to listen was terribly hard," she says.

After that, she began to teach private lessons. She found out she could pass on the skills necessary to do a single flip jump or a single Axel. That's when a career as a coach became a little more interesting. And that's when Ness began to plan her school schedule around the skating lessons she wanted to teach. "I did a lot of manoeuvring, let me tell you," she says. "I'd get the notes and go home and study. It sounds terrible."

By this time, she was teaching from four to five hours a day, making a comfortable living on the side. And her skaters were doing well. One year after she graduated from Berkeley, she had a skater qualify for U.S. championships. Five years later, she coached a skater to win important junior-level competitions in St. Gervais, France, and Obertsdorf, Germany.

Ness built her own reputation, right from the beginning. "I was lucky, because the kids began to do well," she says. When they did, Ness scuttled an idea to go to law school.

"I really enjoyed it," she says. "And I didn't do much else. I didn't take very many vacations – if any. In 1979, a vacation would be a trip to worlds [championships]. I really did learn a lot. To keep up with current trends, you have to keep seeing stuff. If you don't, you become out-dated." On her "vacation," Ness would sit and watch every practice she could. So absorbed was she in what she saw in the rink, she saw little of the cities she visited.

Ness's wanderings brought her to a chance meeting at a training camp with a spindly, wispy skater called Kristi Yamaguchi, who wanted to skate – not necessarily to become an Olympic champion, but because she loved the costumes that went with the job. Like Ness's career, even their relationship began in a low-key manner. When tiny Yamaguchi told Ness her name was Kristi, Ness replied, simply, "My name is

Christy, too." That sealed the beginning of a coaching-student relationship that ended with Yamaguchi winning two world titles and the
Olympic gold medal in 1992.

Ness began teaching Yamaguchi, at age nine, on a part-time basis,
partly because Yamaguchi's previous coach had handed over the torch,
in unusual fashion, to Ness. "Most coaches don't do that," Ness says.
Others had been warning the Yamaguchis that, if she transferred to
Ness, who had built up a lot of students at the time, she would be only
a small fish in a big skating pond, and Ness wouldn't have time to focus
on her talents. "That's because the other coaches wanted to teach her,"
Ness says. "All coaches run into that." In the coaching world, whispers
of advice sometimes carry self-interested biases.

What Ness inherited was a young skater who "cheated" her Axels
and double Salchow jumps – in other words, Yamaguchi would try to
land jumps without completing the rotation. For the first six months
of their relationship, the pair – blonde-haired Ness and dark-eyed
Yamaguchi – worked on jumping during public skating sessions.

"She was minute," Ness recalls of the little girl with braces on her
teeth who weighed all of forty-eight to fifty-two pounds at her first
national championship. "She was funny as could be, just because she
was so minute and so quick. You'd have to slow her down when she
went to a competition, because all of a sudden, she'd speed everything
up. You'd have to actually calm her down." When Yamaguchi started
skating pairs with Rudy Galindo, he would gasp in exasperation. "I
can't keep up," he'd say. She would unexpectedly change rhythms when
the chips were down.

Looking back, it was impossible to determine how far Yamaguchi
would go, Ness says. But she always listened intently to instruction.
Ness would give her a lesson, and, when she met with her the next time,
she could tell that the girl had worked on the skills she had been shown.
"There was some follow-through on the lessons, which doesn't happen
all the time," Ness says.

Then came the week that Yamaguchi won the pairs event with
Galindo one night at the 1988 world junior championship in Brisbane,
Australia, then came back the next night to win the women's title, too.

At that point Ness saw something special in Yamaguchi's eyes. "That was the first time that I saw what inner drive she had," Ness says. "I could just see it in her face. I could just feel it. I had never really seen that strength of determination before. Maybe she had it all along, and I just hadn't seen it."

Coaches live in hope for such determination from a skater. They try, but there is no guarantee that they can instil the quality in their pupils. Over this, they have little control.

Paul Wirtz is not just a coach. He is a coach with family ties. Aggressive and intent, Wirtz has spent years learning the unusual boundaries of his job, training younger brother Kris, a Canadian silver medallist in pairs with partner, Kristy Sargeant. It is a complex relationship, where sibling rivalry and arm-in-arm brotherhood have to take second place to order and discipline, striving and pushing. It is not an easy trade-off.

"It was very difficult for me," Paul says. "I've never been able to be the brother." With three other brothers and a sister, he watched wistfully as a close relationship developed between Kris and a brother who played golf or between Kris and his sister. "I could never get that close," he admits. "If I got that close, I would lose the leadership."

As a young boy, Kris wanted a close relationship with Paul, a skater who was eleven years his senior. It bothered him that Paul put it out of his reach. "He would always complain to my mom that he loved [me], and [that I] would have nothing to do with him."

Kris was an emotional being, like his father, Günter, an amiable German-born entrepreneur with an open heart and a Tyrolean hat that he wears to every competition. Paul, on the other hand, could stick his emotions in a hind pocket when he wanted to. The family dynamics were unusual: there were five children within six years in age, then eleven years later, Kris came along, the youngest, a blond tagalong with a happy spirit.

The age difference between Paul and Kris also worked to separate them emotionally. Paul pursued his skating career in Toronto while his young brother was growing up hundreds of miles away. "When I came home, I hadn't really been a part of who he was," Paul says.

When Paul began to coach his younger brother, he was twenty-three years old, Kris twelve. By the time Kris was sixteen, Paul had already turned him into the novice pairs champion of Canada. But the success didn't come without a lot of family stress. "When I first started, I was very young and inexperienced," Paul says of his coaching exper-tise. "My teaching skills weren't exactly honed, or my managerial skills, or my skills in tact." The brothers Wirtz bumped along, lurching into psychological ruts and potholes for years as they both learned.

Kris had tried everything at once: singles, pairs, dance. He even played hockey for a while. When Paul had returned from Toronto, he had become an itinerant coach in Northern Ontario, bouncing from small town to town to teach a growing number of pupils, and he was not always around to oversee his brother's peripatetic passions. So he had to work quickly and intensely when he was at home in an effort to bring his late-starting brother up to snuff. If Kris hadn't been his brother, he admitted, he couldn't have been so intense about his work.

With Kris, Paul had more control over the way he taught than he had with other students. Rightly or wrongly, he said, he was less afraid to crack the whip at his brother, since he was less apt to lose him as a pupil. And, in the beginning, Paul could get a little aggressive with his brother. For instance, if Kris landed a jump and did not prop-erly point his toe, "he was made to do it," Paul says. Too many skaters fail to point their toe, but by gum, his own brother was not going to fall into that trap.

Paul learned that this method of coaching did not always work the way he had hoped. Kris did not respond at all well to Paul's bearish tack. Kris was a happy-go-lucky type, one who never wished to rock the boat. A late starter in figure skating, he understood that he wanted to reach the upper echelon of skating as quickly as possible, but he was hurt by Paul's manner. "He would shut off," Paul says. "The aggression wasn't good with him, but I would get results." What he didn't get was an easy relationship with his brother.

Had he handled his brother in a less-brusque manner, Paul believes he would also have produced results. "But I think when you're dealing with family, it's very easy to get caught up in it," he admits. "You know you're not going to lose this athlete. You know you want him up there as fast as you can [get him there]. Sometimes coaches don't push skaters as hard because they don't want to lose the athletes. They try to use a little more psychology and work around it."

Paul's aggression arose from his emotions. "Your emotions can get in the way, especially when you're young and inexperienced," he says. Today, if he were to start training Kristy Sargeant's little daughter, Triston, or the children of his other brothers, Paul said he would treat them differently.

The tie that bound the skating family together was Paul and Kris's mother, Jane, a schoolteacher in Northern Ontario. She was a calming influence, a mother who could read hearts. And she understood her role in rocky situations: as a buffer between brothers. Both Paul and Kris turned to her for advice; she had a way with child psychology. "One good thing about my mom and dad that I don't sometimes see in a situation like this, is that they are very loving and understanding people," Paul says.

But it was Jane who understood and cleared the path to growth – for Kris as an athlete and a teenager, for Paul as a teacher. "I'm really lucky that my mother is the person she is," Paul says. "I can always hear her. She would always listen to me when I would get really revved. Then I would cool down and we would talk. And she could show me both sides."

Paul says that he has seen coaches who teach their own children gradually lose their objectivity. They will not hear the "other side." He has heard coaches speak of their skating children constantly, with an obsession that is blatant to everyone but them. "It doesn't even matter if I say that that's happening," Paul says. "When you're in it, you're in it." Sometimes it creeps up on them. It doesn't start out as an obsession. "If she skates, she skates," the coach might say of his daughter. "If she doesn't, she doesn't." No pressure. But when she picks up her shiny white skates and lands the first Axel, the parent-coach's heart swells: he has given birth again.

But the dream doesn't always go smoothly. Paul says he has seen parent-coaches "lose it" so profoundly with their children that they finally turn them over to other coaches. That move sometimes doesn't work either. "When I hear them talk, it's as if they're teaching them anyway," Paul says. Paul's mother was a calm third-party influence, albeit a close one, who could wedge reason between emotion and skater. It is her kind of influence that Surya Bonaly may be lacking in being coached by her mother. "They have not had a control group around them," Paul says. "[Mother] was a soft, quiet control, someone who would always be there when I completely lost it."

And Paul lost it when Kris reached his adventurous teens. At eighteen, Kris wanted a closer look at life. But Paul's expectations of how diligently Kris needed to train did not match his brother's will. And Kris began to question Paul's knowledge of technique. "It was not pretty," Paul says, thinking of a few brotherly dustups in an apartment they shared in Montreal. "Things got physical."

The problems flared up again during the 1995-96 season; Paul was less than happy with his brother's attitude and training habits. But they worked through it. "[Things are] fifty thousand times better than worlds [in Edmonton]," Kris said the following season. "We're working towards a common goal now. Before he used to see something in me and I never felt it. After a little bit of success and a feeling that, geez, I could be in this game, I felt now we were working together.

"He's there for Kristy and me any time. If we have a personal problem bothering us, we just talk to him and he'll listen. He's a great friend. He's not just a coach.

"Like any relationship, we've been through the highs and lows together. We hit a few lows. The highs have been good. All of a sudden, we realize what makes each other tick. We know what ticks each other [off], so we don't push those buttons. He knows how to get the most out of me and Kristy. I could have quit a few years ago with a bad taste in my mouth about my brother and my family, but nope."

But the lows were very nerve-racking for the whole family. The atmosphere became so tense that, several times, the family meetings at Christmas could quickly "turn upside down," Paul says. "It was always my mother who sat back and watched and listened, as I'm sure three or four or five Christmases were ruined."

When the fraternal storms subsided, Jane would calmly deliver her sensible advice, reminding her sons of the steps that they must take in order to progress, that growth was coming, that they should all stay calm and build towards national championships. Collars loosened. Everybody ate cake.

"Then I look at Mrs. Bonaly," Paul says. "She's so caught up in a twist. There was never anybody there close to her to be the buffer. I can see how it can go out of control."

He has seen a parent lose objectivity, firsthand. Kris skated pairs with Stacey Ball, then her sister, Sherry, and ended up in disagreement with their mother, who made all their skating outfits. When Mrs. Ball made Kris a bright-pink tuxedo the year he skated at the Albertville Olympics, Paul flinched. Afterwards, when Paul insisted that he have the outfits designed and made properly, Sherry's mother objected: she did not like the outfits she had not made. There was an uncomfortable stand-off. Paul suggested that he cease coaching the pair and send them instead to an American training centre – on the condition that the parent not live in the same city as the daughter. That was not an option acceptable to the Ball family. The pairs partnership split, basically over a disagreement about costumes.

The situation haunted Paul for several years. "Sometimes I would blame myself," he says.

In the midst of all the drang, however, came Paul's mother's calm voice. "What's best for Kris right now?" she would say. "Do you think it will help him later on in life, with the decision you have made?"

With his mother's help, Paul had to make calm decisions about what was best for his brother. "To actually take that step is a very hard one," Paul admits. "You have to think, 'Maybe I'm on fast-forward here, and this is not going to help anybody.'"

Paul sees that, despite the problems, coaching a family member does have its advantages, however. Paul has found that he can manage the future of his brother's career much more easily than he can with a skater who is not related to him. For example, Paul could see that Kris was no longer going to progress and thrive while competing as a singles skater unless he could master a triple Axel. At the time, Kris had been skating against – and defeating – the likes of Sebastien Britten, Elvis Stojko, and Marcus Christensen. It would have been easy to continue, buoyed by the current results. "I told my parents, it was over, finished," Paul says. "In a couple of years everybody would need triple Axels." He was right. Kris never mastered a triple Axel and the need for one became paramount. Britten and Christensen never mastered the jump either, and never advanced on the world stage, but Stojko did. Parents of another skater might not have been so willing to accept Paul's advice, particularly if the skater had been defeating his opponents – at the moment. Paul was able to steer his brother into another discipline, early enough so that he could succeed in it.

With singles skating no longer a valid option, Paul didn't want to lose any time; he turned Kris into strictly a pairs skater. "There are some calls I would like to make with other skaters, but I know they wouldn't accept it," Paul says. "It would have to be more gradual. With your own brother, you can make those decisions quicker. . . . I was able to manoeuvre [Kris's career]. You can manage them the way you want." Last year, Kris and his partner, Kristy, finished second in the short program of a major international competition, defeating the world's gold and silver medallists. "I think the best years of Kris and Kristy are yet to come," he says.

And so may the best years of the two brothers, knotted together by a sport, whether they like it or not. Right now, they seem to like it. In spite of their difficulties together in the beginning, they have become support systems for each other, probably for life. "[This is] maybe what people would really like their brothers and sisters to be," Paul says. "We're always there for each other. He has more faith in me than he's ever had."

Kris can call Paul at any time of the night. When Paul is in Europe at a competition, Kris looks after his car at home. Every day, Paul sets aside three hours of his time for Kris and his partner. "The trust is there for both of us, and the results are getting better and better," Paul says. It is a family tie that neither wishes to undo.

"I wouldn't have skated without him," Kris says.

All coaches are part-time psychologists, out of necessity. Sometimes they need psychology to inspire a skater. Sometimes they need it for themselves, to deal with problem parents. The skating world has changed so dramatically that it's becoming more difficult for coaches to bring skaters – and their parents – back down to earth, says the PSA's Carole Shulman. "And even if you're not a world-calibre skater, there are parents out there who think their children are. It's very difficult to teach a skater that there is something really important in life, and that it's not skating."

Christy Ness, at least, had some of the necessary tools to cope with these ignominious bumps along a coach's path. She graduated in sociology. It's not surprising that one of her senior papers was entitled "Competitive Figure Skaters and their Parents." In it, she tried to outline why a parent pushes or does not push a child in the sport. Is it because they did not find success in their own lives? she wondered.

"Every coach has dealt with parents they considered pushy, from all walks of life," she says. "From one woman who had a PhD and was really pushy to other people who had no accomplishments of their own. It's hard to tell."

Over the past few years, Ness says she has been very fortunate; she has had no problem parents at all. That may be an indirect result of her experience as a coach. As you get older, she says, it gets a lot easier to deal with parents. "For one thing, you're not younger than they are," Ness points out. "When I first started coaching, I was younger than they were by a lot. . . . As a new coach, it's difficult to get respect."

Ness had some of her most difficult and demanding mothers when she started coaching, she recalls. "They wanted their children to succeed at all costs. They thought they could buy it." At one point, she taught two young skaters who ended up arguing about whose parent had more money to spend on lessons.

Ness says she doesn't mind suggestions from parents, but she had to deal with some parents who interfered with her attempt to do her job. In one case, a skating family turned into skating authorities as soon as their teenaged daughter began to do well at the international level. Nice enough people, Ness muses, but advice started to come from all directions. Every single day, every single session, every single minute, the mother was at the rink to watch the practices.

Some children become so programmed to perform with their parents in the background, Ness says, that they look to their parents after every jump – like Surya Bonaly. When things got hard with one skater she had, it always seemed to be harder when the mother was around. Yet Ness believes that skaters, who eventually have to face the music at centre ice, alone, must learn to think on their own and become self-sufficient.

With all the questioning, doubt is born. "If [parents] don't have faith in the coach, and they keep questioning the coach, so does the child," Ness says. "You have to have that mutual respect and trust. That must be at the core of every relationship. If you don't have that, and it starts to deteriorate, it doesn't work."

Now that Ness is a more experienced coach, she is more apt to walk away from coaching challenges she will not win. "You realize it's not going to work in the end," she says. "It's not worth it."

At one point in his life, Frank Carroll had no telephone. For three years, he lived in utter peace, no ringing interrupting his meals, his music, his time away from the rink. He was the young hotshot coach on the block, producing top skaters, and the peace was just fine with him: it kept overanxious parents from climbing into his private life. Before he had his phone disconnected, he got calls at all hours. Once he got a call at 2:30 A.M. from a mother in the San Fernando Valley, asking if her nine-year-old could take lessons from him.

"Are you crazy?" Carroll said abruptly. "I'm in bed and I have to get up at 4:30."

"I thought this was the only time that I could get through to you," the woman said. That was it, the straw that broke Carroll's patience. "This is nuts, if I can't sleep through the night," he said. His phone was disconnected almost immediately.

Some parents cross a line that Carroll cannot bear, a line that he energetically defends to maintain his sanity. "Some parents are all-consuming if you allow them to be," he says. "They expect you to be devoted twenty-four hours a day and to think about their child like they think about their child. They think you should be worrying about the neckline on her dress. And whether she had a fight with Johnny at the rink and whose fault it was. And is she really psychologically ready to do this, and is her double Axel really rotating properly, or why hasn't she got her double Axel. They would like to discuss this sort of thing with you for hours. A costume can be an hour-long conversation on the phone."

Parents don't understand that these things are out of line, Carroll says. It is up to him to draw the line. And in his mind, Carroll has developed an unusual ability to shut off one part of his life when he enters the other. He owns two homes, one in Palm Springs, California, and the other in Lake Arrowhead, California, where he works at the Ice Castle International Training Center. "They are two places that shall never meet in my mind," he said.

Most of his friends have never seen him on skates, or have never been in an ice rink. When they are together, they do not talk about skating. They are not interested in figure skating. This is fine with Carroll. He would go crazy otherwise, he says.

Being an older coach, Carroll has built up a system, with confidence, to deal with his intense kind of work. "I think when you are young in this sport, [parents] expect you to be there when they snap their fingers," he says. "They expect you to be concerned about everything. But when you get older like I am, or like Carlo Fassi [now deceased], or Peter Burrows, or Carol Heiss, I think we're a little more intimidating, because [we've] done this so long."

As for Carroll, he thinks it would be nice to have another world champion. But if he doesn't, it won't be the end of the world for him. "Life goes on, with or without," he says, a coach who has met all the strange shadows of the sport and lived to talk about them.

Not all coaches think like world pairs champion John Nicks. He trains skaters so that they don't need him any more. Intentionally, he wishes to make himself unnecessary as a coach, to fade further into the background as the years go by. In the general world, coaches are loath to lose clients. But Nicks welcomes it; if he doesn't lose a client he believes that he has not done his job.

Two-time world pairs medallists Jenni Meno and Todd Sand of the United States began to fashion much of their choreography and choose their own music as they became contenders on the international scene. Their coach, John Nicks, who also developed Tai Babilonia and Randy Gardner, didn't mind.

"They know that my coaching philosophy is that . . . a coach's job is to ensure that, as the years go on, the athlete gets more and more independent of the coach, of the parents, of everybody else, until they are an entity in and of themselves. When they get to that stage, they are the complete competitor.

"If you relied on anybody or anything and that's taken away from you, you've got a problem. That starts with a ten-year-old who has a teddy bear at rinkside and then one day it's not there any more and she falls flat on her face six times. The successful athlete is the one who is very self-confident and [relies] only on their own abilities.

"It's very much like if you have children, or young teenagers, you should gradually give them their independence and authority. You can't give it to them all at once. But through those formative years, you teach them how to handle themselves."

A lot of Nicks's colleagues don't agree with his philosophy, perhaps for obvious reasons. But his philosophy makes a lot of sense. The best coach may be one who gradually makes himself obsolete.

Powdered Sugar: Makeup on Ice

Quick as a wink, a puff comes out, plumping its flesh-coloured cargo of powder onto a fresh face, an athletic face. It's makeup time in the figure-skating world. Cosmetic enhancement is an inescapable part of a sport that has become a television darling and a big-business showstopper, bright lights and all. And makeup artist Linda Bradley has watched it grow. From her perch at the makeup table, she has witnessed the launching of a thousand ships.

When Bradley competed as a medal-winning ice dancer in Canada during the 1970s, makeup was almost an afterthought, an impromptu, informal lesson given by a coach before showtime. But now, makeup has become such an integral part of the painted sport, particularly at the élite level, that Bradley has set up her own business, aptly called The Artistic Impression Makeup Company, to give seminars and consultations to skaters, some as young as six years old. A full-time makeup artist at a Toronto television station, Bradley has also developed her own line of cosmetics for skaters.

Bradley affirms that, although there was an emphasis on makeup during her skating heyday, nobody taught skaters how to apply it properly. "We were just going on what the coach said," she notes. "We were always told [by the coach] to put on the red lipstick and the red blush and a little bit of mascara. That was about it."

Often, if the coach were female, she'd rummage through her handbag, pull out her own lipstick tube, and hand it over. Now, the more high-profile the competition, the more exacting the makeup application. Many skaters carry their own makeup kits, juggling skate blades with lipliners and eyeshadows. As surely as the females of the sport learn Axels and Salchows, they also learn to enhance the shape of a cheekbone or a brow. Many become young experts. Most athletes learn how to apply their own makeup, peering into mirrors at makeshift tables, learning the skills from whomever they can. Young, childlike Michelle Kwan emerged from a summer show tour all the wiser, having observed over the shoulders of her older peers, such as Oksana Baiul and Nancy Kerrigan. "I learned from the best," she says, her eyes newly asparkle, her cheeks glowing with soft dust.

As the sport of figure skating has become more popular, so has its image become more important. Fan interest in the sport began to climb in the run-up to the 1988 Olympics in Calgary. And nine years ago – coinciding with that interest – Bradley's seminars started. She would give skaters a list of products to buy to re-create the look she put together in the classroom. But, three years ago, when she discovered that they weren't buying the recommended products, but the cheapest ones they could find in drug stores, she also founded her cosmetics line for skaters. It is Bradley's way of contributing to an artistic impression, that part of skating in which judges look for skills that go beyond technical accomplishments.

Bradley learned all about the skating side of artistic impression while competing in ice-dancing events. In 1970, when she won the Canadian junior title with partner Kevin Cottam, now a well-known choreographer, her name was Linda Roe.

She and Cottam finished fourth at the senior level, but then Cottam called it quits, deciding to pursue a solo career. After that, she teamed up with Michael Bradley, her future husband.

Together, the new partnership finished third at the Canadian championship for three consecutive years until they finally decided they had little incentive to continue. In those days, Canada sent only the top two dance teams to world championships.

At age twenty, they turned professional, declined an offer to skate with Ice Follies in faraway Taiwan, and went to British Columbia to teach for a year. By chance, a Vancouver entrepreneur, with the help of two American backers, formed a touring show called The New Ice Generation. "It was a great concept," Bradley says. "It wasn't a dog-and-pony show like the Ice Capades and the Ice Follies were at that time. We were competitive skaters going into an ice show. We wanted to really skate. This little show offered us the opportunity to do that."

The show toured all the tiny towns in the western Canadian provinces until it folded in 1976. Back the Bradleys went to Toronto, and they were lucky again. A new television show, called "Stars on Ice," began airing on CTV on Tuesday nights. The Bradleys were principal and chorus skaters with the show until 1981.

All the time they were doing the show, working in a television environment, Bradley set her sights on a career in makeup. "I had no experience at all when I started," she admits. "I wanted to get some experience, so I called cosmetic companies. There weren't the schools then that there are now. The only school that offered anything to do with makeup was Seneca [College in Toronto], and it was more of a merchandising course, about how to display cosmetics. It was more for retail. I didn't want that."

These days, the Yellow Pages are chock-full of the names of schools or outfits, many of them private, where prospective makeup artists may learn the trade. But Bradley had no such advantages. So she got creative. She was persistent. It wasn't easy, but she talked someone at the Canadian Broadcasting Corporation into giving her the names of senior makeup artists who worked there. She was lucky enough to be accepted by one of them as an apprentice. Bradley paid for the privilege.

"It was a fabulous, wonderful experience," she says. "It was far more hands-on and intense and shorter than it would have been if I had enrolled in a two-year course in school." Bradley learned her craft the old way, from the ground up. At first she was a gofer, sprinting for sponges and brushes. She was not allowed to do makeup.

That changed when the CBC filmed a production of the National Ballet of Canada. Bradley was ecstatic when she was given the chance to apply the body makeup to principal dancers such as Karen Kain and Frank Augustyn. Body makeup was needed on any exposed skin – other than the face. The former skater was still considered too inexperienced to work on facial makeup.

At the time, Bradley was only a casual worker at CBC. Whenever a staff member was ill, the CBC would give her a call and she would drop everything and head to the studios. Still, she landed plenty of chances to work on CBC's popular television series, such as "Mr. Dressup," "The Tommy Hunter Show," "The King of Kensington," and "Front Page Challenge," during the glory years of the public network.

"It was a great initiation into the business," she says. "It was a good time to be involved with CBC."

Her career in makeup was temporarily put on hold when she and her husband decided to distance themselves from skating. The young couple decided to move back to Linda's hometown of Victoria, B.C., where her husband got "a real job" working with Moore's Business Forms. Linda became a mother, and started a catering business.

"We got completely away from skating for four years," she recalls. "We needed that kind of break. Both of us grew up with skating, then we married each other, and all our friends were skaters. We just needed to get away."

The couple made a major effort to make the break with skating – but weren't entirely successful. Bradley continued to teach skating on weekends, just to make ends meet.

When her husband's firm transferred him back to Toronto, Bradley rejuvenated her cosmetics career, but this time in the tough freelance world, fighting for work on commercial jobs and on some television series. In 1987 she was hired full time by CFTO television, a CTV affiliate in Toronto. She ended up working in the same studio where "Stars on Ice" had been filmed years before. For a makeup artist, the studio environment can be less exciting, but more secure, than the freelance life, a difficult, competitive business indeed, Bradley confirms.

Currently, outside of the studio, Bradley shakes her stardust and friendly advice over the heads of skaters trained by Doug Leigh (coach of Elvis Stojko and 1996 Canadian champion Jennifer Robinson), dance coach Roy Bradshaw, a former British champion, and others. Clubs or coaches call her in to give seminars, so that skaters are well equipped to do their own makeup with a degree of professionalism when competition time rolls around. Some coaches see Bradley's work as yet another aid, another piece of the jigsaw puzzle to be admired by judges and audiences – a small part some of them don't fully comprehend.

"Coaches aren't experts in everything," Bradley says. "They can't be expected to know everything. Some of the women coaches will know more than the men about makeup, obviously, but some of the men coaches know absolutely nothing."

First, Bradley teaches technique to skaters in a group seminar. Afterwards, some skaters request a private, individual consultation, so that Bradley may coordinate their cosmetic look to their costumes.

Bradley brings the best of all worlds to her sideline job. "I know makeup," she says. "I'm a professional makeup artist, and I was a professional skater, so I know what skaters need in terms of intensity of makeup."

Because Bradley also did makeup for the benefit of television cameras, she knows what skaters need during competitions that are widely and increasingly televised. The cameras roll on long, panoramic shots of a skater on the ice: but they also capture facial close-ups, and details, right down to the tears in the kiss-and-cry area, where skaters await their marks. The makeup a skater wears has to work in both situations: making facial expressions visible to people high up in the stands, and yet not caked on in such a heavy, theatrical way that television viewers are taken aback at the sight during close-ups.

In Bradley's eyes, a polished elegance suits a skater who wants to be seen as an athlete, rather than as an entertainer gobbed in greasepaint. After all, athletes compete; they want to be taken seriously by judges, by spectators. Yet, some of the Russian skaters really don't care how theatrical they look, she says. "It's amazing how some of our Canadian teams are wanting to copy what's being done more in the European world, where it seems that the theatrical look is very much in, especially with ice dancers."

Theatrical makeup, Bradley says, is more intense, more like what spectators would see on stage: big eyes, pronounced cheeks, even shading on the men. "It's not called a natural makeup," she adds. Russians Maia Usova and Alexander Zhulin are the perfect examples of skaters who use a theatrical style of makeup.

Bradley's *beau idéal* is a skater with lustre and becoming bloom. Two who have recently made impressive transformations are American Michelle Kwan, during the year she became world champion, and Shae-Lynn Bourne, the Canadian ice dancer who blossomed during the 1996-97 season, with elegant costumes and more-professional makeup. "She's come a long way," Bradley says of Bourne. "She is really looking beautiful."

Kwan now looks "absolutely stunning," says Bradley, in her transformation from little girl with a big bow in her hair to big girl with a sleek, glowing look. Bradley is so impressed with Kwan's appearance that she had assumed the Californian has worked with a professional, when actually she has learned from other skaters. Whatever the source, the end result is pleasing. "I think the goal of skating is to look polished, professional, and classy," Bradley sums up. "And I think she has done all of that. It's not gaudy at all. It's just a very polished, refined look.

"I think it's one thing skaters need to keep in mind – that they are athletes. I try to [stress] that with the kids that I'm doing seminars for. But, unfortunately, it's sometimes the coaches that want them to look more theatrical."

Bradley plies her trade in the world of precision skating as well, and she has plenty of customers. One precision team would fill up a seminar room in a sitting: up to twenty-four skaters make up a crew that strives for unity of movement and the creation of unique patterns on the ice. It is a discipline of skating that has boomed in recent years – so much so that its first world championships will be held in the year 2000. But its direction has gone decidedly theatrical, Bradley said. She is "amazed" at how gaudy their makeup has become during national and international competitions.

"I don't know why," Bradley says. "I guess it's just a whole part of that element of skating. They want it to be very dramatic and theatrical."

Precision judges have told her that they would prefer that competitors move away from the theatrical element, Bradley says. "But as much as they say that, it's the teams that are theatrical that are winning the competitions. So the ones coming up underneath them think that if that's what's winning, then this is what they need to do."

Young girls on teams have taken to dying their hair colour so that they all match. They spray their hair black, or put glitter in their hair. "I guess it's fun for the kids," Bradley says. "When it comes down to it, that's what it's all about. Although when thousands and thousands of dollars are being spent on it, it becomes very competitive. They have international competitions now, and they compete over in Norway, and elsewhere in Europe. We can't just say it's fun any more. It isn't."

Even young children have found that out. Bradley has given makeup seminars to children as young as six years old. And she has given more precise individual makeup consultations to ten-year-olds. "They are all being told to wear makeup," Bradley says. At Skate Canada in Kitchener during the fall of 1996, even the tiny flower retrievers were rouged and puffed. So was one little blond boy.

Bradley says young children who toil at competitions in the television environment with its bright lights need some makeup, because their features tend to be so fair. While skating far out on the ice, their blond eyebrows and eyelashes and light features disappear in the burn of the bright lights shining on white ice. "With young ones like that, it's just a matter of bringing those features out, so that they appear," Bradley says. "It's not to make them look older than their years in any way."

Bradley prefers skaters to look their age. She will not advise a ten-year-old skater to look fifteen. Or a fifteen-year-old to look twenty.

Some fifteen-year-olds already do look twenty, even without makeup, she concedes. "In skating, you're looking at such gorgeous people. And with athletes in general, their skin is always so good and they're always such healthy-looking kids. It's just amazing, when you put a little bit of makeup on them, how gorgeous they look. They're like professional models."

As long as television and showbiz are part of skating, there will always be people like Linda Bradley, imparting her knowledge on mascara and foundation and shadows, stirring up the pot of comeliness.

Judges: In the Hot Seats

*J*udges take a lot of heat. They make winners out of skaters, but they often fight a losing battle – against country, against the International Skating Union (ISU), which has the power to discipline and suspend them, against skaters, against fans, against the media, against referees, even against neighbours and acquaintances. Much of figure skating's most controversial lore has been hatched on the judge's bench, over some placing or another. Judges can be the agents of politics, but they can also be the victims of politics.

German judge Elfriede Beyer has seen much from her perch on the judges' stand. She has doled out marks and placings at ten world championships and two Olympic Games. The tall, slender woman from Frankfurt, whose other passion is flying planes, never shrinks from her duties. "I felt always nervous," she admits. "But it is a great feeling, when you get announced and they say you are the judge from Germany. Also, with the power of the audience, it makes you really proud to be a judge, to say, 'This is the gold medal, this is the silver medal, this is the bronze medal.'"

But there is little doubt that the skating judges of the world sweat it out when they think of their responsibilities. In the early hours of one Calgary Olympic morn, Canadian judge Dennis McFarlane looked at his reflection in a mirror and wondered why he was putting himself through such a pressure cooker, possibly facing the censure of nineteen thousand fans in the Calgary Saddledome, all with opinions and judgements of their own. Yet, he has been a high-level judge for forty years, and has never received a letter of reprimand from the ISU for a questionable mark or placing.

McFarlane was on a panel at the 1992 Albertville Olympics in France when judging controversies rattled viewers back home. When the judges finally returned, their morale was at a all-time low.

"We had a lot of people who got really discouraged afterwards," recalls Jackie Stell-Buckingham, technical director at the Canadian Figure Skating Association (CFSA). "They got dumped on." Their friends, relatives, workmates, and whoever else knew they were judges were all over them, demanding that they justify their decisions.

"Then [the judges] start to think, 'Why do I do this? Am I a mental case? I could take two extra weeks' holidays and spend the time with my family and not get hassled by every person I know.'"

Another Canadian judge, Susan Heffernan, was not enthralled when her mother suggested she become a judge at the age of sixteen. "No way," she said. "Everybody hates judges." But now Heffernan has joined the ranks of the judges who, in most countries, are unpaid volunteers. Although most get their expenses covered at skating events, many forfeit paycheques from regular jobs when they take time off work to go to competitions. Beyer managed by working overtime hours at her job in the personnel department at a bank in Germany. Once, an understanding employer gave her three extra free days to go to an Olympic Games. For Beyer, it was like winning the lottery.

Beyer's enjoyment of small mercies is understandable, considering how difficult it is to become a high-level judge, how exacting and tension-ridden the task is, and how much personal time a would-be judge forfeits to learn the skills necessary to sit on an Olympic panel. It can take twenty-five years to become a judge at the world or Olympic level in Canada – fifteen if the judge already has a skating background. First, they judge primary skating tests, and only gradually advance through the various levels by attending special judges' clinics, taking oral and written tests, acting as trial judges, testing their mettle before they take on the actual task.

Finally, to be allowed to work at a world championship, a judge must have participated in an ISU seminar at least once in four years, and this seminar is a fearsome hurdle to clear. There is a series of tough oral and written tests, on which they must achieve a mark of 84 per cent or higher, and then endure eighteen hours of questioning from top international experts to defend every mark they give during a live judging competition.

Since July 1, 1994, ice-dancing judges who wish to mark the international competitions (events other than world or Olympic competitions) are subject to even more stringent scrutiny because of recent controversies over decisions. New judges are on probation for two years following their first international appointment. After the two-year period is up, the judge must have earned at least one favourable judging report from a referee in an international event, such as Skate Canada or the Cup of Russia, in order to continue judging at that level.

All of these judges must answer to referees, who administer the rules of figure skating at an event. A referee is an experienced judge who graduates to take on ultimate responsibility for the running of the actual competition. To become an international referee, an applicant must have been an international judge for four years (in dance, the requirement is only three).

To oversee the judging of an Olympic or world event (a position referred to as an ISU referee), the would-be referee must have been an Olympic- or world-championship-level judge for four years and an international referee for four years. ISU referees are the most experienced bench-sitters of all, directing the event from their positions in the middle of the judging dais, with judges sitting on either side.

The responsibilities of the referee are many: overseeing the draws for skating positions at an event; checking that the ice is ready; ensuring that each group of skaters gets the proper warm-up time; or making certain that the correct marks flash up on electronic boards. They rule on what skaters do if they encounter problems while performing, such as a broken boot lace or music that stops in mid-routine.

In the interests of skaters' safety, a referee will blow a whistle signalling skaters to stop skating in mid-performance.

Referees also mark each event, along with the judges, although their work does not count in the actual tally. Instead, their marks serve as reference points, to determine if a judge's marks or placings are out of line.

However, to avoid influencing the judges, referees are to keep their marks to themselves until the event is over, when they meet with judges to discuss their work. There, the referee may ask judges for verbal explanations of their marks. Or, if a judge has issued marks that referees feel are unusual, they may ask the judge for a written explanation.

Afterwards, referees do plenty of homework. They pore over each mark issued by every judge and submit reports to the technical committees of the ISU. Some referees have been known to spend up to five hours at this job, all on a volunteer basis. A judge's reputation lies in their hands. The ISU can suspend a judge, basing its decision on information from the reports.

Referees will not always be able to watch every second of a skater's program, like judges do, because they may have to deal with various technical details while a skater is actually performing. Sometimes they may rethink their own marks and evaluations after the heat of the competition; again, their marks and placings serve only as a guide.

"Referees are not meant to be ogres," says one long-time referee. "Their job is to be a manager of people and help them along." Ideally, they put judges at ease, helping them to do their work. And, after an event, they also offer advice to skaters, apprising them of rule infractions or judges' opinions of their skate.

In the end, the fundamental task of judges, with the help of their referees, is to make a judgement of the routines offered up by skaters, using a marking procedure that is a complex system of points and placings. The scale of marks in Olympic-eligible competition ranges from 0.0 (not skated) to 6.0 (perfect and flawless). One of the least-understood aspects of judging is that the mark itself is less important than where a judge actually rates one skater in relation to another. For example, one judge may seem to have given lower marks to a particular skater than other judges on the panel, but the marks may still be the judge's first-place marks; the judge may have used a lower marking scale, tending to hand out low marks to all skaters.

Judges give two marks for each performance: the first for technical merit, the second for presentation or artistic impression, a complex mark that takes into account how a skater interprets the music of the program, using body line and movement. The placement of a skater is determined by adding together the two marks and comparing them to the totals awarded by other judges. These placements are called ordinals.

If at least five of nine judges place a skater first in a segment of a competition, then the skater has finished first in that portion of the event. But the results get more difficult to determine if no skater wins a majority of firsts. The winner is then determined by the number of first- and second-place ordinals they have in relation to another skater. If that doesn't work, the accountants take the sum of the first- and second-place ordinals, and the skater with the lowest sum wins.

In singles and pairs skating, competitors take part in a short program that is about two minutes and forty seconds long and a long program that is four and a half minutes in length. The short program is a tension-filled event, because judges deduct points if skaters fail to complete, or make mistakes on, eight prescribed elements, such as a death spiral, a triple jump, a lift, or a spin.

Judges mark the long program very differently from the short by giving skaters credit for skating skills and abilities, rather than making point deductions. The long program is also called a free-skating program, because a skater can include any element he or she wishes, as long as it is legal. (Back flips, for example, are illegal in Olympic-eligible competition.) The short program is worth one-third of the final mark, while the long is worth two-thirds.

Ice dancing operates under slightly different rules, with one or two compulsory dances done to prescribed steps and music (worth 20 per cent of the final mark), an original dance, skated to an annually prescribed "rhythm" or theme such as jive or waltz (30 per cent), and a free dance, allowing a skater freedom of music choice and rhythms (50 per cent). For the 1997-98 Olympic season, the ISU has changed the name of the original dance to the original set pattern, reflecting yet more restrictions placed on the middle portion of the dance event. Indeed, judges must keep abreast of rules that change year by year.

In light of all of these complexities, judges are under great stress. Judges do more than count up the number of times a skater falls on his or her backside during a competition. They look at a complicated series of skills in order to make their placings – and they get only ten to fifteen seconds to make up their minds about what marks to offer after a skater has taken a final bow.

It is a life of few washroom breaks – particularly in an event with thirty to forty skaters – of long hours of intense concentration, and, other than a few pleasantries, of keeping to themselves. According to ISU rules, judges aren't allowed to speak to each other at skating events. They can discuss the event only with the referee and the assistant referee.

"That means, for obvious reasons, you can't go around trying to influence people," says Canadian judge Sally Rehorick, who started to judge skating more than twenty-five years ago as a way of staying in the sport after her skating career ended. "Judges from twenty to twenty-five years ago all recount these horror stories of the approach behind the scenes: 'If you do this for my skater, I'll do this for yours.' It just doesn't happen now."

Suzanne (Morrow) Francis was a victim of the horror stories when she competed at the Olympics as a singles and pairs skater for Canada in 1948 and 1952. As a pairs skater, with partner Wally Distelmeyer, she won an Olympic bronze medal in 1948; they are credited as being the first to perform a death spiral the way it is seen today, with the woman's head nearly brushing the ice and the man pivoting in a tight circle, acting as the anchor for the woman's sweep.

But in 1948, there were plenty of off-ice rumblings that suggested Morrow and Distelmeyer were victims of alleged judging deals involving Belgian and Austrian pairs. Of course, that meant that Morrow and Distelmeyer's placement was predetermined, at least by some judges, before they set foot on the ice.

Yet Morrow and Distelmeyer were hardly undeserving of a look by honest judges. Highly respected British skating competitor, judge, and author Captain T. D. Richardson wrote in one of his books, *Ice*

Skating (1956), that Morrow and Distelmeyer were "certainly unlucky not to gain a title on this side of the Atlantic." Several non-working judges told newspaper columnists that Morrow and Distelmeyer should have been both Olympic and world champions that year. The skating world often referred to them as the "uncrowned Olympic champions of 1948."

Morrow and Distelmeyer weren't the only ones who apparently found themselves at the short end of the mark hierarchy that season. The father of the top U.S. pair, Karol and Peter Kennedy, was dismayed that his offspring had finished only sixth at the 1948 Olympics in St. Moritz, particularly since they had been good enough to finish second at the world championship the previous year. He set out to prove the marking discrepancies with his camera at the world championship that followed in Davos, Switzerland.

Kennedy told reporters that he had photographed the pairs event and could prove that the winning Belgian pair had fallen, that an Austrian pair had stumbled, and that Morrow and Distelmeyer were flawless. Mysteriously, his camera disappeared from his room and was returned later, but with the film removed. The Belgian judge placed the Canadians fourth at the 1948 Olympics Games, even though an American judge placed them first, and three other judges a clear second. Sadly, the Canadian judge placed Morrow and Distelmeyer in a tie for second, a move which effectively cost them an Olympic silver medal.

At the world championship, the Belgians won, and Morrow and Distelmeyer were third. The Kennedys finished fourth.

At the 1952 Olympic Games in Oslo, the judges were at it again, swapping placements with vigour. In the decade following the Second World War, the Austrians were the brokers of scheming, as they tried desperately to hold onto their fading glory days, during which Austrian skaters had led the sport. Austrian skaters had been winning world medals since the world figure-skating championship was established in 1896.

According to Suzanne Francis, in 1952 an Austrian judge approached her mother – who was Canadian team leader at the time – with a complicated deal. He told her that, if the Canadian judge would

support Austrian skater Helmut Seibt to finish in second place behind
the eventual winner, American Dick Button, he would ensure that a
German–Austrian bloc of judges placed Francis to finish second in the
women's event.

The Austrian said that, if the Canadians were not interested in the
plan, they could make the same deal with American judges to elevate
U.S. skater Tenley Albright to second place, past both Francis and 1951
U.S. champion Sonya Klopfer (now Dunfield), who were both ranked
ahead of Albright.

After discussing the issue with the Canadian judge, Norman
Gregory, Francis's mother told the Austrian that she did not want to
win that way, and refused to participate in the deal. Gregory later wrote
a letter to Francis's mother, telling her that he could not take action
against the Austrian dealing unless she could produce a third-party
witness.

As it turned out, Seibt won the Olympic silver medal behind Button,
although he finished fourth at the world championship the same year.
And Albright won the Olympic silver medal that year, too, behind
British skater Jeannette Altwegg, while Klopfer finished fourth. At the
world championship later that year, Klopfer was second; Albright withdrew partway through. Francis finished sixth at the 1952 Olympics as a
singles skater, and fourth at the world championship.

"It goes on and on," Francis sighs, thinking of the old judging
intrigues.

Most judges now say that the growth of television coverage during
the 1960s and the dropping of compulsory figures after 1990 provided
certain cures for the judging ploys. Compulsory figures are the exacting
tracings that are variations of a figure eight, sometimes even with three
lobes instead of two. A good figure is lined up well, with no lopsided
lobes and each tracing of the figure (up to three) must be exactly on top
of previous tracings. In the years before television, judges could scheme
with impunity, because it was difficult to tell a good figure from a poor
one without going right onto the ice, standing directly over it, and
peering at it closely. Spectators wouldn't make a fuss: they were usually
unaware of the quality of the tracings.

But with growing worldwide audiences watching every move and mark, plotting became more difficult. "Long gone are the days when groups of judges would meet in a room and plan their strategy," Francis says. "And gone are the days of the out-and-out approaches for trading off, at least as far as I know. . . . I know for sure that, in school figures, the business of passing a judge and getting down to examine turns and whispering what mark to give, those days are gone. I really do think they [the ISU] are making an effort to clean things up. They are trying different things. They're going to have to."

But plotting still exists. During the past couple of decades, the pressure has continued to come from Soviet or Russian coaches, and particularly before figures were abolished. Elfriede Beyer judged at two Olympics. At both events, Soviets approached her to ask for favours.

Beyer remembers the 1980 Lake Placid Olympics with some amusement. She was well aware that the fur-capped Soviet contingent wanted to talk with her, to persuade her to look favourably upon multiple world champions Irina Rodnina and Alexander Zaitsev, who had taken the previous year off when Rodnina gave birth to their son. In their absence, American pair Tai Babilonia and Randy Gardner had won the 1979 world championship. The Soviets wanted to ensure there was no contest between the two pairs at the Olympics.

Beyer was assigned to judge the men's event, as well as the pairs, and she also knew the Soviets were anxious to get their first men's Olympic gold medal with Vladimir Kovalev, who had won silver at the previous Olympics. Visions of placements danced in their heads.

"They were trying to get to me, to talk to me and find out what I was thinking about placements," Beyer recalls. "But I would always say, 'I don't have time now. I have to go to practice.'"

Beyer had a good excuse. Although she had originally been assigned to the event as a judge, the West German team leader died ten days before the Olympics started. She and another German judge were pressed into service as team leaders at the last minute, doubling their duties. "So I always said, 'I have to look after the skaters,'" Beyer says with a grin.

Four times the Soviets tried to approach Beyer, and four times she was able to slip away, busier than a centipede on a hunger march. But the fifth time, the Soviet judge cornered her when she was at dinner. She plopped herself beside Beyer and invited her to their bungalow for caviar and champagne. This time, Beyer had no excuses to offer.

Beyer had just enough time to tell the other German judge about her predicament. "Now they've got me," she said. "You know what to do. Pick me up in half an hour."

Off Beyer went to the Soviet lair. The caviar and champagne came out, sparkling in the light. The Soviets were gracious hosts, talking about the events at Lake Placid, "all things around," Beyer recalls. "They talked about everything.

"Suddenly, they wanted to know what I thought about Rodnina and Zaitsev."

At this very moment, the other German judge, as if on cue, knocked on the door. Beyer inwardly rejoiced. The Soviets invited him in, too, but he quickly brushed them aside, saying he and Beyer had to deal with an issue at the athletes' village.

"They never tried it again," Beyer says. "It was over." As it turned out, Babilonia and Gardner withdrew because of injury, and Rodnina and Zaitsev won without obstacle.

Eight years later, Beyer was under pressure again as judge of the men's event at the 1988 Calgary Olympics. The strategies were in full gear, particularly at the compulsory figures event, an event coaches call "the last bastion of manipulation." The Soviet judge tried very hard to persuade Beyer to put Russian Alexander Fadeev, the 1985 world champion, on top. Beyer didn't. She preferred his younger teammate, Victor Petrenko, who happened to be Ukrainian.

"He made me frustrated," Beyer says, speaking of the Soviet judge in Calgary. "He was always saying I had to put his skater in first place or he would put my skater in last place. It was a big pressure."

Petrenko finished third in Calgary, while Fadeev missed the podium. The Soviets never bothered Beyer again. "Maybe they know they can't make the deals with me," she says. "I don't want to have this pressure to give the skater a mark. You don't know what is happening on the ice, when this is happening."

Although many agree there has been a vast improvement in the honesty of judging, deal-making still continues. A small circle of coaches, usually from old Soviet or Eastern bloc countries, still tries to wield influence with judges. As recently as the 1994 Olympics in Lillehammer, a Russian coach approached Canadian coach Louis Stong, asking him to get a favour from a Canadian judge; in return she would ensure that his student, Josée Chouinard, would get a medal in the women's event.

"We don't do that," Stong abruptly told the coach. "If Josée stands up, she doesn't need help. If she falls, then nobody can help her."

Some of the experiences of judges today aren't all so different than they were yesterday, in certain ways. T. D. Richardson laid out the prerequisites in one of his books, *Modern Figure Skating* (1930). To be a judge, one must become, for a time, a "thoroughly obnoxious person," he wrote. "To boil it down, the ideal competition judge is (1) entirely lacking in the bowels of compassion, (2) critical and intolerant, (3) to all intents and purposes completely sexless, (4) disloyal to his friends, and (5) unpatriotic."

If a judge is otherwise, the result is scheming and deal-making and unfair marking. Richardson, who competed in the first Olympic skating event in 1908 and later became an international judge, didn't hold back when he wrote about the scheming. "Generally speaking, throughout living memory, the judges have been assailed, cursed and execrated by successive generations of competitors, supporters and parents alike, until of recent years, were it not extremely annoying and, indeed, at times scandalous, it would be a joke. But to be quite frank, however, very often the indignation and adverse criticism has been more than justified by many of the extremely peculiar decisions given."

Richardson fell afoul of politics against judges after the 1927 world championship in Oslo, the one in which Sonja Henie won her first world title. He objected vociferously and publicly to the result of the men's event, in which Austrians placed first, second, and third – and in which three of the judges on the seven-member panel were

Austrian. Richardson was the British judge on the panel, and he could not understand why British skater John Page finished only fifth, although he had made no mistakes.

Henie also won her first world title in similar fashion: three of five judges were Norwegian. So was Henie.

Richardson thought he had the support of his national association when he made public protests that caused the ISU to create the one-judge-per-country rule. But eighteen months later, a figure committee of the British association suspended him from world and European judging for a year, for "daring to offend my Continental friends," he said. Yet one of the members of the British committee had earlier been vocal about the controversy as well; he had written a letter to a newspaper criticizing the practice and used an assumed name. He was not disciplined. Richardson figured the man even played a part in meting out his punishment.

Suzanne Francis knows how Richardson must have felt. Although she judges at home in Canada, she hasn't judged an international event since June 1993 for a multitude of reasons. Her thirty-five-year international career in the sport has been rent by two suspensions, neither of which she understands. She is outspoken and independent and unafraid and proud of what she does, and that does not always sit well with the ISU brass. Francis has received, perhaps, more Bronx cheers than most, from every corner.

"Judging is governed by fear," she says. "The international judging community is so afraid to step out of line in any direction, even to expressing their own opinions about the judging, through their marks, because they're so afraid they're going to be suspended. Although they're working on and trying to correct the problems in judging, I still feel that any time you have a fear of reprisal, you're not going to get truly honest judging.

"That's not to say judges are dishonest. I think they are afraid."

Francis has always jumped in where most judges fear to tread. "There are very few who march to their own drum," she says. "There are too many who are too afraid to be different. They are afraid they'll be challenged [by ISU referees], and warned, and kicked off the judges' panel. If you place one skater out of line, they're going to challenge you about it, even though referees have advised judges to judge independently."

Francis did just that in 1976 at the Olympic Games in Innsbruck, Austria. She marched briskly to her own beat when she placed Canadian Toller Cranston first in the free-skating event, while all but one of her peers rated Briton John Curry best. Because Francis was Canadian, it appeared that national bias was at work.

A Soviet judge had also been out of step, placing Soviet Vladimir Kovalev first, ahead of Curry. Soviet judges, at the time, were famous for promoting their own skaters – so much so that, in 1978, all Soviet judges were suspended for a year.

But Francis felt she had good reasons for making her placement.

"Suzie, just say you made a mistake," said referees Sonia Bianchetti of Italy and Ben Wright of the United States at the judges' meeting after the event. Francis calls such meetings "the inquisition."

"No," Francis said. "I don't feel I made a mistake. I really believe that, of the two free skaters – although they have different styles – Toller is the better free skater," Francis told Bianchetti and Wright. "Even though Toller missed something, his program was so much more difficult between the elements. It's very easy to execute your jumps if you're doing nothing in your approach to the jumps. You have to look at all the tricky stuff. You have to look at the risk factor."

Later, Curry admitted that, in 1976, he had set out to make difficult moves plainly apparent, rather than camouflaged. He had packaged the jumps with simple music, basic manner, basic steps, and "suddenly it looked difficult," he wrote in his autobiography, *John Curry*. "By aiming low, I had achieved a high from a judging point of view."

But Francis was not fooled. Still, the refrain came. "Suzie, just please say you are sorry and that you made a mistake."

"I won't," she replied. "I believe in what I did."

The ISU suspended her, as well as the Soviet judge. Later Francis bumped into Cranston and told him about her plight. "You're kidding," he said.

A short time later, Bianchetti rushed to Cranston, upset that the

Canadian skater had refused to sign up for the ISU tour through Europe at the end of the amateur season.

"You have to go," Bianchetti told him.

"Why?" Cranston asked.

"Because you're the best free skater in the world and we have sold all the houses in Europe on the strength [of the promise] that you're going to be there," she said.

Cranston looked at her and replied, "If I'm the best free skater in the world, why have you suspended my judge? Why didn't you tell all the other judges on the panel that they were wrong?"

Cranston held his ground and did not go on the ISU tour.

A year later, Dr. Josef Dedic, the Czechoslovakian head of the ISU's technical committee, told Francis that the Czechoslovakian Skating Union used her written dissertation, in which she gave the reasons for the choices she made at the 1976 Olympics, at a seminar on the art of how to judge free skating. By doing so, he was not making any judgement on whether Francis's decision on placements was correct, but was impressed at how she had drawn the comparisons between Cranston and Curry in the free-skating event. They were extremely detailed, move by move. Ironically, Francis, the suspended judge, felt as if she had been given a compliment for her work. Obviously, the comparisons must have been valid and well argued.

"So, when you have judges that are not afraid to stand up, then off they go," she says. "When you have judges that don't stand up, then they stay. I would not change my opinion. If that's what happens when somebody does that, fine. It makes it tough for judges who want to judge independently what they see."

In her own way, Suzanne Francis was a real individual, just like Toller Cranston. She was an original, an independent thinker, right from the beginning of her judging career. She made a big splash in her first international judging assignment, the 1964 Olympics in Innsbruck, Austria. She was hard to miss. She wore a bright-red wool coat. The coat turned into her trademark.

Francis was a very busy official on that first assignment. In Innsbruck, she acted as an assistant team leader for the Canadians, as coach for Canadian champion Charles Snelling – he didn't have a coach with him – and as judge for all three disciplines (ice dancing was not part of the Olympics at the time). "I was like a one-armed paperhanger," she says. The team finally took pity on her and found another Canadian judge, Bill Lewis, up in the stands, attending the Games as a spectator. Organizers enlisted him to take some of the heat off Francis.

Because Francis was the assistant team leader, she lived in the athletes' village, although judges were not supposed to spend any time among the people they were to judge. Because of her living arrangements and her duties, Francis did not get a chance to see any pairs practices, and, at the time, judges did not get protocols (or detailed results sheets) of previous competitions, so that they could become familiar with the range of marks given at the time.

The first pair to take to the ice was the second-ranked West German team of Sonja Pfersdorf and Gunther Matzdorf, who eventually finished fifth at the following world championship. In those days, judges strode out into the centre of the rink to hoist their marks up out of a box when each skater finished. Francis was judge no. 4, and easy to spot in her red coat, and she held up a 4.8 (out of 6.0). She believed it was a fair mark.

But because Francis hadn't seen the protocols or the practices, she did not know where to place the pair, especially since she could not compare them to another couple. Francis's heart sank when she saw her peers' marks pop up: 5.3, 5.4, 5.5. Her mark appeared sadly out of line.

The booing began in earnest, particularly because the West Germans trained in Garmisch, West Germany, only about thirty to forty miles from Innsbruck, and a large proportion of the Olympic skating crowd was German. The spectators showed their disapproval of the red-coated Canadian in no uncertain terms. They hissed and threw eggs, milk cartons, anything they had in their hands, onto the ice, and onto the judges. Abuse rained down upon Francis's blonde head.

Although judge no. 4 appeared terribly out of line, no rule existed to prevent Francis from awarding such a mark. She quickly realized that she would have to mark every skater very low, to keep her placement order intact.

Every time she stepped out on the ice, her marks were almost a full point lower than any of the other judges'. The hissing escalated. The event turned into a day of Olympic proportions, a long day, as rink crewmen hustled constantly to clear off the ice. "This went on into the wee hours of the morning, because they had a lot of extra work to do," Francis recalls.

When the final five skaters came on the ice, Francis knew it was safe to elevate her marks in a range closer to the others because she had plenty of room left to place them in the correct order. While her peers awarded 5.8s and 5.9s to world champions Marika Kilius and Hans-Jurgen Baumler – another West German couple and crowd favourites – Francis held aloft her marks of 5.6.

When Soviets Ludmila and Oleg Protopopov came out to skate, Francis was enthralled. Because Kilius and Baumler had made a mistake, Francis placed the Protopopovs first, ahead of them. She was not alone in making this judgement. So did the Swiss, Czech, American, and (of course) Soviet judges. The Protopopovs had won their first major title by a narrow margin, earning the approval of five judges to the Germans' four. The German crowd was not happy about this turn of events.

And Francis was the only judge to place Canadian pair Debbi Wilkes and Guy Revell ahead of the Germans, too.

"All hell broke loose then," Francis remembers. "The whole arena started chanting, "*Vier aus*! Four out!"

Francis stared in disbelief. "It wasn't very funny judging with all that garbage coming down on my head," she says. She stayed cool through it all, until the worst thing she could have imagined happened: Canadian team manager George Sherwood put his arm around her comfortingly. "Poor thing," he said, away from the crowd. Francis dissolved into tears.

The next day, Francis ended up on a television broadcast shown throughout Europe, alongside the referee of the event, to explain to the world that the range of marks did not determine a winner, but the placements did. Even though her marks seemed low, her placement of skaters was not outrageously out of line, she said.

But life got rough and tough for Francis and her red coat in Innsbruck. The media dubbed her the Red Devil. People would spit on her as she walked downtown. Once, an angry fan threw her off the sidewalk into the street. The situation became so dangerous that Francis was not allowed to walk downtown without an escort. Later, at home, she received mountains of mail, 65 per cent of it abusive and obscene.

Everywhere in Europe, she was known as the Red Devil.

Francis's newfound – and unsought – fame continued for weeks after the Olympics. Unfortunately for her, the world championship that followed shortly afterwards was held in Dortmund, Germany. There, Kilius and Baumler squared off again against the Protopopovs. This time, the Germans won by turning the tables, winning five judges to the Protopopovs' four.

Francis had never been assigned to judge in Dortmund, she says. She attended as a team leader, but, in her red coat, she did not go unnoticed. One day, she decided to have her hair coiffed at a local salon. "I was in one of those cubicles with curtains," she recalls. "I was on my back with my legs up in the air." Suddenly, the curtain ripped back and a horde of paparazzi snapped photos of her – in her vulnerable position – that quickly appeared in German newspapers. "Everywhere I went, I was the Red Devil, even at the Germany embassy," she says.

Because of Francis's 4.8s at Innsbruck, the ISU immediately adopted a new rule that called for the averaging of marks for the first skater in a competition. The marks are averaged before they are released to the public. The averaged marks give judges a reference point for their scale of marks. Even from the beginning, Francis had made a name for herself on the international stage.

Francis returned to Europe two years later to judge at the 1966 world championship in Davos, Switzerland, but the Canadian Figure Skating Association warned her never to wear her red coat again. "They got to you, didn't they?" a Canadian reporter asked her when he spied her in a more modest black pea jacket in Davos.

"I was told never to wear a red coat, but it still doesn't mean I have no red on," Francis said impishly, as she swept open her coat to reveal a scarlet-red lining.

The European newspapers wrote that the Red Devil had changed her colours. But Francis hadn't changed at all. She still wanted to call results as she saw them. However, this time, the ISU officials were lying in wait for her, she says. They had been able to do nothing to suspend Francis at the 1964 Olympics: she had technically done nothing wrong. But they seemed to watch her work with intense scrutiny. (After the 1966 world championship, she got a suspension from the ISU for her efforts at Davos.)

In Davos, Francis was again – ominously – judge no. 4 during the men's event. When she saw eventual world champion Emmerich Danzer of Austria skate his first compulsory figure, she was less than impressed. It didn't help that the judges and skaters had to cope with a snowstorm that dropped wet, sticky, heavy snowflakes on the ice, the skaters, the judges, and the spectators at the outdoor rink. "[Danzer] did this figure and stopped three feet from the centre [when he should have continued through to complete the first tracing of the figure]," Francis recalls. "Then he jumped back to the centre. He did this three times. I couldn't give him a good mark, so I gave him a really low mark."

Danzer had been the European champion for two years running, and the other judges chose to ignore his mistakes. All of the judges but Francis and a Swiss judge placed him first in figures. Instead, both Francis and the Swiss judge placed the second-string Austrian skater, Wolfgang Schwarz, first after compulsories. "He did really nice figures," Francis says.

During a break after the first figure, Francis – who speaks a little German – overheard some officials in the judges' room in a nervous state about the snowfall – and about Danzer's efforts. "We've got to stop this competition," they said. "Because if [Danzer] can't get around a three-lobe figure, he's never going to get around a two-lobe figure and on one foot in this wind and snow."

Francis interrupted and told them in German: "If the other skaters can get around the figure, so can he."

The competition continued. During the freeskating event, Francis carefully watched Gary Visconti, the 1965 U.S. champion, and decided that he was "absolutely to die for." She placed him first in free skating. Although three other judges also placed Visconti first in free skating, Francis was the only judge that rated him first overall. The American judge ranked Visconti second overall, behind Danzer.

Then, "the inquisition" started. At the judges' meeting, the referee assured Francis that he could understand why she had placed Schwarz first in figures. "You were right," he said. "We will support you when the council deals with you."

But Francis ended up getting a suspension for showing national bias. "Why are you suspending me?" she said, remembering that she had placed the Canadian skater, Donald Knight, fifth and he had finished seventh overall – not as serious a transgression as being out of line in medal positions.

Francis told them a more likely candidate for suspension was a Japanese judge who had placed Japanese skater Nobuo Sato (father of Yuka Sato) second, when he finished fifth overall. Francis asked why the Japanese judge was not challenged.

She was told that the referee was being lenient with the Japanese judge because she could not speak English, even though English is the official language of the ISU. "The Japanese got mileage for years out of not being able to understand English," Francis says.

But Francis was really taken aback when she discovered that she was suspended for national bias, primarily because she had placed the American, Visconti, first overall. (He won the bronze medal.) "The last time I noticed, we [Canadians] weren't the 49th state of the United States," she said.

The referee had been European.

Francis continued on her honestly swashbuckling way, however. And, in doing so, she has created other rule changes. At the 1988 world championship in Budapest, she watched in astonishment as American pair Jill Watson and Peter Oppegard, who had been Olympic bronze medallists a month earlier in Calgary, missed forty-five seconds of their free skate. From her rinkside seat, the confusion was obvious after they had missed a manoeuvre. The Americans seemed to be arguing. Finally, after a long, aimless drift across the ice, Watson looked as if she wanted to stomp off. But they continued and finished sixth overall.

Francis plunged ahead, unafraid to mark what she saw. Watson and Oppegard finished seventh in the free skate, but Francis was the only judge to place them as low as ninth. "Oh, you're going to get it for this," her peers told her. But she didn't. "I took a huge deduction from them," Francis said. "You can't miss one-fifth of your program and still be marked out of 6.0."

Instead, the referee told Francis that she was the only one that judged the Watson–Oppegard incident correctly. The following year, the ISU adopted a guideline for judges on how to deal with a long interruption.

But wherever Francis went, her placements often caused disagreement among officials. She and Canadian judge Bill McLachlan were the only two Canadian judges who placed Isabelle and Paul Duchesnay ahead of Karyn and Rod Garossino in ice dancing at the 1984 Canadian championship. "They thought we were crazy," Francis says. "People were blasting us about it in the judges' meeting. But we said, 'You watch, they will be world champions someday.'" Francis didn't get another chance to judge the Duchesnays, however. They left the country to skate for France, and won the world championship in 1991.

The whole incident led Francis to think very hard about how events should be judged. "Judges are not there to just be mechanical pushers of marks," she says. "You have to have a little bit of vision and appreciation of the whole of what you're seeing, and not be so technical that you're counting the number of turns and you lose track of the beauty of the whole. Timing is important in dancing, but it's not the only thing."

Canadian judges, she says, are known for being too technical.

Francis liked the Duchesnays because they were "individuals" and their presentation was exceptional. "I always had them down in the first mark [technical mark], but I always had them up in the second [presentation]," she says. "I liked their creativity, their originality, their speed. If I wanted to find negatives, their timing and sometimes their stroking – like Toller's – wasn't the best. Toller wasn't the best stroking creature, but it didn't take away from the fact that he was a wonderful free skater for his time."

Francis also liked Natalia Bestemianova and Andrei Bukin, the Soviets who won the 1988 Olympic gold medal, because of their emotions, their fiery presentation, their passion and creativity, and something extra that Francis calls "soul."

"For me, ice dancing has to show soul and passion," she says. "It has to come from within. It can't be mechanical."

Currently, Francis's favourite Russian ice dancers are 1996 world silver medallists Anjelika Krylova and Oleg Ovsiannikov. "I saw her and her former partner in a spring competition in France years ago," Francis says. "I went to the coach [Natalia Linichuk] and I said this team is wonderful. This girl is so exceptional that she, I think, will be world champion one day. But I'm not sure it's going to be with this partner."

Francis said the couple did a routine to the theme from *Spartacus* that was just "spellbinding." Krylova won a world bronze medal in 1993 with that partner, Vladimir Fedorov, then split with him to join Ovsiannikov. Krylova and Ovsiannikov's 1997 free dance, to "The Masquerade Suite," "catches me deep inside my emotional being," Francis says. "There's a certain sense of drama that all the Russian skaters have that make it to the top. Not the girls [singles skaters], but the men and the dancers seem to be able to exhibit it.

"I think the Russian dancers have very fleet feet, very tricky feet. Yet they are able to work their upper bodies so that every little nuance of the music is portrayed."

The *Carmen* program that Bestemianova and Bukin did was the best *Carmen* she ever saw, Francis says. It's music that has been used widely – by 1962 world champion Donald Jackson of Canada, by 1988 Olympic gold medallist Katarina Witt of Germany, by Debi Thomas of the United States, by Alexei Yagudin of Russia, and many others.

Francis's vast experience has given her a pair of sharp eyes that pick up many skating nuances. But they did not prevent her from getting into trouble at the 1988 Olympics with the referee at the post-event judges' meetings. She was the only one who noticed that, in the pairs event, Russian skater Elena Valova – who eventually finished second with partner Oleg Vasiliev – had improperly touched her head down onto the ice during a death spiral, and that, during that move, she had also slipped off her blade and was riding in an arc around her partner on the side of her boot. After all, Francis had been a pairs skater herself; she knew what to look for. Francis made deductions for the errors, and, when the referee looked at a video replay after the event, she noted that Francis was correct. The referee told the other judges to watch for such errors.

However, at the same time, Francis had to defend herself about why she had placed a Canadian pair higher than the rest of the panel. Yet, during the actual event, Francis was soundly booed by the large crowd for not giving them a higher mark. "All of the Calgary arena was booing me," she recalls. The next day, the local paper printed a sarcastic cartoon about her. She couldn't win.

Judges are caught between all kinds of ironies. On the one hand, the ISU scrutinizes their work and tries to put a stop to poor results. One of their criteria is to examine a placement that is strangely out of line. How can it be correct if it is so out of line? How could all the other judges be wrong? On the other hand, ice-dance results in particular have come under criticism because the placements have rarely varied from event to event, from compulsory to free skate.

Suzanne Francis's work was refreshing in one way: she was one judge who never followed the protocol. Although she'd been in trouble many times, a bad referee's report that she received in the fall of 1992 at Skate Canada in Victoria, B.C., proved to be the last straw in her international judging career. In June 1993, she resigned from judging international events.

At Skate Canada, she and American judge Linda Leaver were the only two judges who noticed a major timing error made by Russian competitors Icoslava Nechaeva and Yrie Chesnichenko during the first compulsory dance. Almost all of the rest of the judges placed them second in both compulsory dances. In the first, both Francis and Leaver placed them eighth out of ten couples.

The second dance was a little rocky, too. Most judges placed them second. Francis placed them fifth, Leaver sixth. Francis was also less than pleased by their original dance and placed them fourth, while the others placed them first or second.

In the free dance, Francis obviously held nothing against them. She placed the Russians first, along with two other judges. The Russians eventually won the silver medal behind the favoured Finnish team of Susanna Rahkamo and Petri Kokko.

"Don't worry," the referee told Francis at the time of the first compulsory. "You . . . caught the mistake in the timing with that team. You were absolutely right." When Francis asked him where he had placed the Russians, the referee told her that he had placed the skaters in a similar order.

Three days later, it appeared that the referee had changed his mind about the Russian team – much to her surprise, Francis says. "When he had 'the inquisition' afterwards, all of a sudden I was wrong. Referees, too, can be swayed by majority rule and are often afraid to support the out-of-line judge, declaring others wrong."

It was the referee's job to hand in a written report to the ISU's ice-dancing committee about the efforts of the judges on his panel. Under ISU rules, Francis got a copy of his report, and was shocked at what she saw. The referee had judged Francis and deemed that her judging performance in compulsory dances was "poor."

Judging for the original dance? Fair.

Judging in the free skate? Poor.

Her oral and written explanations for her decisions? Unsatisfactory.

"I regret to say that Mrs. Francis is out of touch," the referee wrote.

The report came as a major blow to Francis, who, three months earlier, was sent to Quebec to do a dance seminar for judges, coaches, and skaters to bring them up to date on a number of rule changes for the season. Six years earlier, the Skate Canada referee had told the then president of the Canadian Figure Skating Association that Francis was the best dance judge Canada had ever produced.

Francis considers herself very knowledgeable technically. She has served on most of the technical committees in Canada. "To say I'm out of touch is a little weird," she says.

Francis's judging of the Russians may not have been the only issue that rankled the referee in the competition. She placed Canadian dance champions Jacqueline Petr and Mark Janoschak third in the free skate – higher than her peers on the panel – even after the couple hit blades and Janoschak tumbled at one end of the ice during a simple crosscut. The Canadians were not able to resume their imaginative court-dance routine until they had skated to the other end of the ice, a major interruption in the program. Most of the other judges dropped them to sixth or seventh because of the miscue.

Francis also gave high marks to the young, new Canadian team, Shae-Lynn Bourne and Victor Kraatz, who were competing in their first season as senior skaters. They finished sixth overall in the event, but Francis had marked them third in both the compulsories and the original dance. In the free dance, Francis also rated them higher than her colleagues did, in fourth behind Petr and Janoschak, although she said their so-called hydroblading moves – stretching low to the ice – are pairlike tricks, not dance moves, she says.

It appeared that Francis was strangely out of line and blatantly nationalistic. But not according to the placements laid out by both the referee and assistant referee, who are experienced judges, she says. Post-meeting notes showed that both the referee and his assistant had placed Petr and Janoschak third overall in their own marking examples during the competition.

As for Bourne and Kraatz, the referee had placed them third in the original dance. The assistant had them fourth.

In the first compulsory dance, Francis had Bourne and Kraatz fifth; the referees agreed. In the judges' meeting, she was not asked to explain her placements of the Canadians, nor was she cited for showing national bias, "so the referee must have agreed," she says.

During the meeting, the referee said he could not argue with Francis's fourth for the Russians in original dance, according to Francis; his report said otherwise.

Also, Czechoslovakian skaters Katerina Mrazova and Martin Simecek finished third in the free dance. Francis was the only judge to place them as low as sixth; others placed them anywhere from first to third. Post-meeting notes showed that both referees placed the Czechs seventh. While on the surface, it appeared Francis had lost her way during the competition, her judgements were in step with those of some of the most experienced in the process.

Francis was incensed that the referee had given her such a poor report, yet had been telling her all week that she had been making the right judgements. "I always said if I got a bad referee report, I'd quit," she says. "My pride wouldn't let me go on."

But this was different; Francis thought the report unjust. She approached the Canadian association and asked them to stand behind her. "My shoulders are broad enough," she said. "I would like to make a test case out of this. This is the kind of action by a referee they're trying to abolish. This to me was one of the most blatant examples of referees saying one thing to your face at a meeting and then changing when they write the reports.

"I don't think any judge that gets to that level should be considered incompetent or out of touch," Francis says. "They should have been weeded out long before."

The CFSA wouldn't fight her case.

Eight months after Skate Canada, Francis resigned. "I no longer wanted to be subjected to what I call hypocritical referees," she says. "I'm proud of what I did in my skating life and I don't need this any more."

But the poor report wasn't the only factor that pushed Francis to the decision. She also disliked the rule changes made to ice dancing that restricted the kind of music skaters could use that season. (Ballet music was out, and music had to have a definite beat.) "In my opinion, they set ice dancing back thirty years," she says. "I'm very much in the school of allowing free expression for the free dance."

At the same time, in the period leading to the 1994 Olympics in Lillehammer, Francis was also not in favour of allowing the reinstatement of professionals, such as Brian Boitano and Katarina Witt and Jayne Torvill and Christopher Dean, so that they could compete again in world championships and Olympic Games.

And, physically, she wasn't up to it for a time. Francis underwent quadruple heart-bypass surgery several years ago. Now, with renewed vigour, she has turned her interests elsewhere, and she just doesn't have time to judge skating, even at home. She's been too busy exhibiting at dog shows across the country. "When I was nine years old, I was given two presents: a pair of skates and a little Scottie dog," she says. "Those two things shaped my life. I've been involved in both things all my life."

Because of her work as a figure-skating judge, she had to put her interests in dogs on hold. It's different, now, however. During the 1996-97 season, Francis did not judge figure skating at all. When she's not showing her own dog – Francis is a part-owner of the top hound in the country, her gift to herself when she retired as a veterinarian – she's judging dog shows. Francis has gone from wet knees to wet noses, without a moment's hesitation.

In many ways, Francis finds the dog-judging world preferable, although not without its tense moments. A month after the Calgary Olympics, when boos dogged Francis everywhere, she stepped outside an arena where she had been judging a dog show and met another unwelcoming chorus. A dog owner, furious at where Francis had placed his prized pooch, started to scream at her: "You're no better a judge of dogs than you are of figure skating!"

The man was reprimanded for displaying an indignity to a judge. But there are no such protective rules for figure-skating judges.

Far from the wagging tails of her canine crew and the unsmiling faces of judging referees was the home reaction to Francis's stormy calls. Francis's daughter, Kristen, was "mortified" at the flurry of controversies over her forthright decisions. "She'd say, 'Mom, why do you always have to be different? I'm getting teased at school. I'm getting teased at work. People don't understand the marking system. Why do you always have to be low?'"

So, at one competition, Francis decided she would no longer mark low. "I can be the highest," she says. "I can judge between 5.6 and 6.0, if they want everybody up there. There's something like fifty computations between those two numbers."

After all, years ago, Francis was the judge who devised a chart indicating how many mark combinations existed, to prevent judges from getting themselves boxed in. Francis wasn't the type to get boxed in, just the type to get roasted.

If Suzanne Francis's life in a judge's seat was like a magnetic storm, Elfriede Beyer's career has been like a calm shore. Beyer said she hasn't been booed that often, not at major events anyway. She has enjoyed a long and relatively incident-free judging career. She has never been suspended, although once she got a letter from American Ben Wright, who had been acting as a referee at a competition. Incredibly, Wright questioned her placement of sixteenth for a skater who had finished twentieth, although it's not common for a referee to worry about lower placements.

Even Beyer's climb up the ladder was virtually free of the multitude of tension-ridden examinations and tests. Beyer, who started out as a rollerskating judge, rose quickly up figure-skating's judging ladder in the late 1950s and 1960s and never had to write an examination. She was only a recreational skater herself; in wartime Europe, her family had little money to pay for tests or ice time or for club fees for either rollerskating or figure skating. Beyer was also lucky in that she came from an area of Germany that had few judges; she could ascend the ranks quickly.

Every judge's nightmare is placing skaters out of line with their peers, but few of Beyer's placements seem to have been wildly controversial. At the 1994 world championship in Japan, Beyer placed Michelle Kwan ninth in the technical program – her highest placing – while one other judge placed her as low as nineteenth. One referee was about to challenge Beyer's placing at the judge's meeting, but the other deemed it was satisfactory, because Kwan had shown good technical skills. Overall, Kwan came eleventh in the technical (or short) program. It pleased Beyer that Kwan only two years later became a world champion; it vindicated her placing.

But falling out of line is a major worry for judges. "When I give more marks than the other judges, then there is applause," Beyer says. "But I'm not feeling well with this. If you are extremely out of line, it makes you nervous."

At the 1984 world championship in Ottawa, Beyer recalls facing the spectre of national bias – or being out of line for a patriotic reason – while judging two German competitors, Katarina Witt from East Germany and Manuela Ruben from West Germany. When Ruben landed a smattering of triple jumps well, Beyer marked her almost as high as Witt technically, although much lower artistically. In the free skate, she ranked Ruben fifth, although Ruben finished sixth overall.

When Anna Kondreshova from the Soviet Union skated, she was "sitting on the ice more than skating." Although she eventually won the silver medal, Beyer placed her only sixth in the free skate.

But when another Soviet skater, Kira Ivanova, came to skate, Beyer got worried, fearing she'd be accused of national bias because she had Ruben so high. Although the panel collectively placed Ivanova seventh in the free skate, Beyer placed her in third spot, above Ruben.

Not surprisingly, the referee approached Beyer and asked her if she had received any pressure from the Russian judge. "Why did you put this skater before all the others?" he asked.

"I said to him that I was so afraid to have national bias [with Ruben]," Beyer says. "Since this time, they didn't ask me if I had national bias."

Beyer is all too familiar with the quandary in which judges often find themselves: steering away from charges of national bias, yet also satisfying their own federations about where they place their skaters. In most disciplines, one placement can determine whether a country may send one or two or three skaters to the next world championship. Because a country may send, for example, two skaters to a world championship if it has a skater finish in the top ten the previous year, there is always pressure on a judge to push up a skater who is lying eleventh. "If they would like the skater to finish in tenth place and you have them eleventh, that is the pressure you face from your federation," Beyer explains.

Susan Heffernan, who judges for Canada, says judges walk a fine line whenever a skater from their country steps onto the ice. "Sometimes you get a bit annoyed, when you feel it's right and it's not a national bias at all," she says. "But if the referee doesn't agree with you, you're up for disciplinary action."

Judges facing censure from the referee at a review meeting may have to write a letter of explanation for a decision that differs from everyone else's. The ISU might send the judge a letter. "They've got grades of letters, depending on the seriousness of the errors," said Jackie Stell-Buckingham, technical coordinator of the Canadian Figure Skating Association. "Once you get a couple of those on your record, they can actually suspend you from judging internationally.

"For judges to go out on a limb and do something they might believe in, but they're really not sure – they don't do it very often."

As a German judge, Beyer faces a unique problem that squeezes both skaters and judges from her country. When East and West Germany merged into a unified country in 1990, the marriage stripped the total number of judges and skaters Germany was allowed to field at competitions. It is the exact opposite of the phenomenon that has struck the former Soviet Union: because so many of its countries have split off to form separate republics, many skaters or judges who never got a chance to get out of the country have seen the vistas open up.

Currently, the ISU allows accreditation to Germany of only twelve world championship or Olympic judges, twelve international judges, and six referees, like any single country. For a year, the ISU gave Germany some leeway, allowing eight referees, or about fifteen championship judges.

But gradually, through attrition, the numbers have dwindled to the allotted amount. Still, Beyer sees a danger. Young judges who would like to take tests and move into the ranks at the top must wait until there is an opening. "We have one judge who has done the exam, but there is no place on the list for him and he will have to wait." There is a danger that young judges could get discouraged and give up, Beyer says.

"We are a very big country now," Beyer says. "We have a lot of judges to make places for and small countries, such as the Netherlands, have the same number of places as countries like the United States and Canada and Germany. Maybe now there should be a decision about this."

She said many judges from the former German Democratic Republic (East Germany) have stopped judging. They are focusing more on their own lives and are busy trying to find work, particularly because new freedoms allow them to leave the country. Before the tumbling of the Berlin Wall, many East German judges rarely left the country, perhaps doing so only if there was a competition in Moscow. Only a few were allowed to leave.

Beyer remembers with amazement the judge from the other side of the Wall whose federation sent him to every competition that Katarina Witt entered – even though the country had many, many judges to choose from. Unlike Witt's judge, Beyer says she is relieved that she did not have to judge only one event. She is a qualified judge for both singles skating and pairs. "It's much better," she says. "Otherwise, you get tunnel vision."

Beyer, at age sixty, has ten years left in her judging career. She currently works in administration for her federation, and has acted as a team leader as well. She is a popular judge, known to give parties for her peers at events in Germany. She has made special efforts to include ice-dancing judges who sometimes get left out of the social loop.

Her memories of judging include experiences many judges have faced: unusual roommates and unforgettable events and decisions. At the Calgary Olympics in 1988, she was judge no. 1 for the men's event, which featured the Battle of the Brians, between Canadian champion Brian Orser and U.S. champion Brian Boitano. Boitano won by a vote of only one judge, earning the favour of five judges to Orser's four in the long program. Beyer was one of the four who voted for Orser.

"I liked the skating of Brian Orser," she says. "I liked it more. I agree that Brian Boitano was also very good. The referee told us that both of them could have been first."

Several years later, Beyer met Boitano when he skated at an exhibition with Witt in Beyer's hometown of Frankfurt. Sheepishly, she remembered where she slotted him at the Olympics.

"That night, I didn't give you the top place," she admitted to him.

"I know," Boitano replied. "I remember, but it was okay."

Some of Beyer's most unusual adventures occurred at the Lake

Placid Olympics in 1980. Even at the Olympics, the judges don't have a chance to be alone in the room: they bunk up with their peers. Beyer was assigned to a suite with two bedrooms that she had to share with three other people. She arrived with a sinus infection, and was told to go to bed by the team doctor.

When she awakened, groggy, she made out the shape of a man standing close to her bed, staring at her. She stared back. He was Oriental. She turned over and tried to sleep.

The next morning, she saw another judge and tried to explain to him what she had seen. "I can't stay in that room. There was a man in my room," she told him.

"No, that can't be," he said.

"I was not dreaming," Beyer insisted. "I saw this man."

Together, they went to the room and there he was, sitting in a chair. "He was laughing and thinking it was fine to be there," Beyer said. He spoke no English.

The organizers allowed her to move to another suite, which she was to share with an Australian and French judge. She left her nightclothes on her bed and went to watch a practice.

When she returned, she found somebody lying in her bed, on her nightclothes. It was a Canadian judge this time. Beyer hustled to the front desk, where they discovered they had given the Canadian a phone extension number instead of the correct room number. The phone number just happened to be the same as Beyer's room number.

With judges, a sense of humour is a necessity. T. D. Richardson forgot to mention it in his list of judging musts. Suzanne Francis is determined to keep hers. Swing open her closets at home, and red is everywhere. It is her favourite colour, as irrepressible a hue as she can find. Someday, she vows, she will buy a red car and get a licence plate to match: RED DVL, it may say.

Aside from her dogs, Francis can take comfort in the quiet support she gets from her peers. She still has a letter tucked away from another judge who told her: "You've been a great example for me, and I hope in my judging career that I can judge as you did, and call what you see and not be afraid of the consequences."

As for Elfriede Beyer, she plans to build a flaming red fire, if she has to. "If I ever get a letter or a suspension, I will take all my rulebooks, make a nice fire, warm up my hands, and go as a tourist," she says.

It's one way of taking the heat.

Music: The Speech of Angels

Leonore Kay is master of all she surveys: stacks of compact discs piled merrily to the ceiling, in a house stuffed with more than ten thousand albums. It is a house that bursts with song, and some of figure skating's top artists, such as Michelle Kwan and Daniel Hollander, have heard its beckoning. The sound of music has drawn them to Kay's door in Newmarket, Ontario.

Kay represents a recent phenomenon in the increasingly complex world of figure skating, in which detail is everything and specialists are becoming part of the game – and not only at the élite level. It is Kay's job to find just the right music for skaters, music that fits them like a glove. Then she pieces and patches it all together, shapes it and moulds it into a down-to-the-second program, with musical waves that punch out jumps and plead for spins.

In the past, coaches were the ones who chose the music and devised the routines from it. But these days, few coaches have the time to devote to such intense, picky work. "Many coaches find getting music for their skaters extremely difficult and time-consuming," says Kay in a rare moment of repose. "Although some coaches love to do it, it's not a job that all coaches like." After all, if a coach teaches, say, thirty-five students in a year, he or she, under the traditional process, would have to devise two programs – a short and a long – for each. That means finding music for seventy programs, some of which have two or three different pieces of music in them. "It's a nightmare," says former coach Louis Stong.

Under these conditions, it wouldn't be surprising if some of the musical selections were less than *à propos*. Even at the élite level, there are many poor choices of music. On the other hand, Kay figures it took eighty hours of work to find and edit the unusual music Kwan used for her Taj Mahal program during the 1996-97 season. Actually, she figures eighty hours is an underestimate.

It's no wonder that a specialist such as Kay spends so much of her time searching for the right piece: music is all-important to skating programs. Most people don't give it the time it deserves. Music choice is so crucial because all of the choreography and program design – and even costume design – flows from it. And it is a major contributor to the mark judges give for presentation, which is, to put it simply, how well a skater interprets and uses the music. Choosing music is the most difficult element of coaching, Stong says. "The hardest thing is [this] decision every year. It ain't easy. And a lot of people don't have the background or the resources. You've got to listen, listen, listen."

Stong's wife, Marijane Stong, is probably one of the best music selectors, so good that she is currently carving out a business plan to become a music specialist, in addition to her work as a coach. Marijane was the one who found the music for Brian Boitano's 1988 Olympic gold-medal-winning program to the film score from *Napoleon*, for Kurt Browning's famous *Casablanca* routine, for Josée Chouinard's delightful "Comme Çi, Comme Ça" number that she used for her short program during her 1995-96 season. Marijane will be at the forefront of a new skating trend: there just aren't many music specialists in the field – yet.

"Music is ultimately important," Marijane says. "If all your tricks work and your music is terrible, you can be okay. But if your tricks don't work and your music is terrible, you can drop several places. If some of your tricks don't work, but the whole package is still really wonderful, you can come up with a great second mark [for presentation, rather than technical merit] and be okay. Good music is very important for the top skater."

But it is also important for a very young skater to have well-rounded programs, with tasteful music, Marijane says. Early influences can create the music choosers of the future. From the time she was a little girl, Marijane was surrounded by music. She started ballet lessons at age three. She took piano lessons from age five. Her grandmother played the piano, too, and her mother played violin and took joy in her collection of classical and Latin American music. Marijane's skating teacher, Liliane De Kresz, a Hungarian skating champion who had emigrated to Canada, was also a pianist with a tasteful knowledge of music and had a sister who was a singer. And Marijane's husband, Louis, is an opera buff. "If I wasn't involved with the people I was and didn't have such good choices in music – for me – I may never have been able to do what I do now," she says.

The Stongs have about three thousand albums in their home and steep themselves in music at every opportunity, even while travelling in the car. The television is on only if the program being broadcast contributes to a musical idea. They constantly change radio stations in order to hear a wide variety of music. Marijane keeps a pen and pad in her car at all times, just in case she hears something special on the radio. "Sometimes in the past, I've missed something really good by not being able to write it down right away," she says.

As a coach, Marijane has been searching for music for her ice-dancing pupils since 1967. Because ice dancing is hidebound in rules and restrictions, the music search can be a most frustrating and lengthy process in this discipline in which edges, footwork, and musical approach are all-important. (Ice dancing does not include jumps, spins, death spirals, or throws. Judges compare skaters' edge quality, patterns on the ice, positions, turns, timing to the music on steps, and even whether the music is suitable.) Yet, this is where Marijane started, in her quest to find the right music.

The only part of an ice-dancing competition about which coaches – or music specialists – don't have to worry is the compulsory dances, with their prescribed moves and steps and patterns over the ice. The

International Skating Union dictates what specific music is to be used by all skaters for compulsory dances.

However, choosing music for the original dance – comparable to the short program in other disciplines – is extremely difficult. For each season, the ISU assigns a particular "rhythm" to the original dance, such as a *paso doble* rhythm or a jive or a waltz. Dancers must not only skate to music that fits the assignment, but they must also show the flavour or character of the dance. Judges may deduct from 01. to 0.4 for inappropriate musical selection in the original program – if the music does not fit the ISU guidelines that define what is, for example, a real polka, tango, or samba.

For the 1997-98 season, coaches were faced with a new problem: the ISU decided to change the original dance back into something called the original set pattern – which is what it was called, for the last time, during the 1989-90 season. An original set pattern imposes yet more restrictions on a skater and the music. In the original set pattern, the designer of a skater's program must map out a pattern on the ice, and then the pattern must be repeated two or three times, depending on the decree of the ISU. The music, of course, is also repeated and edited so that the repetition seems natural. In the original dance, which existed for seven years, skaters could flow over the ice in any pattern they liked, with no repetitions. Because of this freedom, skating insiders would refer to the original dance as a mini free dance. (Free dances are different in that no rhythm is prescribed, although the music still must have a discernible beat.)

Faced with the growing restrictions on finding music for this original set pattern, Marijane developed an idea. She had known for two seasons that the rhythm for the original dance or original set pattern for the 1998 Olympic season was to be a jive. In her research, she found that all the best jive music had vocals in it, but, under ISU rules, vocal music is not permitted. So Marijane and another coach suggested that the top skating body allow vocals in music only for the jive program. For the first time in its history, the ISU agreed.

"Now I think they're opening the doors again a little bit, gradually," Marijane says. "I think they want ice dancing to be a great hit at the Olympics."

Marijane found herself up to her ankles in trouble years ago in 1967, when she first started, by using forbidden vocal music for a program she designed for her ice-dancing brother, Bruce Lennie, and his partner, Donna Taylor. In fact, Taylor and Lennie won the Canadian junior title that year, while skating their free dance to Tony Bennett singing "I Left My Heart in San Francisco."

"The audience loved it," she recalls. The following season, Marijane decided to keep a section of the Bennett song in their senior free dance. But, when Taylor and Lennie finished second at the Canadian championship and earned a spot on the world team, she was forced to change a section of the music, since she was advised that international judges would take a dim view of vocals.

Coaches have traditionally been the selectors of music for a skater's program, but with the increasingly common use of choreographers, the burden of music choice has sometimes shifted to the person who actually designs the routine. There are no written rules regarding who undertakes the task. Sometimes a choreographer insists on choosing the music in order to have total artistic input. When he worked as a choreographer, Toller Cranston would arbitrarily assign a music choice, with no input from the skater. Most often, however, the choreographer works in close concert with the coach and the skater to agree on a choice. "Some choreographers want the whole basket," says Louis Stong, who tended to work with Toronto choreographer Sandra Bezic. "But what we're finding nowadays is that people are just glad that somebody else is going to help. And the more help you get, the better."

Marijane was not the coach or choreographer of record for Boitano, Browning, or Chouinard – all singles skaters rather than ice dancers – but she played a vital role in their programs, just by helping out her husband and Bezic with their music searches. She stumbled on Boitano's Olympic music quite by accident, while looking for free-dance music for one of her own students. One day she went to a library – something she rarely does in her music hunts – and just happened to see the album cover for the soundtrack of the film *Napoleon*. It struck her immediately that the photo of Napoleon on the cover, decked out in a regal hat, even looked like Boitano.

Intrigued, she wondered if the music would fulfil the ideas of Bezic, who had been hired to design Boitano's programs that year. Bezic had told Marijane that she wanted music that was completely different from what he had previously used: contemporary, dancey kinds of tunes. The key to the search had been to find something totally opposite to what she figured Boitano's arch-rival Brian Orser would use. Bezic pictured Orser skating to something softer, more lyrical, and with plenty of musical opportunities for his fast footwork. Boitano, a tall skater, needed something dramatic and powerful. Marijane signed out the album and made a few rough copies of the music. The *Napoleon* soundtrack turned out to be such a natural link to Boitano's abilities that Bezic was able to choreograph about half of Boitano's long program in one evening.

Marijane played more of an overall role with Chouinard's "Comme Çi, Comme Ça" program, but the music was also more difficult and time-consuming to track down. Marijane heard the music while driving in her car and listening to radio station CFMX-FM, based in Cobourg, Ontario, which played a variety of music but catered strongly to a classical audience.

As soon as she heard it, Marijane knew it was perfect for the French-Canadian Chouinard, who was her husband's pupil. "I just felt it was French; it was sweet; it was strong; it was flirtatious. It was kind of settled; it didn't rush, rush, rush. It would give her time to do everything properly." And Chouinard loved it. Her mother remembered hearing the piece when she was a little girl. But finding the piece, written at the turn of the century, turned into a frustrating chore.

Husband Louis made an extensive search in HMV music stores, a chain that allows customers to listen before they buy. No luck. He turned to a coach who also works in the head office of the chain to see if she could find it further afield. No luck. "It was absolutely unavailable," he recalls. In desperation, Louis phoned the radio station to see if he could borrow their record. But the station had a policy that it does not lend music. However, when Louis told them that the music was to be used for a skating program for three-time Canadian champion Chouinard, they bent their rules: Louis was allowed to borrow the album for one hour – only.

Having found the music, the Stongs turned it over to Bezic, whose busy schedule perhaps made her reluctant to go through the laborious process of editing it to fit the two-minute-forty-second length of the short program, and then dreaming up the choreography. She preferred that Chouinard keep the outstanding short program, from the ballet *La Fille Mal Gardée* from her previous season. But when Louis urged her to time the "Comme Çi, Comme Ça" piece, Bezic found that it was exactly two minutes and forty seconds long. "That's it. We're using it," Bezic said.

The group moved on to finish the project. While Bezic was tied up elsewhere, Marijane took on a role that involved more than just finding the music. Although her husband was the coach, she and Chouinard "marked" the program. In other words, they decided the best spots to place the eight required elements of the short program so that they fit well with the music. "She felt the music so naturally, it was very easy to set it," Marijane says.

Together, Marijane and Chouinard created a footwork sequence to fit the music. Then Bezic stepped in when she was available to work and filled in the rest of the moves, from the beginning. For example, Bezic created the required spiral sequence. "We knew where it was going to go, but we didn't do it," Marijane says. The creation of the program, complete with the choosing of the music, was a group effort. But Marijane had set everything in motion, starting with her ear for tasteful and suitable music.

Over the years, Marijane has learned what kind of music tends to work in competitive programs. In ice dancing, with all of its restrictions and rules, it takes a real skill to search out appropriate music. In singles and pairs skating, without any of the restrictions of ice dancing, the choice still requires sensitivity and taste. It is not the function of judges to slam a program because they dislike the music. Ideally, music is a vehicle used to show off the skater's skills and abilities. Still, some music choices are blatantly unfortunate, unsuitable for the personality and style of the skater, or uninspiring and unappealing, or "something that's really weird or obscure or that doesn't really say anything," Marijane says. "Music with a beautiful rhythm and melody can take you some-where, and can actually say something. If it's just a lot of noise, it may entertain some people, but, generally, it's not going to give you a feeling of gliding and flow and beautiful lines."

Marijane avoids synthesized music, which may be interesting for some young skaters, particularly young boys. "But for the upper echelon, it would not be a good way to go," she says.

One of the most notable users of synthesized music is Ukrainian skater Dmitri Dmitrenko, who has found his niche composing his own routines in a music studio, with the help of two friends back in Kiev. "Some of it I like," Marijane admits. "Some of it I don't. But he creates it himself, and it's personal. He takes a chance, but I think people wait for it now, because they know he creates it."

Dmitrenko's fertile imagination comes up with the concept for the music. In 1994, he shed Debussy and Beethoven and created a highly unusual tune that he called "The Fly" for his short program. At first, he said, he told his astonished coach, Ada Minevich, that he wanted to play the role of the fly, but his choreographer, Elena Gudnichak, talked him out of it. Instead, Dmitrenko played a more normal role in which he "killed" the fly partway through the routine, slapping his hands together.

When he appeared at Skate Canada in Red Deer, Alberta, in 1994, the official word was that he would skate his own long program to his own piece, "Don't." Dmitrenko said later that there had been something lost in translation, however, because he had actually called the wonky music "I Did." Few could tell the difference, but Dmitrenko used his music to communicate a lighter side that nobody had seen when he had won the world junior championship in 1992 and the European championship in 1993. "I think I just amuse myself," Dmitrenko said of his composing sideline.

He likes to write his own music, because he says he can feel it and understand it better. And he can compose it to exact specifications. He does not want to look like another skater. He wants a different style. Writing his own music ensures that.

During the 1996-97 season, Dmitrenko unleashed another short program with music he composed. He called it "Short Game Program," and it was, not surprisingly, a clever play on concepts that turned his short program into a video game. He glued a compact disc to his costume ("First one I found," he said) and delighted anybody who could figure out what he was doing. "I wanted to make a program like a video game, and I wanted to write music with my own voice. I wrote the music last year, and I thought it would be for exhibition. But when I started work for the short program, I put all these ideas together."

In the undertones of the music, Dmitrenko's own synthesized voice drones out skating elements or other simple statements in either Russian or English. "Let's go," the voice says at the beginning, in Russian. Because Dmitrenko wrote the music before he knew what his combination jump was, he simply intoned "combination." At the end, he says, "Game over." When Dmitrenko used the program for the first time, at the Skate Israel competition in the fall of 1996, he asked international judges if the voices were indeed legal, because of the ISU rule that vocal music is prohibited. The judges deemed Dmitrenko would have no problem with his unusual music: the voices were not really vocal, but synthesized.

Dmitrenko created about 60 per cent of the choreography in the program, but deferred to a professional to tie it all together. With pupils like Dmitrenko, coaches or choreographers don't have to spend much time rooting through the music bins.

Leonore Kay takes a different tack, obviously. She was the one who discovered the unusual music for Michelle Kwan's long program, music composed by an unknown Azerbaijan musician and performed by the Moscow Radio and Television Symphonic Orchestra. At first, Kay was attracted by the brilliant hues of reds, oranges, and yellows of the Middle Eastern scene on the liner of the compact disc. "Talk about judging a book by its cover," she admits. She didn't buy it immediately, not until after she noticed that a music store, which happened to be one of her prime sources of good skating music, was having a closing-out sale.

Kay lost no time parking her car. When she spotted the disc, she decided to give it a listen.

"I thought, 'Wow, this may not be what we are looking for, but it is tremendous music,'" she says. "I snapped that up." She was so excited by her find that she forgot to go to the rink on the way home. "I zoomed right past the exit," she says.

The find was important. The music search for a skater such as Kwan – a world champion – is difficult, because "we know that we want something really different and distinctive, and that's really hard to come by," Kay says. "It had gotten to the point that one day I thought, 'I have nothing here [in my collection]' – and I have ten thousand albums."

But the real work had only just begun. Kay played the music for Kwan's choreographer, Lori Nichol, then made a tape to send to coach Frank Carroll and to Kwan. The response from all corners was enthusiastic. The rest of the process involved teamwork among all four parties, although Kay is not as involved in the final product – the complete designed routine – as Marijane Stong.

While Nichol developed the idea of what she wanted to do with the music, Kay began to plan how to shorten the length of the piece from sixteen minutes to about four, the required length for the women's long program. (The long programs of men, pairs, and dancers are four and a half minutes long.) "You have to weed out what's really interesting and what really works," she says. "And it didn't have everything we needed. We had to go somewhere else for the slow part. That was a chore trying to find something that complements it. But you don't want it to blend so much, you fall asleep."

Carroll's attentive ear finally discovered the slow part they needed. He had found a cassette with music called "Lion of the Desert," but, at a crucial point, the tape sputtered and garbled the music. He and Nichol called Kay. By chance, several thousand miles away, she found the music in her own library on compact disc, which offers a higher-quality recording than cassettes anyway. "I couldn't believe it," she says. "And I'd had it for years. I'd never used it, so it was just sitting there."

Kay did about six or seven rough cuts before she sent the music by courier to California, where Carroll works. "By the time you finish, it gets so nitpicky," she says. "As Lori was choreographing it, there was a portion where there wasn't enough music – I'm talking two seconds – just to finish a spin or some other move. I had to find a way of accommodating her for that."

Kay did it by repeating half a phrase of music. In all, there are thirteen edits in Kwan's long program. "That's a lot of cuts," Kay says. "It boggles the mind sometimes. You just keep picking away at it."

Musical nitpicking is a way of life for Kay now, especially since she decided to hang up her coaching furs about nine years ago. A former skater who passed her gold figure, gold free skate, and gold dance tests, Kay was burned out from long, cold days coaching at rinks.

Kay's husband, Bill, an editor with a broadcast news service in Canada, first suggested that she give up coaching and just find music for other coaches. When he first brought it up, Kay says she thought he'd "totally lost his marbles," even though the response to her music choices in the past when she had been a coach had always been favourable.

Kay had no extensive musical background, but she did have a sensitive ear, and her husband had been an avid collector of music since he was in his teens. "I have the source material," Kay says. "That and my knowledge of skating is what sets me apart."

The Kays had so many albums that, as soon as they moved into their home in Newmarket, the first task was to build shelves to hold them all. "It's getting to crisis proportions here," she says. "I'm not too sure what we're going to do next." She has also lost her dining room to a vast collection of reference books about music and movies.

"This is not a one-man operation by any means," she admits. "It's very involved. I'm very fortunate that I have my husband. He's sort of an encyclopedia. If he doesn't know something, he knows where to go to look for it."

To top up her own musical knowledge, Kay has been taking music lessons, mostly to understand how music is built and how sounds work and grow together. "I don't see the end of it," she says. Her teacher is a patient graduate of the University of Toronto's music program who has his own recording studio.

Kay is an unusual musical specialist. There are many music technicians who tape and record music for skaters with great success. But, because of her vast library, Kay is more than a technician who edits together musical selections.

Just in time for the 1996-97 season, Kay expanded her ability to edit music by leaping into the computer age: after a good deal of research, she bought a sophisticated software program that allows her great versatility and speed in constructing music. It was a remarkable change from the previous season, when she had constructed Kwan's *Salome* music with old-fashioned reel-to-reel tapes.

"I'm very glad I had the experience on the reel-to-reel," Kay says. "It really makes you listen to what you're doing, because, if you make a mistake on reel-to-reel, you have to start all over again."

Her music teacher found her a computer wizard to help her learn how to use the editing software. Luckily, Kay found someone who had the same software package to take her through it step by step, right from firing up the monitor. It took him almost six hours to show Kay the ins and outs of the program.

"Digital editing on the computer is non-destructive," she says. "It doesn't matter how many mistakes you make, you just keep doing it until you get it right. You have to think it through, obviously. . . . You can do more, more quickly. I can do fades and cross-fades and overdubs instantaneously. It's as quick as I can work. [Digital editing] just opens up a lot more creativity."

Even with the sophisticated computer equipment, the job of building a well-constructed musical routine of exactly the right length can be very time-consuming. "A lot of time goes into finding the right piece of music and the right pieces," Kay says. "A great deal of care and thought is put into these programs. It's a funny thing. The better you are at doing the job of editing, the more unaware people are, because everything runs so smoothly."

Kay soon found that she had a job on her hands that was more than full time. Originally, she started to help out young coaches who couldn't afford to buy armloads of compact discs, which were very expensive several years ago. But her work has darted out in all kinds of unusual directions. She has created music programs for synchronized swimmers, baton twirlers, the odd gymnast, and even horses.

The first person who ever called Kay was a female dressage rider who blurted: "I don't have a daughter who skates. I have a son, but he doesn't skate. But I have a horse."

"Okay, I'll do it," Kay said. "I had no idea what she was going to ask me to do, but I said I'd do it." The rider's babysitter had been one of Kay's skating students.

Musical freestyle programs, called kurs, are becoming more of an important part of dressage as the sport seeks ways to attract television audiences and follows the lead of figure skating. For the first time, kurs became part of Olympic dressage competitions only as recently as the 1996 Games in Atlanta.

Unlike horses, skaters, judges, and audiences respond to music's cadences and subtle moods; it's up to Kay to decide what's suitable for a particular skater, what works for their ears and senses. She designs music not only for élite skaters, but for young skaters, too. For the novice who steps into her musical haven and is unsure of his or her musical way, Kay pulls out an array of styles: movie soundtracks, classical music, some Broadway tunes. Almost intuitively, she gets a feel for the kind of music that attracts them. "When their eyes start smiling, you know you've got the right piece," she says.

Kay's job is to understand the rules of skating, some written, some unwritten, and make sure the skater gets a three- or four-minute program with, for example, a change in tempo. A good, solid, basic traditional program will go fast-slow-fast, with interesting ripples of notes for a footwork sequence, usually after the slow section, she says. "That's not exactly what you have to have," she says. "But you'll never ever go wrong with that."

Kay will look for a piece of music that has plenty of highlights in it, in order to fit in the various jumps and moves. "Does the music say, 'This is an opening,' and then does it calm down and do a slow part?" she ponders. "If it's a tall, willowy person, you're not going to give them something that's so incredibly fast that their feet can't keep up. It can be difficult for someone with a long stride."

If a skater is talented at doing certain "field movements," such as spreadeagles or spirals, it's a clever idea to stretch out the slow part to feature their strengths. It's unwise to use music that emphasizes frailties. Kay keeps all of these things in mind when she's searching.

To make wise choices on what kind of music suits a skater's personality, it also helps Kay to get to know her clients. Kay met Michelle Kwan during the summer of 1995 when the American skater came to Toronto to work on her new programs (including "Salome's Dance") with music that Kay had set aside several years before. "We just never had anybody we thought could handle it," she says. But that year, when Kwan set out to transform her image from a precocious little girl to a more mature one, Kay knew the music was a natural for her: it was about a young girl with qualities that were distinctly unchildlike, and, in fact, sinister rather than innocent. "I got to know her a little bit," Kay says. "She's a funny girl, very bright. She's probably capable of doing anything."

Kay has left behind those cold, dark rinks on which she coached long ago. Instead, she is often bound to her home, tied to the computer by unseen muses. For one thing, she feels warmer, she admits. She's definitely up to her musical ears in melodies and pianissimos and boogie-woogie. These days, her work schedule varies from exhaustingly busy to steady, almost year-round. "If there's a [slow] cycle in there somewhere, I'm missing it," she says.

Kay's busiest season doesn't necessarily correspond to the height of the competition season, because her work involves preparing programs for the following season. Usually, a skater and coach begin to think about programs for the next season as soon as the current season ends. For those who don't go on to world championships, the season ends after a national championship in January or February. Yet all skaters are ready to start again by late summer, or early September, when the competition season starts again. From mid-February until August, Kay works almost non-stop, making as many as three appointments a day, working from 7 or 7:30 A.M. and on into the evening, usually about nine hours a day in all. Once, when a coach arrived from out of town after a long drive with a handful of skaters, Kay felt compelled to push herself to work twelve hours, with a half-hour break for pizza. "That just killed me," she says. "And I couldn't hear for three days."

After all, Kay had to test out the music to hear what it would sound like in the rink, at full volume. "It's okay if you're trying to do a quiet mix," she says. "But this coach had three or four competitors with her, and you can't just do really quiet music."

As Kay cuts and edits and builds and searches, almost full-out for months, the outer world chugs on without her. A social life is a forgotten luxury. She and her husband, who works shifts, don't have 9-to-5 friends. Kay cuts loose on Fridays, doing errands and – ending up at a rink. "I love skating," she says. "You can't tear me away from it."

Sometimes Kay shares a gentle joke with choreographer Lori Nichol that their social lives are getting in the way of their work. Last season, Kay and her husband took a break, a vacation to Florida, but somehow they ended up in a music shop, fingering through compact discs, grabbing some earphones for a listen. "It used to be that my husband would drag me into record stores, and I'd sort of tap my feet and tap my fingers," she says. "I'm afraid now that the position has reversed somewhat."

Because of her workload, Kay rarely gets a chance to actually watch a competition, although she did make it to the 1996 world championship in Edmonton and to the 1997 U.S. championship in Nashville, to see her work come to life in a rink. Last season was particularly harried. Finally one Saturday, she said, she put her foot down, closed down shop, and headed for a Canadian sectional competition. She spent the day cruising from rink to rink, a sightseer, inspector, and kid in a frosty candyshop. There were so many young people skating to her work that she couldn't possibly see them all. Usually, she catches up on the results of her work during their practice days.

Her rewards are immediate, however. "The kids are super," she says. "Once you deliver the music, it's instant gratification. You've given them what they want and their eyes light up and they go 'wow.' Who wouldn't like that?

"Some of the younger skaters come here and they leave with their eyes shining. Some of them don't say too much when they arrive, but by the time they're leaving, they open up a bit. I remember taking a program into the rink one day last year, and this skater came up to me and said, 'Did you do his music? That's so awesome. I really like that.' And [the skater] was [a] kid who thanked me for his music three weeks earlier."

Kay often has amusing adventures dealing with young up-and-comers. Last season, she provided the music for five or six Canadian novice men. One by one, they called her up and asked to skate to the same piece of music. When Kay informed them of this, they, like seasoned music experts, would ask which track or selection the other was using, or, without missing a beat, whether their opponent was using the music in the short or the long program.

"Oh my word," Kay said to herself, recognizing one pint-sized skater who seemed to have the nimble smarts to act as his own agent in the future. In the end, it all worked out.

For Kay, music is a universal language, a magical tool. And for figure-skating programs, not just any music will do. "Music has to appeal to the audience the instant they hear it," Kay says. "And it has to appeal to the skater the instant he or she hears it.

"If it doesn't say something, then it's time to get a hot dog."

It's the fundamental question Kay and other hunters of music ask themselves about their music choices. "If you heard that music, would you stop and listen?" Kay queries. "Or would you go and get a hot dog?"

It is Kay's job to make sure the fans stay fastened to their seats.

The Magic Floor:
The Choreographer's Workplace

*I*n the eyes of a choreographer, a skating rink is not just a cold, hard rectangular surface. It is a magic floor.

Nobody knows this better than Osborne Colson, an eightysome-thing, nattily attired, gravel-voiced seeker of soul, who was inducted into Canada's figure-skating hall of fame in 1996. A coach-choreographer who trained and directed Barbara Ann Scott's first all-Canadian tour in the 1950s, Colson has eyes that do not see merely a staid ice-chip-white surface when he looks at a rink. He envisions a palette of colour, with countless possibilities. His magic floor has life. It has hues. It has texture. It is a place for form and movement. It is art. To a chore-ographer, vision is everything.

Today, choreography in figure skating is more important than ever, an indispensable factor in a final result or a pleasing performance. Choreography gives a reason for all the stroking and jumping and spin-ning. It creates feeling and form and establishes a goal. It ties the high-flying technical elements into a point of view, a thought, an expression of life's varied path.

"Choreography is not just smiling for the judges," said Ellen Burka, who coached – and created choreography for – her daughter, the 1965 world champion, Petra Burka, for 1976 Olympic bronze medallist Toller

Cranston, for five-time Canadian pairs champions Sandra and Val Bezic, for two-time Canadian champion Karen Preston, even for Elvis Stojko until he was fifteen. She also choreographed part of the long program that helped Dorothy Hamill win the 1976 Olympics, as well as her short program.

"Don't forget the fingers," Hamill remembers Burka telling her in her autobiography, *On and Off the Ice*. "The hands. The arms. Feel the music in every part of you. Let it flow out of your fingers."

As Michelle Kwan grew into a polished teenager, she gradually realized that choreography meant more than smiling through a spiral – so much so that she created her own exhibition routine in the season following her world-championship win. At only sixteen, Kwan had learned her lessons well. Her sessions in choreography with Lori Nichol were not just a matter of setting steps for her programs, but were lessons in art and movement, rhythm and dynamics, whisper and mystery.

Indeed, choreography on ice is not all that different from the design of line and resonance and rhythm and pattern in other arts. Only the medium and the vocabulary are unique. Colson, a painter of body movement, knows this well. For eleven years, back in the 1970s, he set up a summer skating school in conjunction with the Banff School of Fine Arts in Alberta, because he always felt that skating and the arts world were interrelated.

For six years, one of his students at the school was Sarah Kawahara, who started there when she was eleven. She had first started working with Colson in Toronto at the age of nine. Now, Kawahara is spreading Colson's teachings and ideas as far and wide as she can. She is one of the busiest and most successful choreographers on the planet. Some describe Kawahara as Colson's unfinished symphony; neither ceases to learn. Across a continent, they still talk, share new visions.

"We would have lectures from the different departments [at the Banff school], whether it was costuming, music, theatre, or dance," explains Kawahara, who is based in Los Angeles. "I think all of that really affected the way that the creative process was born for me in my formative years. I have used every iota of it in my independent life. To this day, I refer to him [Colson] in everything I do. He germinated everything for me."

Several years ago, Kawahara and Colson were together again, presenting a seminar on choreography for the Professional Skaters Association. They called the seminar "Palette of Colour." Colson explained his approach, in which the ice is a palette of distinct hues, with a blue section, or a magenta section, or a green section. "Skate as if you arc blue," he will tell a skater. Skate the way the colour feels, he will say. Imagine how it feels. Find your mood and colour inside your mind. Spotlights aren't needed. Spotlights can be conjured from the strength and the fertility of the imagination. In Colson's world, colour is a feeling and a movement and an emotion.

"In the movement of skating, there are many different textures and colours within what you do," Kawahara explains. "And the movement can have hard edges, with bold colours. You want to complement that with the opposite, juxtapose it with a rounder edge in front of a hard edge. It's very much like painting, and music is formed that way, too. All of the arts have this in common, different textures and colourations. They all have shape. It's design in space. The medium is different, that's all."

Kawahara learned her lessons well, too. As an amateur, she was known as a graceful artistic skater, in the vein of 1968 Olympic champion Peggy Fleming, at a time when expression and art in skating were relatively unsung concepts. From the time she joined Ice Capades at age seventeen, she put her Colson-born theories to work, and eventually became a choreographer for the once-vibrant company. Since then, her charmed choreographic life has led her to create ice palettes for the best and most interesting in the business: Scott Hamilton, Dorothy Hamill, John Curry, Toller Cranston, Chen Lu, Surya Bonaly, Christopher Bowman, Tai Babilonia and Randy Gardner, Charlie Tickner, Peggy Fleming. One of her most recent projects was to design the complex weavings of forty-five skaters for "Pocahontas," a Kenneth Feld production for Walt Disney's World on Ice.

Kawahara learned her choreographic ABCs from Colson and from experience, but generally, there aren't schools for figure-skating choreography. The former Soviet Union perhaps came closest with its state-supported system of art, sport, and education. It produced Marina Zoueva, whose spellbinding work propelled her best-known students, Ekaterina Gordeeva and the late Sergei Grinkov, to superstar status.

Zoueva has a university degree in choreography from a Moscow university. But well-known choreographers, such as 1960 Olympic pairs champion Bob Paul, often do not. Paul relied on instinctive feel and past experience when he designed programs for Peggy Fleming, Dorothy Hamill, Linda Fratianne, Walt Disney's World on Ice, and even Donny and Marie Osmond's television show.

Choreographer Lori Nichol's primary skating school was the U.S.-based John Curry Skating Company, with which she performed for several years. She learned from the best teachers, in an informal way, while employed by Curry, but she also soaked up knowledge from every artistically minded coach or choreographer she met or worked with from her early skating days. When she was an amateur skater in the United States, she learned about choreography when her coach, Don Laws – later coach of Scott Hamilton – designed her programs for her. Laws had a certain flair for art. Nichol was also exposed to the work of other choreographic skating experts, such as Ricky Harris, a former professional skater who has university degrees in drama and dance choreography, and the late André Denis, a Canadian choreographer who was a force during the 1980s, before he died of AIDS. Nichol also drew inspiration from Colson and Burka, whom she met and watched and with whom she shared information after she moved to Canada as a coach. Her heart beats in rhythm with art.

As mentioned, if there was anywhere in the world that a skater was apt to have formal training in choreography, it was in Russia (the former Soviet Union). Zoueva, a former Soviet ice dancer who finished fifth at the 1977 world championship with partner Andrei Vitman, decided to learn dance choreography when she finished her amateur career, and studied at the University of Art in Moscow. Because Zoueva had been a skater, she was at a distinct advantage when it came to translating her university studies onto the ice. Many dance choreographers try their hand at designing skating programs, but have to relearn the kinds of movement that come from gliding on blades across a slippery surface, rather than moving across a floor. Dance choreographers who have experience with skating are welcomed in the dance world.

Zoueva reached right into the world of art for her inspiration and made practical use of her university studies, on the spot, with skaters. About the time Gordeeva and Grinkov were first paired together, Zoueva was studying for her final examinations in 1984, for which she had to produce choreographed routines for ballet – a solo and a *pas de deux*. She enlisted the help of three Moscow skaters: Gordeeva and Grinkov and Elena Voderezova, who had already become the first Soviet woman to win a world championship medal – a bronze – in 1983.

The examination committee gave Zoueva the highest marks possible for the *pas de deux* she devised for Gordeeva and Grinkov, which eventually became one of their exhibition numbers. The fledgling couple had explained Zoueva's concept very well, the exam committee told her. Gordeeva was only thirteen years old at the time, Grinkov, seventeen.

"I used them as an example to make a little choreography on the floor, not the ice," Zoueva says. But it was only one more small step to take the choreography to the ice. For example, she would study adagio (a ballet dance in slow tempo), then transform what she learned onto glinting steel blades.

During the early 1980s in the Soviet Union, life was good for artists and for students in Moscow who wanted to learn. Zoueva had student passes for all the Russian ballet theatres and used them extensively. "I had a lot of ideas [for ice choreography], because I studied at the university of art," Zoueva says. "I had good communication with artists and drama students and ballroom people. I worked in a normal theatre, and I worked in a children's dance theatre in Moscow. I made the connection between many things. It gave me lots of power."

She took the exercises from her university classes back to the rink and tried them out on skaters in her group. Among them were Elena Leonova and Gennadi Krasnitski, who would win the world junior pairs championship in Kitchener, Ontario, in 1987, and Ekaterina Muruguva and Artem Torgashev, who would take the silver, as well as 1985 world champion Alexander Fadeev and Anna Kondreshova, a world silver medallist in 1984. "It was a great time for work, to be creative, to be happy, and to have lots of enthusiasm," she recalls.

Zoueva taught drama classes and exercises to the members of her skating group, who benefited immediately from her study. "We make some poses from pictures," she says. "We do some animal movements. We make situations for people if they love each other, or don't want to talk. We did exercises on what happens if it rains or there is sunshine, how people fight, what it is like to be friendly. They were like exercises in life."

All along, Zoueva was studying how to teach her skating students. The first program she created for Gordeeva and Grinkov was quite simple, but she could see they were "very talented for movement." Although Zoueva has a library of music styles stored in her head, she had to take what music the school assigned her for this program, done to a disco beat. "I just make parallel movement," she says. "It was not great choreography, but it was a wonderful exercise for pairs skating, how to do parallel movements.

"After this program, I think, *mama mia*, I should do something else for the kids. I think they were so nice, all smiles, all fresh. They worked very easy, very lightly."

This time, she chose piano music by Claude Bolling and added bird sounds. "My feeling about them was that they were so light and fresh," Zoueva says. "They make it fun for people who look at them. Katya had a nice smile and Sergei had excellent hand movements. He had amazing hands.

"It is a problem that choreographers have. Some people just can't use their hands. It was natural for Sergei. Of course, we teach this, and correct it, but for some people, it doesn't matter how much you train. If you have talent, you have to improve the talent."

It is up to a coach or choreographer to find the strongest talent of a skater and improve it, channel it, and give it direction, Zoueva says. Sarah Kawahara agrees. Zoueva has an eye for hidden talents and gently draws them into the light.

Zoueva has a gift for finding just the right music for a skater, too, and it is music that asks for line and expression and – if you're talking to Colson – colour. Alexander Fadeev says this gift of Zoueva's is one of her strongest assets. She gets inside the skater and inside the music and matches them together, emotionally, intuitively. Then she assembles her creative movements at high speed, astonishing skaters who have worked with her. The ideas tumble out of her fertile imagination like polished pearls from a whimsically upturned basket.

The moment Gordeeva first set foot in Zoueva's apartment in Ottawa after Grinkov's death, with daughter, Daria, at her side, Zoueva knew instantly what music to use for two programs Gordeeva would do at her husband's tribute in Hartford, Connecticut, in early 1996. She chose the Adagietto from Gustav Mahler's Symphony No. 5 and the *Serenade* for strings by Peter Tchaikovsky, the Russian composer who saw the truths of his generation crumbling and strung together notes of romantic melancholy.

Mahler was a composer who touched the soul by weaving his personal emotion into the music's beats and bars and rhythms. Zoueva chose his work because of the feeling it created when she heard it. "Everyone has in his life some moment when they feel down," she says, speaking of the symphony. "And everyone should find some power in life to get up and do it again and give something to someone else. It is not in life, only to do good for yourself, but to give somebody else more. We wanted to show to the audience that everywhere you can find this feeling to be strong again."

The music was right for Gordeeva, Zoueva felt, because of what she could see in her face when she came to her. "It's because she wanted to do [the Celebration of Life tribute] for Sergei, for only this one reason. I saw it. It gave me lots of power and I had lots of ideas."

Zoueva had never used the music before. No one in figure skating had, she says. It was even more appealing because Zoueva knew that, after Mahler composed the piece, he had signed it personally and sent it to his fiancé. With knowledge of this loving gesture, Zoueva felt inspired to give it to Gordeeva, because it spoke of the Russian couple's attachment to each other on the ice and in life.

The music was also perfect because it had a tragic, minor tone. But a sub-melody lurking beneath it breathed a spirit of romance, even a celebration of romance, and with it, hope. "There are many streams in the music," Zoueva said.

Throughout their career, Zoueva created programs for Gordeeva and Grinkov that matched the tenor of their lives at the time. With each one, there was a progression in feeling, a reason for its existence. In 1990, when it was becoming clear there was a romance between the two skaters, Zoueva gave them *Romeo and Juliet*. "Sergei was recognizing that Katya was probably a woman," she says.

Four years later, after the couple had married, had a child, and performed as professionals, Zoueva brought forth Beethoven's *Moonlight Sonata* to use as their long program at the 1994 Olympics. It was as if the music had been created specifically for them: strong and delicate, reverent, pale and clear, ghostlike. "I saw how they had matured," Zoueva says. "And how Sergei so much respected Katya and how Katya respected him as a man. They loved each other, and they respected each other. That was very important. I made the program as if he was on his knee in front of the Madonna and baby. She was really woman. He was really man."

During the professional career that followed, Zoueva used a Rachmaninoff composition and created a tableau in which the pair skated like Rodin sculptures. "Sergei's body was so perfect, like a Greek god," she says. "And Katya's body was like sculpture. You can't add anything to them. I wanted to take what they had and fix it in time forever, the moment how people love each other." Grinkov particularly loved the Rachmaninoff number.

Zoueva's creation of their last competitive routine, to Verdi's *Requiem*, was an artistic invention of another level. She wanted the Russian couple to portray an idea of love that goes beyond the love between man and woman. "It's because I think they grow," Zoueva says. "It is a serious idea, not just movement."

The Verdi music was first brought to Zoueva's attention while she was still living in Russia by Moscow ballet choreographer Vladimir Kostin, who told her he had the perfect music for Alexander Fadeev. It was an aria from *Requiem* that had a very masculine tone. Zoueva listened to it, researched it, but she did not feel it was right for Fadeev.

For five years, she put it aside and kept it in a box. After she moved to Canada, Zoueva pulled it out of the box again for Gordeeva and Grinkov, but she used three completely different sections of the composition than the ones suggested by Kostin. The idea that Gordeeva and Grinkov were to portray in *Requiem* dealt with the ugly feelings welling up inside of people, but also the desire for good. Through a heartfelt appeal to God, asking for forgiveness, one can find peace, harmony, and love in one's soul.

The first part of the music that Zoueva used is warlike, when the devil drags down the human spirit. The second is the emotion of weeping, regretting, asking for forgiveness. The third is music of peace and sanctuary, as man turns from evil to good. A serious idea, indeed. Their choreographer had taken Gordeeva and Grinkov's performances to an intellectual level, far beyond the Lucky Luke routines of Philippe Candeloro, *Rocky* soundtracks, "The Flight of the Bumble Bee," or other boogie-woogie routines often seen in skating. Her work was high art.

Yet there is a place for boogie-woogie and uninhibited fun in skating, and, as a director of choreography of Disney skating productions for sixteen years, Bob Paul has become an expert in how to design the ebb and flow of genies, dwarfs, and princes charming their way across unusual sizes of ice surfaces. Paul, an Olympic champion and four-time world champion with Canadian partner Barbara Wagner, had none of the formal training of Marina Zoueva, but a long history of carnival performances, and even some acting, singing, and dancing lessons spurred him on. "My choreography came by the seat of my pants," he admits. "I did it instinctively. My musicality was what I had naturally."

If Paul had any training at all, it began extremely early. He grew up in the days of the travelling carnival extravaganzas in Canada, a skating phenomenon that started during the 1930s. He first skated at a complex called Icelandia in downtown Toronto, at a site that is now a large parking garage. Icelandia was the place to go for children who did not belong to clubs. In Toronto during the 1940s, there were only three artificial rinks in the city and no artificial rinks in parks. But Paul was keen enough that he found Icelandia, which was so organized that it staged modest skating shows. Its volunteers even took the shows to small towns lacking the resources to present their own, ferrying busloads of young skaters all over the province. Paul was one of the kids on these buses, and, at age ten, he was doing his own choreography with a flourish. "They probably were silly," Paul admits.

Paul may have created by instinct, but later in his skating career he had an expert to show him the way. His coach, Sheldon Galbraith, who had a good eye for body line, always choreographed his competitive numbers. Paul learned from Galbraith's example and had a chance to try out all the ideas on his own because Galbraith always assigned his pupils to create their own exhibitions. When Wagner and Paul joined Ice Capades after they left the amateur world behind, they carried on the tradition. They choreographed their own routines.

When his professional career came to an end, Paul headed to Los Angeles to become an actor, but to earn a living he taught skating on the side. His first student was Peggy Fleming, who at fifteen was "a gangly little junior," Paul recalls. But while he was teaching her, he was also learning valuable lessons. He did what all aspiring young actors do. He took acting classes, signed up for small workshops, pounded the pavement, tried to find agents. He studied singing and jazz dance. The work got him only so far in his acting career. He once landed a part on a "Bewitched" episode on television, although he was rather typecast: he played the part of a skating teacher. But his classes and his work as an actor served to enhance his work as a choreographer. Almost without breaking a sweat, Paul's bread-and-butter career in skating took off. He followed its lead.

Paul was on the cusp of a significant trend in skating: the importance of choreography to programs. He was part of it. He was one of the first to do specialized work as a skating choreographer during the mid-1960s, working alongside a coach who took care of the technical concerns.

"Everybody [who was a coach] did everything at that point," Paul says, speaking of the traditional practice of coaches who designed programs as well as teaching skills to skaters. "I think they just took [choreography] for granted, that it would just be there. I think they relied on personality more than choreography. If you happened to get a good blend of both, then you were on top of it."

In the years after the Second World War, choreography had been something of a happenstance practice. Galbraith and Swiss-born coach Gustave Lussi paid particular attention to it, figured it was just as important as the skills. Sonja Henie fused her love of ballet with skating as early as 1928 when she linked the disparate skating elements into a flowing whole. But not every coach considered choreography necessary or even desirable. Otto Gold, a European-born coach who worked in Canada, was a stern taskmaster who disliked frills and furbelows in music, skating patterns, and costume. Barbara Ann Scott, who trained with him for years before she worked with Galbraith, recalled that, if she or one of her peers moved their arms like a ballet dancer, he'd throw his gloves at them. To Gold, choreography was a sin. To Galbraith, choreography was one of the saving graces.

A tall man, draped in a great coat and beaver hat, Galbraith was an imposing presence as he worked with tiny Scott on ice, imitating feminine ways of moving with short steps and flowery pirouettes. No doubt, he amused some spectators, but he changed Scott's career and set new priorities in skating. Bob Paul also carried the Galbraith torch and was able to take it a step further, making a career of it beyond coaching.

Paul's career as a choreographer started because of a chance meeting with Peggy Fleming in 1964. His partner, Barbara Wagner, introduced him to the young American during a summer exhibition in Sun Valley, Idaho. Fleming was a guest skater. So were Wagner and Paul – one last time. After the show, Paul intended to hustle over to Los Angeles to begin his acting career. When he met Fleming in Idaho, she was in the midst of changing coaches. "Mrs. Fleming [Peggy's mother] had a habit of changing coaches frequently," Paul remembers.

By coincidence, Paul bumped into the Flemings again in Los Angeles a week after he arrived. He was looking for work as a coach in the city of dreams, and the Flemings were looking for a coach. It was a match made in lotus land. The Flemings hired him.

Under his guidance, Fleming finished third at the 1965 world championship, but, true to form, the Flemings left Paul a year later to work with Carlo Fassi, an Italian who had won two European titles in

1953 and 1954. Fassi, who was considered a master coach, had just set up shop in Colorado Springs, and he did a courageous thing for a coach. He asked Paul to handle Fleming's choreography, instead of doing it himself, to exercise complete control over his skater. It was the beginning of a trend that exists today.

"I think it was brave of him to do that, because of the egos that exist in figure skating," Paul says. "There's a lot more cooperation with coaches sharing students today. The specializing is much more prominent today, although egos still exist. But specialization did not exist then. Because I was pursuing the acting, I was quite pleased just to do the choreography."

Even today, not every skater can afford a specialist. Out of necessity, many of the rank-and-file skaters use their coaches as choreographers. Some coaches are blessed with a talent for choreography, but there is no guarantee. "You can have a brilliant coach, but that doesn't mean they're musical or have ideas creatively for choreography," Paul says. Coaches who would rather defer to the expert may only go so far as to determine the order of jumps in a skater's routines, then let a choreographer create the collection of steps and moves and body lines and moods, all in harmony with the music.

Paul's choreographic career was sealed with the work he did for Fleming, however. He did what all good choreographers do today: he took a gangly teenager, all legs and arms, and transformed her into an elegant vision on ice, a finished, polished masterpiece. While Fassi gave Fleming the technical tools, the confidence, and the advice, Paul gave her a presence on the ice, so that her programs were more than a collection of elements. She was already a U.S. champion before Paul had met her, but at the time, he says, the skating world thought "she was just a flash in the pan." The sentiment was that she had simply stepped into a void left after the air crash that wiped out the American figure-skating team heading for the 1961 world championship in Prague. Fleming and Paul proved the naysayers wrong. "With the work that I did with her in one year, she totally changed from a young girl into a mature young lady," Paul says. It was a Michelle Kwan-like transformation.

"She was so naturally classical that we always tried to find a number that fit her classically," he says, speaking of her long, balletic lines and pure, clear movement. "A lot of it was God-given, and I just enhanced it. There are certain bodies that just have it naturally, and she had one of them. It had to be brought out and defined and refined, and that's what I did."

Paul was not one to choreograph from the sidelines. He strapped on his skates when he worked with Fleming. "I always chased her around the ice and talked to her, not yelled at her, but talked, while she was doing the routine," he recalls. "Then, just before the elements, I would keep quiet, so she could concentrate. And then all the in-between stuff is what makes up the program. I'd constantly talk to her, to remind her, do this, do that. Even after she turned pro, if you see a video of her winning the [1968] Olympics, and then you see her ten years later, she matured a lot even then, yet she never went to a heck of a lot of classes. It was her skills in observation. Whatever she looked at, she imitated, and it developed on its own."

When Fleming won her first world title in 1966, defeating defending champion Petra Burka of Canada, she was coached by Fassi, but it was Paul who created the memorable choreography. For her long program, he used Tchaikovsky's *Pathétique* symphony, an unusual work that the Russian composed during the last year of his life. The piece was meant to be an enigma, penetrated by subjective sentiment. Fleming created sentiment of her own, in an enigmatic way. She skated like a ballerina, but with a lucky chewing-gum wrapper folded inside her glove. She was only seventeen.

Paul's choreography also helped Fleming to win the Olympic gold medal in 1968 in Grenoble, France, only eight years after he himself had won Olympic gold as a pairs skater. From the very beginning, Paul's choreographic career had swept him to the top in a rush, like a giant Ferris wheel, and he wasn't close to being finished after Fleming's retirement from amateur competition. Television became a major force during the 1960s, and Fleming created the first figure-skating television special. She did others, too. And she wanted Paul to do the choreography for them, as well as for her personal appearances

and other exhibitions. Paul choreographed five television specials for
Fleming.

Paul tackled the jobs with zest. Producers and directors of television
shows wanted six or seven routines. "Then you could take liberties and
do something that was a little more mellow, because, unlike live audiences in arenas, you didn't have to expect an audience to give you a
standing ovation," he says. "You could do something more lyrical and
subtle.

"I think it's more difficult for a lady to get applause than a pair,
which is spectacular with their lifts, and men who are obviously more
athletic," he says. "It's a tough challenge for a lady. Ladies like to do
lovely soft numbers, but soft numbers just don't get applause. That was
always the challenge, to get a variety in a live show, to make a skater
look different from one act to another."

When Fleming was an amateur, Paul had sought variety by pushing
her to do upbeat routines for her exhibitions, or non-competitive routines. Once, he had her skate to Tom Jones's "What's New Pussycat?"
in which he tried to bring the modern dance steps of the day onto the
ice. The music was not complicated, but the choreographic creation
was, he says.

Bob Paul opened up new horizons for Peggy Fleming, but new horizons also opened up quickly for a man who had a flair for choreography.
When Fleming skated as a guest with Ice Follies, she introduced Paul
to the show's owner, Irving Feld. Within six months, Feld hired Paul as
choreographer. When Feld reached an agreement with the Disney corporation to produce Walt Disney's World on Ice, Paul was busy for
years as its director of skating and choreography. With Paul's roots in
carnivals, he was a natural for directing Disney creations.

"My first show was a regular ice show," Paul recalls. "Instinctively, I
felt I knew what to do, because I had been an observer of ice shows
since I was a kid. I just loved the ice shows. I went to them all." One
year, when Paul was a young boy, four ice shows came to Toronto,
including the Hollywood Ice Revue, in which Barbara Ann Scott had
taken over the starring role from Sonja Henie, as well as Holiday on

Ice, Ice Capades, and Ice Follies. On top of those treats, Paul watched an extravagant carnival production put on by the Toronto Skating Club. "Kids just belonged to the club because of the shows," Paul says. "They thought the people that competed were crazy."

Later, the professional shows, such as Ice Follies, took inspiration from the large amateur shows, such as the Toronto Skating Club's carnival, but decided to take it to the road, and tour, all year long. In 1936, Ice Follies became the first touring ice show. The touring Disney shows, which began about a decade ago, offered a different challenge, because its choreographers had to work from a specific story script and bring to life an animated cartoon, without losing its charm. And it wasn't enough to have chorus skaters flash their blades, as in an ice show. Paul had to integrate characters and lead roles into the mix, and work all the moves around dialogue sequences.

In the first year or two, Paul would first lay out the routines in his mind, then work in the steps of the characters later. He gradually came to see that the stars of the productions had to be integrated into the choreography, right from the beginning. And he had to create choreography to take into account the costumes of the characters, which had a limiting effect on movement. Some of them strove to be athletic, but not if their costumes were so bulky that they toppled over. Paul remembers the complications he faced when a bulging rack full of costumes arrived for the genies only a week before the opening show – and they didn't fit. "Nobody could see out of the heads," he recalls. "It was a totally different challenge. The main thing to do is go in with a plan. It can be very chaotic if you don't approach it in a very organized way." Rehearsals can stretch into fifteen- to sixteen-hour days, as skaters synchronize ice movement with dialogue and lead characters reprise their roles, sometimes learning how to act as they do so.

Portraying emotion is an elemental function of choreography. Without it, choreography seems flat and lifeless, like a wound-down gramophone. The Disney productions, out of necessity, are affairs of the heart and require the very things that Marina Zoueva taught her skaters to express from the beginning. Elementary feelings: fear, hate,

love, grumpiness, bashfulness, dopiness. "The emotional part of choreography is something that is hard to train," Paul says. Some have it,
others don't. The ones who don't have to learn to let loose so that they
can enhance the choreography. "I've seen great choreographers do
numbers for people who don't have that God-given gift, and then the
choreography doesn't look so good," Paul says. "We've all had those."

What they're missing, according to Sarah Kawahara, is the inflection in their skating speech. Choreography is like speech; it needs
inflection to become interesting. Without it, speakers are like robots;
skaters are too. When skaters use choreography with inflection, they
are interpreting the tools; inflection is "the mood of how you say it, and
how you express it," she says. Sometimes amateur skaters ignore the
inflection, at the cost of the whole.

The trick to being a Disney choreographer is to be able to choose
skaters who have an aptitude for dangling emotions – and inflection –
on their sleeves as easily as doing a crossover. This ability, says Paul,
who also acted as a talent scout for Disney, is more crucial than landing
triple jumps. The most important factor in searching out a skater who
would be successful in Disney shows are "people with good personalities," Paul says. "That's the levelling factor when you get into show
business." It is necessary, Paul says, to find a skater who can evoke the
emotion of the number. And, in Disney shows, the skater has to bring
to life the personality of the character out of the animated feature film.
Even if the skater is lip-synching Snow White's dialogue, she must still
portray emotion. "Some of them were just scared to death of learning
that, and they only had five weeks to do it," Paul says.

Paul's toughest job was to convince former competitive skaters to
take a Disney character into their souls so convincingly that they could
maintain it no matter what they had to do on ice. It wasn't easy. Skaters
learn by rote, a method that is necessary to win competitions: every
move is so well honed and reworked and repeated that a skater almost
switches onto auto-pilot during a routine. This will not do in a Disney
production. "It's very hard to break the habit," Paul explains. "You can't
all of a sudden break into a competitive spirit. You must do all the competitive tricks, but you must have the same feeling that you are still the
same person."

Paul has had to work very hard with some skaters to change their ways, reminding them at every turn to remember their roles. "They'd take that first crossover in the solo, and all of a sudden, they were the competitor again," he says.

Dance choreographers do not run into such problems. Dancers are trained to match their movement to emotion from the time they are children, Paul says. Skaters are not. Skaters are trained to be athletes, to win the Olympics with a series of tricks. Only a handful come equipped with the emotional gear to excel as naturally as they draw breath. Paul says four-time world champion Kurt Browning is the best of the lot from Canada, because he can portray any style: humorous, dramatic, classical – right down to the proper line – or even a Gene Kelly dance routine. "That's a God-given thing," Paul says. Some can learn how to use body language somewhat, but many are moulded to only one emotional interpretation, and cannot go further. To do choreography for a pliable skater like Browning, who opens his skating heart to all, would be a real joy, Paul says. But Paul and Browning moved in different worlds.

As a Disney talent scout, Paul was always on the lookout for skaters with gifts of line, and feeling, and colour, while attending most world championships. He has never lost touch with the current generation of performers. The most impressive interpreters of emotion and feeling in the past decade, he says, are 1984 Olympic champions Jayne Torvill and Christopher Dean. Another he admires is 1980 Olympic champion Robin Cousins, also a choreographer. Gordeeva and Grinkov were high on his list. Gordeeva, as a soloist, has passed Paul's inspection with flying colours, a weightless body lighting up a rink with a delicate emotion and touch.

Western culture is not alone in producing skaters with a rich lode of emotional ability to interpret choreography. Paul is astounded by the talent of Yuka Sato, a shining chameleonlike Japanese wonder who won the 1994 world championship. "She is incredible," Paul says. "Torvill and Dean and Cousins interpreted their own choreography, and Sato interprets what somebody gives her. But even on television, which tends to neutralize the emotions of a piece, you can see her emotions. I haven't seen her perform in person. But there is something obviously inside of her that has really allowed her to let loose. There are certain ones that affect me emotionally, and she certainly does."

With his experienced and discerning eye, Bob Paul scouted out Canadians Jaimee Eggleton and Karen Preston to play the lead roles in "Aladdin" and "Snow White and the Seven Dwarfs," respectively. But his work as a choreographer for Disney was far from complete. Like a maestro who hears every note, Paul had to organize the flow and patterns of forty-five skaters in each routine. It's a complicated, daunting procedure. While the world outside was basking in sunshine on a spring day in 1994, Paul was huddled over an enormous book of diagrams in an empty rink in California, as he designed the "Snow White" production. His work was so complex that he had to record it all, lest he forget.

The book was hundreds of pages thick, a detailed working outline of every nuance in the "Snow White" production. On every page, Paul had jotted – crammed – a series of skating patterns. He had already watched the original Disney movie, gleaning from it inspiration, studying it to determine which parts would flow onto an ice format. With all this in mind, Paul designed every moment of each of the forty-five skaters in his massive notebook, taking into account every beat of the music in each scene. The task was so complicated that for a single production number he sketched thirty-three pages of diagrams.

Before he presented the complex notation to the skaters, he watched with a steady eye as his assistant, Jill Shipstead Thomas, tried out the choreography for various roles on ice. He kept watch over the diagrams in his notebook and sometimes joined her on the ice. Eventually, he taught all the moves and routines to the show's performance director and to male and female line captains. After six weeks' of rehearsals in Florida, the group of five then taught the choreography to the cast.

Like Bob Paul, Sarah Kawahara is an expert at designing the choreography for large groups of skaters, all searching for a spot to turn out a toe, creating movement *en masse*. In true Osborne Colson form, Kawahara sees the task in musical terms. "When I did "Pocahontas" for Kenneth Feld, working with forty-five people, it's like forty-five instruments," she says. "It's an orchestration of movement, really. When you are working with the music, you try to ally yourself with how the music is orchestrated."

Kawahara's musical instruments are the skaters. She selects them carefully, matching the skater with the movement that expresses the music. For a lyrical piece, she chooses a skater with lyrical qualities, who has the gift of melting feeling into lyrical body line. Sometimes she chooses an athletic skater for a powerful section. Perhaps pairs skaters could be used for another part, with music that has points and counterpoints. With these expressive instruments, Kawahara creates levels of meaning and feeling.

Kawahara revels in her work with big production numbers. At forty-two, she has found joy in the many aspects of her life, made more full by her marriage to actor-comedian Jamie Alcroft and the bustle of three children: Alysse, ten, intrigued by art and gymnastics, Hayley, a five-year-old karate chopper, and son Thatcher, three. "I do love to have a lot of layers in my life," Kawahara says. "It's very interesting, the nooks and crannies and turns and mazes." So, when she steps out the door of her Los Angeles home, she seeks to create more. Big production numbers give her the opportunity.

"When you work with groups of people, it's very dimensional," she says. Like a gifted artisan, she weaves all of the individual movements together, layer upon layer. Yet, they are part of Kawahara's whole, sculpturally connected, visually complex, emotionally varied.

Kawahara has worked with some of the best solo skaters in the business, but she can scout out the complex levels in their souls as well – and is fascinated by them. An individual has many sides to his or her personality: Kawahara finds them and explores them, and makes a choreographic piece of work that is as complex as an individual can handle.

For more than a decade, she has created the choreography for 1984 Olympic champion Scott Hamilton, perhaps the most natural showman of all. Or so it appears. Kawahara has tended to the vision with great care. "Working with all the facets of his talent has been very, very rewarding," she says. "It's gone far beyond any dimension I saw in the beginning."

Most of all, Kawahara gave a point of view, a single purpose with a unified theme, to Hamilton's programs. A stickler for detail, she made them exceedingly difficult as well, playing up his ability to flash quick and dazzling footwork. While it is possible to construct an abstract program, Kawahara feels better armed to do her work if she can create a point of view, an idea, a thematic suggestion. "I feel I can make a stronger statement," she says.

Hamilton had been a professional skater for two years before he teamed up with Kawahara. "While I felt he had a comic flair, his programs didn't have a point of view," she said. "It wasn't good enough just to be cute and funny and still be a good jumper. If he was going to last, there had to be a reason."

Now, Hamilton can immerse and lose himself in a character, unafraid of showing different aspects of life and its frailties, Kawahara says. Before, he feared that the public would not accept him if he abandoned what he had been, a generally likeable, nimble-footed champ, bouncing over the ice to "The Flight of the Bumble Bee." Kawahara persuaded him that the public could grow tired of him if he did not offer something new. "They've seen all of that before," she said. "If you're going to last, you're going to have to show them other facets of yourself and take them with you.

"They will come with you, if you present it," she told him.

Once persuaded, Hamilton got a bagful of fast-moving, imaginative, busy routines with hardly a spot to rest, presenting memorable characters like Wayne Fontaine, a lounge lizard (a string of lights flash up the side of each leg at the end of a routine, Las Vegas personified), or a hippy-turned-yuppie who goes through ingenious costume changes as he ages throughout the program, or Cuban Pete, or a sabre dancer. One recent example of a Hamilton–Kawahara masterpiece is their spoof on the comic opera, *The Barber of Seville*, in which the Olympic champion appears in velvet knee-knocker britches and white jabot. The routine is a humorous caricature of polite eighteenth-century life. "It's fun and it's consistent all the way through," Kawahara says proudly of the routine. Indeed, it had a memorable point of view: a caricature that never lost its purpose.

"If you look at some programs, they're not consistent," Kawahara points out. "They may start in a character, and end back in a character, but they lose it in the middle. It's really important, if you're going to take a stand, you don't start with a hat, throw it away, and then pick it up in the end. It's important to weave it all the way through, and every move that you make should be of the same breath of the person you started with."

The pre-Kawahara Hamilton used to be guilty of such choreographic *faux pas*. Often in the heat of the performance, Hamilton would lose his character – just like the Disney skater who has forgotten he is no longer a competitor – then pick it up when he remembered. "He figured that was good enough," Kawahara says. "But that's really an amateur mentality." She pushed him to create ideas and characters from beginning to end. She brooked no compromise.

The programs that Kawahara designs for Hamilton are not simple slapstick show pieces. They are a display of virtuosity, of difficult, challenging movements, complex in their combinations. "She's very intricate, and it takes a long time to handle her way of movement," Hamilton says. "Like rubbing your stomach and patting your head. It took me forever to get my feet and my upper body to do that."

Hamilton first practised Kawahara's footwork sequence laid out at the beginning of *Sabre Dance*, but it was so difficult, with its twisting movements, that he had to set it aside for a time because he just could not master it. Kawahara had given Hamilton a daunting task, asking him to move his upper body in certain ways at the same time his lower body was turning in and out. "It was really tough," Hamilton admits. "She'll give me something that's the universe, and I'll just try to pick out the moon and the stars."

Kawahara's work is seen more often in the professional world than the amateur, perhaps for good reason. It is so complex that there would be little room for the eight triple jumps needed to land the marks for a competition victory. Every jump requires seconds of preparation time, precious moments often lost to choreography. "If the amateur world would let her, she could do things that would blow the judges away," Hamilton says. But the jumps have become too important.

Sarah Kawahara is best known for her work with professional skaters, however she has also worked with amateur or Olympic-eligible skaters. Ironically, in 1993, Kawahara won the Paul McGrath Award for her choreography, an honour bestowed on her by about fifteen élite coaches of the United States Figure Skating Association's coaching committee, an amateur body. Occasionally, Kawahara's spirit has strayed into the Olympic-eligible world. She designed the programs for Chen Lu the year the Chinese skater won a world bronze medal.

The amateur, or eligible, world imposes restraints on the work of a choreographer. In a short program, a skater is required to do eight elements, say a triple-jump combination or a certain kind of spin, or, if it is pairs skating, a specific kind of lift, within a two-minute-forty-second time frame. Original dance is ice-dancing's version of a short program, and in it choreographers must take into account the prescribed rhythm, such as a polka, jive, or tango, and the character of the dance, set annually by the International Skating Union. Choreographers rarely fiddle with compulsory dances: both the music and the steps are predetermined by the international association. They may seek ways to enhance some upper-body movements, however.

A long program in any discipline calls for no required elements, but everybody knows a skater has to show off technical wizardry to even be considered among the top. Therefore, choreographers must build their work around the technical tricks that a coach teaches his or her students: jumps, spins, lifts, and death spirals. And they have to limit the program to four and one-half minutes (four minutes for women's singles). There are no such limits to professional skating. Choreographers like Kawahara find most freedom in the professional world.

A couple of forays into the amateur or Olympic-eligible world proved to be frustrating adventures for Kawahara, but not because of the rule restrictions. Christopher Bowman used Kawahara's choreography to win the 1989 U.S. title and a world silver medal, but he also became her "pet peeve," she says. "It was hard to get him to lock into anything, to stay with a pattern and not change it," Kawahara says of the skater, a self-described Hans Brinker from Hell. Bowman was well known for abandoning his choreography and ad libbing his own content.

Kawahara said he used her program for two or three years, although most skaters show off new programs each year. "I always thought that worked in his favour, with his personality," she says. "He did a lot of ad libbing, but when he had that program for three years, the ad libbing was reduced down to the showman part of him." For that, Kawahara was thankful: the showman part is like the icing on a competitor's cake. Any skater needs the content and the tools, and that little bit of extra that creates awe is the icing, the skater's inner soul on display. But Bowman was so undisciplined that his personality couldn't carry him to victory in the amateur world. It wasn't enough. "When you don't know your program, like air to breathe, then for him the ad libbing would take over, and the content would go out."

Kawahara found it difficult to get Bowman to change his outlook, so lacking in responsibility and seriousness. "When I work with people, I expect them to take it seriously," Kawahara says. "Otherwise, why be there? I have other things to do and so do they. It's a profession for me." "I've never met anybody who was so intense about choreography," says Karen Preston, who approached Kawahara to do some professional competitive programs for her in 1996.

But Kawahara knows how vital good choreography is to a memorable performance, one that counts. She was bewildered and foiled in her attempts to convince the Bonalys of that when they approached her several years ago to design the choreography for Surya's programs. Surya's coach-mother, Suzanne, is "very sports-minded," Kawahara says. "It's hard for her to set aside the importance of doing ten jumps in two minutes – and doing them – against doing only five jumps in three minutes – and letting the jumps speak, and to feel it, feel the full impact of what you're doing," she explains. "Doing a circle of movement would be wonderful. I remember I fought and fought and fought for that. But to them, skating a whole circle on the ice without doing a jump was totally unthinkable."

Surya, she said, is quite capable of carrying out her choreography. She is musical. She can hear its call, answer its dynamics. Although her body is muscular, like that of a toned boxer, it has "a lyrical way to it," Kawahara says. She shows very poor stroking quality and uninspiring edges, but "she can stroke differently. She can hold edges. She's capable.

"But when push comes to shove and she's not thinking about what she's doing, she does this twelve-year-old little-kid thing," Kawahara says, speaking of the French skater's immature style, with non-existent choreography, and her lack of care about the finer details of basic skating. "She skates like a little kid, but she's not a little kid any more. She could change it in a second. She's got that much talent."

The problem, Kawahara concludes, is Surya's guidance from her mother. "I'm sure her mother means well. But she can only see certain things. Her guidance is narrow, and it's narrower than the amount of [Surya's] talent."

Still, Kawahara watched the French skater in amazement, landing jump after jump. She also watched, with some awe, how Surya performed in a television special on which she worked several years ago. While other skaters needed five, six, seven takes to reach perfection, Surya accomplished her tasks – with an entirely new look – the first time, every time. "It was amazing," Kawahara says.

But Kawahara was even more astounded at what happened afterwards. Surya had attained the brass ring in her television performance. She had found her skating zenith. "When you reach this place, your life should have changed and you can't go backwards," Kawahara says. "But I don't know what has happened. She went backwards."

In skating, it is not enough to land a triple-triple combination in every practice, Kawahara says. It is just as important to do the movements correctly, but movement and line and grace and beauty has never been top priority for the Bonalys. It is as if they had arrived at Kawahara's doorstep, needing "a spruce up," rather like a car needs an oil change, before a competition. But "[choreography] is not decoration," Kawahara says. "It can't be at this stage.

"You have to remind [Surya] about that all the time. There has to be a point where you commit yourself to it, believe in it, and work through the rusty time and train it and get it. If you don't, it falls short, or it's a hodge-podge of a lot of cooks.

"When it becomes important to her, she'll do it."

If Surya Bonaly is a diamond in the rough, John Curry was the most brilliant of jewels, blending the arts into a magic potion. To perform or to work with Curry was an education in choreography, all on its own. As an amateur skater, Curry ushered in a brilliant era of art on ice during the 1970s. He brought dance onto the ice, in its most glorious form. His first love was ballet, and when his father disapproved of his wish to become a ballet dancer, Curry turned to figure skating instead. As a professional, he was able to use his win at the Olympic Games in 1976 to make the world sit up and take notice of his ideas of putting dance and theatre on ice, and all the while paying strict attention to fine body lines, to portraying the most delicate of emotions, to pushing elegantly across the ice, and to becoming one with the music. Today, some of the sport's best choreographers have followed his lead and learned from him. Both Sarah Kawahara and Lori Nichol have spread the gospel of John Curry far and wide.

Kawahara first met Curry when he asked her to perform in his professional production of "Peter and the Wolf," and he was so impressed with her spirit that he asked her to choreograph a routine for him. They spoke the same body language. Although Curry was known to be moody, prickly, and unpredictable at times, Kawahara always had an easy relationship with the 1976 Olympic champion.

"He really created by trying to ally himself with the music," she recalls. "He was the first person that I felt tried to assimilate with the music. In 'Peter and the Wolf,' he really gave great thought to different body language [for] each character. I was the bird. Many of the skaters were all hunters, and they had a different body language."

Ideologically, they were on a similar wavelength. Kawahara's mentor, Osborne Colson, always takes keen note of a skater's body language, how they speak with movement. He also taught Kawahara how to work with both sides of her body, to master feats as well with the left as the right. Kawahara listened so well, she is now ambidextrous

– rather like Curry, who could rotate spins or perform jumps in both directions. Kawahara could do steps with both sides of her body. The ability led to a creative string of choreography.

"You don't run into too many people that work both sides of their body," Kawahara says. "Mr. C. [Colson] taught me right from the beginning. You'd feel a difference. And then I learned how to break down the movement on the opposite side of my body to try and make it work better. That's when you really learn what your body can do."

Sarah Kawahara considers herself lucky that she had a chance to work with Curry, founder of the world's first artistic ice ensemble. Lori Nichol, who worked in the ensemble for several years, considers John Curry a genius. She was a nineteen-year-old skater when she joined his troupe, "blown away" at the idea of skating with its famous members. Two of her idols had been Dorothy Hamill and Janet Lynn, who periodically performed with the Curry company. Suddenly, she found herself skating alongside them.

Nichol got an education in a hurry. Her early days with Curry's company were a trial by fire. She had won a Canadian professional competition on a Saturday night, got a job offer from Curry, reported for rehearsals on Monday, and performed on a Wednesday night. "I learned four numbers in two days," Nichol says. During the show, her peers understandingly whispered instructions to her on what came next. Fortunately, Nichol has a photographic memory for dance steps, a trait that sometimes hinders her in her current career as a choreographer. If a skater presents Nichol with music with which she has already designed a program, Nichol has to work to block out the memories of her earlier work.

Curry was a brilliant enigma, who lived on the edge of his art. While working in his company, Nichol had an interesting peek at the manner of the man. "He could be many different things in the flash of a moment," she recalls. "He could be incredibly inspiring, gentle, and giving. The next moment, he could be angrier than I have ever seen anyone. I was seeing all of this through a nineteen-year-old's eyes. I was seeing things I was not prepared for. I was really pressed into an art world, not necessarily just a powerful skating world. I had my eyes opened in many good ways and many bad ways. I'm very grateful I had the wonderful experience of working with him, because it certainly did change my life."

Curry was very demanding, Nichol remembers. One of her favourite memories occurred when Curry was choreographing a routine to Stravinsky's *The Firebird*. She followed Curry down the ice, copying a multitude of steps. Then he asked her to do a double Axel. "By that time, I had been with him for a few years, so I understood just to keep my mouth shut," she says. "He wanted me to do a double Axel in the reverse direction. By that point, I had learned that he just wasn't in the mood [to discuss it], so I just didn't say anything, and just quickly did a double Axel in the direction I could do it.

"It was the epitome of what it was like working with him. He would be just furious with ideas, they were coming out so fast. So you had to think really quickly." Luckily, Nichol, with her photographic memory for steps, could keep pace with him. Her nickname had been Feet, because of her gift.

Curry's job offer was an honour. There were only thirteen members in his company. And while she performed under his banner, Nichol received an enviable education in artistic creation and line and any kind of mood-colour imaginable, all vital components of choreography. Curry brought in choreographers from the New York dance world with the highest of reputations: Jean-Pierre Bonnefous; Peter Martins, a gifted ballet dancer, who became artistic director of the New York City Ballet and who created Curry's famous Tango Tango routine; Eliot Feld, who designed Curry's professional hit Moonskate; Twyla Tharp; and Laura Dean, who was intrigued by rotation and the fact that it worked better on the ice than on her normal medium, a dance floor. Nichol had a front-row seat for all of it.

Curry's troupe would start their rehearsals in the morning with a one-hour, off-ice ballet class, then move to the ice for at least another hour. This was Curry's creation: an on-ice ballet class "with edges and lines and turns." The quality of Nichol's skating improved immensely because of the classes, she says. "We all did it in formation, so we all learned each other's timing for each set. We got a sense of performing with others after being singles skaters all our lives."

Only after the classes would the members of the troupe actually go into rehearsals, and Nichol remembers keeping her skates on for ten to twelve hours at a time. The rehearsals would turn into time-consuming experiments as the dance choreographers kept trying things. Painstakingly they learned from scratch how a skate blade creates movement that dancers on the floor could not achieve. In a way, the dance choreographers felt as if they were dreaming, that they had found magic. "Wouldn't it be neat if we could cover this amount of space as dancers?" they would say.

While the free-flowing movement of the blade seemed to open up endless new possibilities, these starry-eyed dance choreographers had to learn that certain dance movements could not be done, because a skater would be flowing across the ice all the while. Nichol was fascinated by their experiments and learned from them.

Under Curry's direction, perfection of design was all. Once, Laura Dean walked into rehearsals only three weeks before the group was to perform – on ice – at the Metropolitan Opera House in New York, and told them to forget everything they had practised so far. She was starting over, undaunted in her search for unique expression. The experiment began anew. "She had us doing channees [turns] for almost the entire piece," Nichol recalls. "In all directions, creating formations. We'd create patterns on the ice while rotating."

John Curry died of AIDS in April 1994, but Lori Nichol has carried on Curry's work, in her own way, as a choreographer. After suffering an injury while skating with the Curry group, Nichol began a coaching career in Canada, where she married professional musician John Bonvivere. She really didn't want to be a coach, but for several weeks she played substitute teacher for close friend Sean McGill, who had also been part of the Curry troupe. Nichol took over McGill's work after he was enlisted to skate with the Jayne Torvill and Christopher Dean world tour in 1985.

"I started coaching without rhyme or reason, until I thought I might have a natural talent for teaching," Nichol says. She also discovered she had a talent for choreography, armed as she was with the teachings of a wide variety of artists. Ten years before Nichol ever began designing programs for Michelle Kwan, she was working out choreography for young Canadians almost every day – not only for her own students but for those of other coaches as well.

Nichol carried on the Curry vision in her own small corner of the world. "I taught a version of the John Curry skating class in honour of John at the Upper Canada Figure Skating Club [near Toronto] a couple of times a week," she says. "We would finish an on-ice ballet class with a creative movement session, where we'd just listen to music. All the skaters were allowed to explore that aspect of themselves."

And Nichol taught them how to explore it. But too few skaters learn to plumb the artistic side of skating, the side that makes choreography come alive, the side that creates it in the first place. For many of them, there just isn't time: they're too busy learning the jumps they need to progress up the placement ladder, and leaving their training venues to take part in shows or new competitions. "Skaters have very little time to listen to music and just skate to it," Nichol says. "But it is a very important part of becoming a true artist on the ice."

Nichol found this out one summer day when 1996 U.S. champion Rudy Galindo asked her to design his short program routine for the following season. (He later decided to turn professional and abandon the race to the 1998 Olympics). "I had never really met him before," Nichol says. "I remember thinking he was very funny and quick-witted, and not quite knowing what I was going to do with that. It was frightening. It's very difficult to work with someone for the first time."

When they stepped onto the ice to work, and Nichol asked Galindo to show her some movements, the American skater seemed stumped. Nichol told him she was going to play the music he had chosen. She just wanted to see him skate to it. Galindo started to laugh. "I don't do that," he said. "You just tell me what to do and I'll do it."

They both broke into laughter. But as the hours went by, Galindo began to experiment, she says. He would do one step, then joke around with another. "I would get an idea from that, so the choreographic process started to happen," Nichol says.

On the opposite side of the coin is the more experienced Barbara Underhill, a world pairs champion with partner Paul Martini in 1984. The pair approached Nichol in 1996 to design a professional routine for them. Just as Nichol turned away to replay the music, out of the corner of her eye she saw Underhill display a creative movement. "As soon as there is even a thirty-second lull when they're not doing anything, she'll just start to skate on her own. She loves it so much," Nichol says of Underhill. "She'll just start to move. She's definitely someone who has spent time skating on [her] own to music. She just started messing around and a wonderful idea came out of that."

"What did you do?" Nichol asked her.

"I don't know," Underhill replied. "I have no idea."

It is Nichol's task to duplicate the moves she sees in experiments and adapt them into the choreography. Again, her photographic memory is an asset.

"I had a picture in my head of what I thought I saw her do," Nichol says. Underhill had just caused what Nichol calls "a divine accident," an unintentional jewel of movement that is fresh, new, and fitting. Together, skater and choreographer work out the moves on ice, committing the best parts to memory, aided by the dynamics of the music. The creative process is a holy step towards the connection between body and mind. Nichol starts it by meditation.

Like most choreographers, Nichol says it is best to know the skater first, how their body moves, how they think, what they like. Once a suitable piece of music is found, Nichol retires to a dark, quiet room and "meditates" with the music, not in the yoga vein, but silently and carefully for many hours by herself. "I get the technical sense of the music, the count and the phrasing," she says. "But then I just let my imagination go with a body on the ice. It's always a good sign if I immediately see that skater to that music. Over the years, I've been able to develop quite a clear picture in my head of the skater I'm going to work with and how they move, their movement patterns and little idiosyncracies."

She does not set a program in her head, but she gets a feeling for what she wants to bring out about the skater, what point of view to take, what colours, how to work in the technical fireworks. "I just let my mind run free with it," she adds.

On the ice, it's play time. Sometimes she and the skater spend hours playing with the music. See how the skater wants to move to it. Show the skater an idea. Perhaps the skater messes up the idea, and causes an accident made in heaven. "Something crazy pops into your head and you try it," Nichol says. "The skater tries to imitate it and ends up on the wrong foot or on the wrong edge and it ends up looking better than your original idea. The ideas start flowing."

Then Nichol sets to work, designing the routine from the first few counts of music, chronologically to the end. "I go note by note," she says. "I believe that doing it that way gives a much better flow to the program." The hardest part occurs at the end, if Nichol has to switch some moves around to fit in a technical necessity. "Sometimes the flow is lost," she says. "So I try to be very immaculate while I'm doing it."

Nichol's students call her the pickiest person they have ever met, because every movement has to sing before she goes on to the next. "Quite often that movement inspires the next movement." This way, she creates a natural flow to the program.

So far, Michelle Kwan has been Lori Nichol's master painting, a sweet pixie transformed into a femme fatale. The transformation wasn't as sudden as most think. Nichol carefully laid the groundwork for Kwan's development as an artist from the moment she began to work with the California girl during the 1993-94 season.

During a remarkable season, when Kwan was a thirteen-year-old flower bud, a world junior champion, Nichol created a short program to "Song of India" and a long program that included music from *East of Eden* and *The Man from Snowy River*. But the programs that year, and even the next year, when Kwan finished fourth at the world (senior) championship, were not really about artistry so much as about what Nichol calls the technical aspects of artistry.

Nichol's work with Kwan that year was all about developing musicality, phrasing, correct turnout of the foot, and proper body line from head to toe, head angles, and presenting the different parts of the body to their best advantage. Nichol, living in Canada, could not give Kwan daily sessions on technical exercises in artistry, so she built the lessons into her choreography in a way that would not compromise Kwan's struggle to master technical feats, such as triple Lutzes and loops. For example, when Kwan landed a double Axel, Nichol would instruct her to hold her landing position in an artistically pleasing way, with leg outstretched and toe pointed. Yet it was all part of the jump landing. The jump had to be well landed in order to execute the artistic position into which it evolved.

Mastering the technical skills in a young skater comes first, in Nichol's mind. "I think if it gets too artsy before the technical is sound enough, then it can backfire," Nichol explains. A case in point is fifteen-year-old Fumie Suguri, ranked fourth in Japan at the senior level in 1995-96. The young skater came to Nichol for help only a year after mastering triple jumps. "I don't think the jumps are in place well enough to make a big move artistically," Nichol says. "She needs some time under her belt to get used to both aspects."

Suguri is a young, untouched talent, perfect for Nichol's moulding hand. Although Nichol has done choreography for U.S. senior skaters Jere Michael and Michael Chack, she is not accustomed to working with skaters who are already developed. But Suguri is only beginning her journey on the international stage, and has little training in the finer points of choreography. The Kwans got to know the young skater when Michelle competed at the 1994 world championship in Japan. While she was training in a nearby Tokyo rink, Suguri liked what she saw, and before long, she arrived at Nichol's doorstep, with no dance training and halting English, presenting new challenges to a choreographer. They both found that choreography is a universal language, to a point. Although Suguri had been learning English in Japan and quickly picked up a lot of key words within the first week she worked with Nichol, many of the important nuances and meanings of words were lost on her. Still, choreography is about the body. Through body language, they connected.

Nichol also tried to explain to Suguri that it would take many years to develop the artistry of a Michelle Kwan. "She wants of course to be another Michelle Kwan and have a transformation like Michelle had," Nichol says. "I was trying to explain that the transformation she saw in one year actually took four years – not to mention that this is an entirely different person with an entirely different path. We're trying to discover what's right for her."

These days, Kwan handles artistic demands like a professional, stretching her horizons, looking for light in shade, shade in light. The season in which Nichol let Kwan loose artistically was 1995-96, with her Romanza and Salome's Dance routines. "Everything went together so easily, it was shocking," Nichol says.

But during the 1996-97 season, Nichol had a more challenging job, because the music, discovered by specialist Leonore Kay, was so unusual, the colours of it so unclear and unknown. (All of the key people – coach, choreographer, and Kwan herself – had input on the choice of the music. They agreed to use it, savouring its unusual qualities.) The main section of music for the long program was an Azerbaijan creation called "Gyulistan Bayaty Shiraz," defined technically as a symphonic *mugam*. But nobody, including Nichol's husband, who has degrees in composition, voice, piano, and guitar from the Royal Conservatory of Music in Canada, knew exactly what a *mugam* was. Nichol set to work to research the music, but various music teachers had never heard of it either. The little bit of information she could dig up – in English – was contradictory. But it was clear that the construction of the music and its rhythm patterns were unique. Nichol was frustrated. To this day, Nichol cannot explain precisely what a *mugam* is.

"Ultimately, you have to trust yourself," she says. "I had analysed it so much that I was starting to lose the essence of the piece. I just stopped and said, 'You know, I have to feel this music. If everybody disagrees on what this music is, I have to adhere to the phrasing that I hear.' It's not your typical 'Sleeping Beauty' that everybody has heard and loved about a thousand times."

The process of finding and editing the music and designing the programs took most of the previous season. Already, by the fall of 1996,

Nichol was working on music that will probably become Kwan's Olympic program for 1998.

Through it all, Nichol has watched Kwan blossom from a smiling little girl wearing a big ribbon in her hair to a mesmerizing artist who won a world championship with two perfect marks of 6.0 for presentation. She has looked inside and seen budding strength in a young woman. "I think Michelle is one of the toughest people I have ever met," Nichol says. "She was born to do this. She's so strong a character. She's spiritually strong. She's emotionally strong. She's physically strong. She's impeccably trained." In a rink full of shadows and doubt, Kwan is pure colour.

Peter Oppegard, a young choreographer with a difference, comes to his job with an unusual and interesting set of tools. He does not consider himself a musical expert, nor a dance expert, yet he has an uncanny feeling for the message of music and how to transform it into body movement. He is not just a choreographer. He is a one-stop shopping centre for his students: he is also a coach, and searches out the music for his students himself.

Although Oppegard was not a student of Curry or Colson, or Galbraith or even Kawahara, choreography is his first passion, and he paints movement and emotion onto the ice with an unmistakable flair. His vision as a choreographer was nurtured by the experiences of his life – as a young boy in a family of seven children who breathed music, as an Olympic pairs bronze medallist for the United States, and as a skating student who was taken by surprise when a ballet teacher inspired him.

His canvas is the ice, his brushes are Stephanie Stiegler and John Zimmerman iv, who won bronze medals in the pairs event at the 1997 U.S. championship in only their second season together. Under Oppegard's guidance, Stiegler and Zimmerman wove a spell over audiences with their "Sorcerer's Apprentice" routine, perhaps the most cohesively emotional and dramatic of all the long programs seen in Nashville that week. The program was crafted like a novel, but its images were delivered in movement. Even a racing pair spin became a symbol of high emotions whirling out of control.

At age thirty-seven, Oppegard is a bright, emerging talent, a relatively new face on the teaching scene. It wasn't easy to start as a choreographer, in spite of his competitive credentials or the history he had built up creating his own artistic work as a competitor. "At first I thought, you put a sign out that said: 'Olympic medallist for hire,'" he says. "It doesn't work that way. You have to show that you can do it for someone else before you get the respect in the industry. It was a little frustrating in the beginning."

But then he realized the recognition was quite a gift, an acknowledgement from critics who were bound to look more closely at him because he had just recently been an Olympian. He accepted the fact that he'd be judged for better or for worse for what he had produced.

Oppegard won his Olympic bronze medal at the 1988 Calgary Games with partner Jill Watson, with whom he also skated for two years as a professional. When Watson decided to retire, Oppegard found a new professional partner, Cindy Landry, a Canadian who had won a world silver medal in 1989 with partner Lyndon Johnston. Although they had a good measure of success, and proved to be an exciting partnership, the work offers did not pour in. Because Landry and Oppegard had won their amateur medals with different partners, promoters did not readily recognize them as an entity.

"We had to earn our position," Oppegard says. During their down times, Oppegard started to coach. He wanted to begin with world-level athletes, but it didn't work out that way. Instead, he took on a tiny five- and seven-year-old pair, Tiffany and Johnnie Stiegler. In the end, it proved to be the perfect way to start. "The fact that I started at the lower levels took a lot of pressure off me," he says.

But for the first two years of his coaching-choreographic life, Oppegard had only these two young pupils, the younger siblings of Stephanie Stiegler. He was able to focus intensely on their careers, and the results were impressive. The blond Stieglers won a national novice title in 1995 and the junior title in 1997, with Oppegard's polished, adorable programs to grown-up themes, such as a tango or

Swan Lake. Their programs were so mature and so artistically arresting that, though they were still barely out of the novice division, they found themselves performing skating exhibitions at major venues such as Sun Valley, Idaho.

Through the young Stieglers, Oppegard was finally able to show what he could do for others. Finally, a handful of new students followed. Still, Oppegard works with only a small number of skaters.

The seeds of Oppegard's choreographic career began after he and Watson had lost their title at the 1986 U.S. championship. "We decided we had to do something different," Oppegard says. "Things weren't going the way we wanted them to go. The first couple of years as a champion, you follow in the footsteps of those who had come before you. We made a conscious decision to branch out and do our own things. I had some ideas, and Jill kind of let me roll with it."

But within that season, Oppegard learned something very important during exhibitions in front of a full, live orchestra. Coach Don Laws chose the music, Stravinsky's *The Firebird*, while Oppegard conjured up the moves. But when he asked Laws if they could cut the four and a half minutes of music to do a show program, Laws said no. "He thought the full orchestration with the full orchestra would be really interesting," Oppegard says.

"It made me start to rethink choreography in terms of a complete act, a complete story," he says. "*Firebird* lent itself to that because it was a complete ballet. So I took one segment of that and started developing it from there. It turned out to be a great launching point for us, because there was this strong masculine role in it, and there was this great role for Jill of the Firebird. That was the first time she got to play something other than Jill Watson. And me also."

Watson and Oppegard won their U.S. title back with the lessons they learned from their *Firebird* routine. The following year, Oppegard did his own choreography again. "We wanted to be leaders, not followers," he says.

As a professional with Watson, Oppegard again tried to branch out and experiment with choreography, but he was never happy with his own style. "I always felt I had a lot more to learn," he says. With

Landry, he got the chance. "What we wanted to develop was a more modern, sultry style, and a little less classical. She really took to that."

When Oppegard began to train the Stieglers, he was able to experiment more, to develop musicality and line in the children, moulding their artistic knowledge from the ground up. He put them on the fast track. "I started working on their lines, their understanding of movement, their understanding of music. The only downside of starting someone that young is that it's a gamble. You don't know how they're going to develop physically and jump-wise. But they've done quite well."

Oppegard quickly learned to teach the young very differently from the way he'd guide an older student. "I mix it up with play, so that they don't know if they're playing or learning." He decided to give them a psychologically safe environment to experiment with music. If they tried something silly, in an attempt to copy him, he never laughed at them. In that way, he tried to show them that none of their attempts was a mistake. When he thought they were old enough to understand, he told them that, if no artistic attempts are wrong, then they were free to try out any idea that came to mind, then just eliminate the ones that didn't work.

In the meantime, Oppegard began to work with the pair's older sister, Stephanie. Through the skating of Stephanie and John Zimmerman, Oppegard has been able to express himself best. When they skate, he does, too, from the other side of the rink boards. His emotion is there for all to see. And yet, he hopes that his skaters exhibit a style that is not attributable to him. His job, he says, is to enhance his skaters' natural gifts.

Zimmerman was a raw, unrefined talent when he first came to Oppegard, but he had a reasonably good awareness of his body and how it moved, Oppegard says. "Because he was older and had not worked in an intensive way, he had real troubles with consistency [technically]." His first task was to nail this down.

"But he came to me with the one thing that I ask of all my skaters: an open mind for learning," Oppegard says. "That's all I wanted to see. Every day, he would drink in as much as he could. When he first started, that wasn't much. His saturation level was very short. I tried to push that envelope."

Oppegard had to balance two completely different tasks to draw out the best from the pair. As a coach, he taught technique, which has strict parameters of skills. As a choreographer, there were no parameters at all: no expression of movement and music was wrong. Oppegard can't choose which function he prefers: coach or choreographer. Both suit different sides of his personality, he says.

"When I'm in the coaching mood, I'm not interested in choreography at all," he says. "It's like I'm two completely different people. Partway through the season, I can't believe I did the choreography. It seems like a completely different person who did it. I'm fully removed from the artistic process. It's difficult for me to remember where I came up with the idea.

"Then, when I'm in the artistic phase, I find it difficult to work in the technical vein. I do the artistry in a completely different time period." When Zimmerman's technique became consistent, Oppegard switched to his artistic side, adding levels of music and performance to the pair's mix. And he discovered something important about Zimmerman. "He's a performer," Oppegard says. "You don't really know that going in. And Stephanie is an amazing performer. . . . Often Stephanie is directing the show on the ice."

What Oppegard brings to the creative table is his sensitivity to music, and an ability to use movement to portray emotion. He admits he does not have a huge musical or dance background.

"I'd love to tell you I took ballet," he says, but admits that, though he took ballet on and off for nine years, "a lot of those years [were] off." Ballet was a chore, until Oppegard was nineteen and met ballet instructor John Renn, who inspired him. Renn also made Oppegard see that, if he did not learn ballet, his future would be limited in the sport. "He was an amazing talent, and he made me understand that ballet was interesting and masculine and it was impressive to be able to do these kind of things," Oppegard says. "He just gave me a great enthusiasm for it."

Oppegard took some acting lessons as well, but when he heard his peers say that all they ever wanted to do was act – and Oppegard had no

Todd Eldredge and parents, John and Ruth, celebrate after he won his world title in 1996. Todd has just placed his gold medal around his mother's neck at rinkside.

Beverley Smith

Beverley Smith

At age ninety-three, John Knebli was still doing what he loved best: making custom hand-made boots in his quaint Toronto shop. *Top left*: His wife, Elizabeth.

Beverley Smith

Coach Frank Carroll believes in standing by the rinkboards and using his hands to instruct pupil Michelle Kwan. Between them stands Kwan's choreographer, Lori Nichol.

Collection of Christy Ness

Above: Coach Christy Ness and Olympic champion Kristi Yamaguchi proved to be a successful team. *Bottom left*: Christopher Bowman was a coaching nightmare. *Bottom right*: Ekaterina Gordeeva and Sergei Grinkov excelled under Marina Zoueva's guidance.

Cam Silverson

Kathy Goedeken

Top: Choreographer Sarah Kawahara was a major force behind the success of the pro career of Scott Hamilton (*bottom left*). *Bottom right*: Kurt Browning is a choreographer's dream, according to Bob Paul.

George Rossano

Top: Coach-choreographer Peter Oppegard speaks to his top pupils
Stephanie Stiegler and John Zimmerman IV, as they practise their Sorcerer's
Apprentice routine. *Bottom right*: Stiegler and Zimmerman in full flight.
Bottom left: Josée Chouinard benefited from the musical choices of
Marijane Stong.

Kathy Goedeken

Kathy Goedeken

Top left: Jaimee Eggleton was well-known as Aladdin in Disney's World on Ice. *Top right*: Karen Preston finds happiness playing Snow White. *Bottom*: Dr. Robert Lee tends to a young patient in his Waterloo clinic.

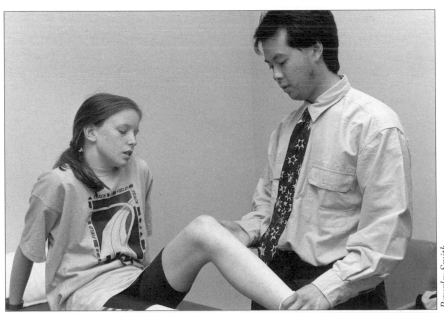

Cam Silverson

Top: The Canadian SpecSkaters, clad in shocking pink sweaters, amuse their neighbours at Skate Canada in Kitchener, Ontario. *Bottom*: Gary Beacom plays at what he does best, standing the skating world on its head.

Kathy Goedeken

such enduring life revelations – he knew he would never be an actor. But the lessons couldn't help but give him more insight into expression.

And although Oppegard played the trumpet until he was fifteen, blasting away in the family basement while a sister played a clarinet upstairs, he does not know the technical side of a note. All five of his sisters played instruments, so the sounds of music were always alive in the Oppegard household. All five of them took ballet, too, so form was not foreign either. Young Oppegard developed an ear for music, and played from memory. Sight reading was not his forte. Nor is music history. "When I hear a classical piece, I couldn't tell you who did it," he admits. "I really like rock and roll better." As a youngster, when the rink was his babysitter, music from the 1960s would sweep the arena. Oppegard skated to every piece that came on. It was his introduction to interpreting music.

All of these experiences he brought to Stiegler and Zimmerman. Oppegard is one choreographer who likes to choose his own music for the programs of his students. He picked the unusual Argentine tango music for their explosive short program, after hearing it quite by accident while driving home from dinner one night. He had been listening to a local semi-classical radio station, which was playing a number by Astor Piazzolla, an Argentine-born composer of modern tango music. "Who is Astor Piazzolla?" he asked himself, unfamiliar with the man who spent most of his life in the United States. But something about the music caught his ear.

But it didn't catch everybody's ear, at first. "I suppose for some people in the early stages, when they just heard the music by itself, it resembled a musical version of a headache," Oppegard says. "There were quite a few people that thought I was off my rocker when I started that piece. Even I began to question it."

But the music had made such an impression on Oppegard that he felt that if he could choreograph it the way he envisioned it in his head, it would make an impression on audiences, too. Oppegard likes to use music to deliver an emotion. The music had enormous power, but little musical structure. That intrigued Oppegard, too. Why not ignore the standard process of choreography by creating a routine without a sense of beginning, middle, or end? Oppegard flouted all the rules when he set to work.

Unlike most other choreographers, Oppegard started to create not at the beginning of the piece, but at a musical highlight. It's a process that can lead a choreographer to paint himself into a corner. But Oppegard's instincts drove him on. "It's all by feel," Oppegard says. "I put it together like a puzzle, piece by piece, with the idea that I've got to carry that emotion through the whole piece."

Instead of tying the main musical highlight to a big skating move, like a twist or a jump, Oppegard decided to have Stiegler and Zimmerman skate a spiral sequence through the music that had the most impact. "Most spiral sequences that I've seen have been so average," he says. "It just became a move that people had to do." Oppegard didn't want any kind of average move.

And because the spiral was to become allied with a highlight, Oppegard knew he had to unearth an impressive, original sequence to match the music. He and his skaters went out on the ice with absolutely no idea what that spiral move would be. But the music told him, and Oppegard fashioned moves that fit the mood of the piece.

The next-most-impressive piece of music came just before the highlight. Oppegard tied a tangolike footwork sequence to it, always mindful that the meat of the program was the tango. Other moves that are required in pairs short programs fell into the remaining spots, like smaller pieces of the puzzle, and then Oppegard worked to connect them. Because he had not carved out a beginning, middle, or end, he had to hope he had enough music left to perform other required moves. This is the part that is not quite as much fun, says Oppegard, the part where creativity is subjected to technical need.

However, when Oppegard created Stiegler and Zimmerman's long program, he resorted to different tactics, more standard methods of choreography. He divided the musical selection into various sections, spotting big technical moves in the first part and tailoring the kind of physical exertion required in the second part to the amount of energy a skater has left. Often the last thing Oppegard creates is the very first position a skater takes on the ice at the beginning of a routine, because "I'm not exactly sure how the character is going to develop through the course of the piece. I just have an idea. At the end, I'd have much more of an idea of what one starting position represents of what they're doing out there."

Oppegard's creation of Stiegler and Zimmerman's long program, which helped send them to their first world championship in Lausanne, Switzerland, in March 1997, was born of his own complex vision of "The Sorcerer's Apprentice." Oppegard had created something quite different for the pair the previous year, an elegant, soft program. "I was not entirely happy with the direction I went last year in their long program," he admits.

"Although they can both be very elegant, the program didn't lend itself emotionally to being more than a very good performance. I wanted to enhance their abilities. They have so much natural ability to handle music. I wanted to impress them with the fact that, if they took it up a number of notches, they would be more recognized at a world level." He was right.

So when Oppegard listened to the music made famous by Disney's *Fantasia*, he felt there was a place in it for both Stiegler and Zimmerman. He decided to try something new: he created his own complex story for the music. "I had never worked this way before," he says. "I had to put a story together in my mind because I knew everybody else had the story of the dancing brooms. Well, I certainly wasn't going to make Stephanie an inanimate object. I know people have done that with capes, but what's more interesting than a relationship?"

Oppegard knew only a portion of his complex story would be understood by an audience; the rest would become a tool for the skaters to convey emotion through their movement. Before he began to work on the choreography, he sat his pair down and explained their roles: that Zimmerman was to be a complex person, a prince of darkness with unusual powers who, quick to decide what he wants, sees Stiegler and immediately wishes to possess her, own her, have her.

During the opening segment, Zimmerman pulls Stiegler close to him and, in an unsophisticated way, attempts to make her his own. Frightened, she resists and flees, at the same time showing her own sense of strength. Zimmerman grabs for her again, wrapping his arms around her. Stiegler, showing equal strength, unwraps the arms. They stop.

The music becomes soft and slow. They start their dance of life over again, from a different point of view, but with a little more sophistication and complex emotion. Zimmerman takes her measure. He knows he's found his match. It is not going to be easy to possess Stiegler.

They repeat the same moves as in the first section, but in opposite positions, more face to face. In more lyrical fashion, Zimmerman resorts to putting her into a trance. For a short time, the spell works. When she starts to come out of the spell, he teases her, tries to win her. The music changes, and Zimmerman starts a light-hearted dance that reaches its height with a throw triple toe loop.

But as Zimmerman tosses her, his sense of frustration takes over. He starts wild lurches and jumps. He goes increasingly mad. During a spin "when things are symbolically whipping into a frenzy," the program reaches its climax and scurries along into a footwork sequence. Zimmerman jumps and jumps and preens for Stiegler. It becomes almost a dance to the death. Both are worn out.

He puts one last spell on Stiegler, but she hides from him and it fails to work. Maddened, he pulls her around and tries one last time.

In the last forty seconds of the program, Zimmerman's character shows his only sincere moments. Stiegler leans forward, with her arms back, symbolizing that she has completely given herself over to him – as Oppegard ties ideas to movement. Zimmerman tenderly touches the back of Stiegler's head. For the first and only time in the program, they are together, as one.

After the final death spiral, Zimmerman, angry and tired of the chase, knocks her out. It is over.

"It just developed and the kids understood it," says Oppegard of Stiegler, seventeen, and Zimmerman, twenty-four. "I told them there would be layer upon layer for their characters. That's how they learn. I try to choreograph a shoe size too big early in the year. By the end of the year, hopefully, they understand what I was after."

With the program, Stiegler and Zimmerman finished third at Skate America in Springfield, Massachusetts, in the fall of 1996, even though the music stopped because of a mechanical failure about forty seconds towards the end of the program, lopping off the skaters' symbolic moment of union. When they eventually continued, the ovation was thunderous.

Both short and long programs gave Zimmerman a chance to show off his dramatic style and Stiegler a chance to show a new maturity. Oppegard's vision worked. When they skated, the ice floor became a magic place. The colour of complex emotions was their best tool. And Oppegard had led them there.

Lori Nichol takes her work seriously. No less than one and a half years before the Olympic Games, she was scanning audio tapes and compact discs for just the right music for Kwan. Time passed. She awakened at 2 A.M. to discover she had fallen asleep with her head on the table and earphones still on her head.

Nichol is no longer a coach, but she continues to take Canada's coaching certification courses. One of the courses deals with choreography and music. But there are others, like understanding the physiological demands put upon a skater's body. "The courses have given me an insight into developing my own philosophies," she says. Nichol has finally found a niche, a centre for her energy. It is art, and the skating of it.

It is difficult for Nichol to imagine a skater who does not just go into a rink, turn on the music, and skate for the love of movement. It is what the presentation mark is all about. In fact, there are eight or nine components to the presentation mark, says Nichol, who is preparing a paper outlining them for the International Skating Union. Presentation, formerly called artistic impression, is the second mark given by a panel of judges, the first being for technical merit. Presentation involves harmonious composition, variation of speed, use of the ice surface, good-quality skating in time to the music, carriage and style and body line, originality, expression of the character of the music, and even unison, whenever two people are skating together. "To truly understand and be educated to the point of recognizing all of [the components] within the four-minute time frame is a lifelong process of learning," Nichol says. "There's a lot involved."

Coaches, choreographers, and judges have many years to learn all of the elements of presentation, from pianissimo to fortissimo. Skaters have much less time. Yet their audiences and spectators are showing a hunger and a knowledge about presentation, Nichol says. The Internet is alive with opinions about the artistic merit of skaters. And time and time again, skaters are finding that the artistic side of their programs is the final, important link to the podium; it is not enough to string together a series of powerful jumps and elements. "This presents skaters with a very serious challenge," Nichol says.

Thus, the race begins to find the movement, the *style du jour* to win the approval of the judges. Is ballet the only way to go, with limbs festooned in frills? Are other modes of artistic expression on the endangered list? "Some believe skating is based on proper line, as denoted by classical ballet," Nichol explains. "Some feel they have discovered a new way of movement, of motion."

The ISU rules on presentation states that skaters are allowed freedom of motion. Yet, another component of presentation suggests a restriction of movement, limiting it to motion found in the world of dance. "I don't think it's something we're ever going to solve," says Nichol. "But I don't think it's fair to say that there is no other way [than ballet]."

Nichol's heart and theory lie in classical dance, like her teacher, John Curry. To her, classical dance is a vital starting point. "It's a learning tool. It's your base, how you learn to move your body," she says. "From there, you are set free. No matter who you are, you have to have some foundation of movement, with body line."

It's hard to convince some skaters, particularly males, that ballet is an important, basic component of figure skating. As mentioned earlier, Peter Oppegard cared little for ballet when he was a young skater. To him, ballet was "stretching on a barre, nothing else," he says. But one enthusiastic ballet dancer changed his mind. The ballet teacher filled in the blanks he needed to progress in his career, making movement a motive.

The only answer, Nichol says, is to educate both judges and skaters about every aspect of movement, so they can distinguish all of its varied colours, lines, and nuances. The popular myth in skating is that judges make subjective judgements about artistry, applauding one over another because they prefer the style, because they cannot really compare apples to oranges. But Nichol feels judges can make valid comparisons between opposing styles. Preferring one style over another is not an option for judges.

"I say you can compare a really good orange to a really good apple," Nichol says. "Or a really bad apple to a really good orange. To me, it's possible to compare the two things, if you know what makes a really good apple and what makes a really good orange. You can do it if you are knowledgeable."

If skaters and judges follow this line of thinking, choreography will be set free. The most creative of choreographers love freedom of expression, variety, life. In an interview Curry gave before he died in 1994 of AIDS, he said, "Young artists must free their minds and their bodies so they can create work which is unique. They must be true to themselves and bring to the skating palette their own special colours. That is what will make the art form grow."

The ideas come from a place Nichol cannot define. When she finds it, she says she is "in the zone."

"I don't [think] there's a choreographer I've ever talked to that really knows. It's like asking, 'Where does love come from?'

"It's just something inside of yourself," Nichol says thoughtfully. "I believe that everyone has a degree of creativity within them. It's just a matter of getting in touch with it, and not being afraid of it. Delving into the arts world is not a risk, but it's difficult and challenging, and it can open things you didn't know you felt before or thought before. It can be emotionally very difficult. To be open enough to be an artist, you have to be very sensitive. Sometimes the seeds of doubt can get in there. That's all part of being an artist."

And it's magical. And colourful.

A Whole New World:
Backstage with Disney on Ice

*D*isney on Ice is not child's play, really.

Beyond the tented curtains of Toronto's SkyDome, behind the quaint cottage of the seven dwarfs and the Hollywood sparkle of the genie's lair, is a jumble of elephantine electrical cords, about a dozen hulking transport trailers, countless rows of giant trunks, and an itinerant village of skaters, searching for – sometimes finding – themselves on the road. They live landloping, rootless, workbound, icebound, absurd lives, on the move for eleven months of the year, dwelling out of enormous suitcases. It seems an abnormal existence, but only to those who aren't part of it.

The life of the roving Aladdin or Snow White or Cinderella, stardust on the outside, wanderlust on the inside, is normal to the skaters of Disney fables. It is a life of impermanence, in a big way. Eighteen travelling crew members spend about twelve to fourteen hours to set up each show, only four to five to tear it down. They pack away about 150 prop pieces and squeeze colossal sets into the trailers. The weight of the jealous queen's castle in "Snow White and the Seven Dwarfs" is 3,000 pounds alone. Grumpy's pipe organ weighs another 2,500 pounds, and is crafted so sturdily that it can hold 3,500 pounds of dancing skaters on its lid. After all, it has to hold twenty-four of them.

Organizers of the Stars on Ice tours, made up of the best-known professional skaters, such as Scott Hamilton, Kurt Browning, even Jayne Torvill and Christopher Dean, have less worries about such daunting logistics; their sets are much less extravagant. In many cases, the Disney tours even cart around their own ice tanks, so that they can play in unusual spots like theatres, tennis pavilions, swimming pools, gigantic tents, or even bullrings in non-skating countries of the world, such as Venezuela, Mexico, Egypt, Singapore.

From its base in Vienna, Virginia, a Disney on Ice ensemble is a small roving village of workers, skaters, support administration, such as payroll clerks, publicity organizers, tour coordinators, and employees in charge of lighting, costumes, makeup, sound, and anything directly related to putting on a show. Counting all the employees, the travelling Disney village can swell to 80 people, sometimes as many as 120.

Choreographers (such as Bob Paul, discussed earlier) do their work before the tours start. And skaters for new productions to be staged in the future are hired through the auditions Disney on Ice holds in every city in which they play. At the auditions, a talent scout looks over the prospects, searching for overall talent, style, presentation, good quality of skating edges, an ability to portray characters, and, most importantly, enthusiasm.

Yet Disney skaters are often the forgotten professionals, the faceless unknowns of the post-amateur world. They are often seen as the second cousins of the toe-pick set, as if skating arm in arm with an animated character reduces the respectability quotient a few notches. But to a host of professional skaters, Disney on Ice is no sidestreet show. It is the largest employer of skaters in the world, having hired about 450 skaters for 10 different productions that play in more than 40 countries. In "Snow White," there are 45 skaters in all, a little more than two-thirds of them women, with an average age of 22. In "Aladdin," the cast balloons to about 60, with a need for a seemingly endless line of blue-hued genies during certain numbers.

The Disney productions – which are owned by Ice Follies–Holiday on Ice proprietor Kenneth Feld, who buys the licence rights to use the Disney name – amass large numbers of chorus skaters, and a few talented stars, who work diligently for their pay. Chorus skaters earn about $500 (U.S.) a week, and have their travelling expenses and accommodation paid for. They even have medical and dental benefits. "Times are changing," says Disney star Jaimee Eggleton, a Canadian skater who has played Peter Pan and Aladdin for more than eight years. "The money is a lot better now. Five hundred dollars a week is pretty good money."

Neither Eggleton nor Karen Preston, a two-time Canadian champion who stars as Snow White, will even whisper what they earn as the headliners in their productions. "It's not the Gold Championship," Preston says. "You're not going to get a quarter of a million dollars for one night's work. But compared to other people my age who have just graduated from university, I'm making more than they are. I'm not really worried about that. The fact that I'm enjoying what I'm doing is more important."

It's unlikely, however, that even the principal skaters earn sums remotely close to their celebrated peers in tours such as Stars on Ice or the annual tour that Elvis Stojko does in a handful of top cities across Canada. Skaters on other tours speculate that Disney principals earn as little as $600 a week, perhaps as much as $1,000 a week, if they are really spectacular, well-known skaters. Some skaters on tours are not even this lucky. Many tours take advantage of Russians desperately seeking to find any kind of employment outside their economically troubled country; some are paid as little as $20 a show, with no benefits. And some of the skaters on tours are forced to do the manual labour as well, putting up the sets, taking them down, and driving the trucks themselves through the night to the next city on their schedule. By contrast, Disney skaters get a bonus at the end of the tour, usually about $2,000.

Whatever amount of money Eggleton and Preston make, however, chances are that they earn every penny of it. Because of their lead roles, Eggleton and Preston perform on ice for about one and a half hours of each two-hour show. The cast members may do up to twelve shows a week, sometimes three a day. In Japan, where Disney on Ice shows are wildly popular, Eggleton did thirty-two shows in twelve days in Osaka alone. More often than not, he would do all three shows in one day, without relying on his understudy. After that marathon run, Eggleton spent one day travelling to the next Japanese city, had one day off, then did another twenty-two shows in nine days.

Although working more than twelve shows a week, or more than seven consecutive days, puts extra money in his pocket, Eggleton admits it's a "brutal" schedule. "We are the workhorses of the entertainment business," he says.

By contrast, Stars on Ice skaters might do from four to six shows a week, but always in a different city in the United States, during a three-month run. Eggleton says he has missed skating only twice in eight years, although he is apparently not counting the time he once crashed while playing Peter Pan, along with a sky-born gondola, and broke both legs. "I work hard for my money and I appreciate it," he says.

Eggleton says he has invested his earnings so well that he could retire "in a couple of years" (by the time he is forty), but he has no desire to leave his life of adventure. He is now thirty-three years old, with a perpetually boyish look, and has already endured the dreaded Disney skating-cast ritual of the over-thirty birthday party. "It's a tradition," he says cheerfully. "It's like the end of your life when you turn thirty. They recite funeral chants and pick a tombstone."

Some of the cast members stay only a year or two. Having had their post-high-school adventure, they quit to go on to college or university or they set out to make new, less-hectic, less-transient lives. Some stay for ten years, and work their way into management positions in the company. Some leave to get married. On average, a skater sticks to Feld's travelling road show for three or four years. Not Eggleton. "I want to do this for as long as I can, until my body quits," he says. "It's the best job in the world."

Indeed, the job comes with a few extras that appeal to an extrovert such as Eggleton. "Things that the other shows don't have," he says. For instance, Feld whisked him off to Japan for five and a half weeks on a publicity tour, in which he went to a different city every two days, chatting up television hosts and newspaper reporters and generally being a good-will ambassador for the show. It is a role in which he thrives. "They took care of me like royalty, because I was the star of the show," he says.

And he was loving it. He found himself being invited to ten-course dinners. He accepted graciously. "You'd offend them if you didn't eat," he explains. He golfed eleven times, at some of the most exclusive, expensive golf courses in Japan. A wealthy businessman took Eggleton under his wing, and, when he discovered the high-flying skater played golf, they went to a course where, Eggleton says, the membership dues were $1 million a year. He also treated the skater to an expensive Kobe steak.

"A lot of Japanese don't ever experience one of those," Eggleton says. "You're getting paid to have fun and travel like a tourist. And for five and a half weeks, [you're] treated like a king. The best part of the job is that you're extremely privileged. I never take it for granted how privileged I am. I wish everyone in the world could do it."

Eggleton loves to tell stories. And he loves to tell *these* stories.

The other perk of the skating-tour world is the sense of family on the road, according to its stars. The troupe is together at Christmas, Easter, Hallowe'en. "A lot of my closest friends are on the road," says Karen Preston, who joined the "Snow White" cast during the summer of 1994. "They have become like a surrogate family to me. My boyfriend is there, all my closest friends. It will be difficult to leave if I ever have to leave."

For a Canadian born into a blustery winter climate, Preston has no difficulties with the idea of spending Christmas in a hot one. On Christmas Eve 1995, Preston flew out of Toronto and headed for Los Angeles, the city she now calls home. "People have this terrible vision of [us] sitting alone in a hotel room around Christmas," she says. "It doesn't happen like that. There are all the other skaters, the crew, the staff. All of them are in the same situation. When you travel together, you become very close. You are more than friends. All my friends were there in L.A. People I care about."

Eggleton, in a different show, different company, does the same thing. "I have my family here," he says. His surrogate family all flew into Toronto on Christmas Day 1995 to do the opening show of "Aladdin" at SkyDome, then had dinner together. For the crew, it's just another way of celebrating. "We spend Thanksgiving together. We have Hallowe'en parties where we dress up. [Eggleton confides that he does not go as Aladdin, but as a clown or a hobo.] We have secret Santa gifts.

"But there are no secrets in an ice show. If you think there is a secret, you're dreaming."

For Eggleton, it's not just the people within the company that he comes to regard as family. "There is a community with people you meet on the road who touch your soul and your life in a way," he says. "Meeting people is the best part. I have friends everywhere, all over the world. Anywhere in the world, I could call people up. It's a whole new small world."

Wandering the world gets under the skin, Preston has found. As an amateur skater, she was one of the lucky ones. She trained with coaches in her hometown and lived with her parents in Mississauga, Ontario, for the duration of her amateur career. Since she has joined Feld's productions, her life has taken a dramatic turn, but she has found the footloose lifestyle to her liking.

"I love it," said Preston during a stop at home during Christmas 1996. "I've been home for less than a month and I'm itching to get going again. This is the longest I've been at home in Toronto in over two and a half years. Normally, I'm home for an eight-day stay. You either get bitten by the tour bug or you don't. You love it or you don't. I guess I just had it in my blood. I love to skate and I'm travelling the world, which I always wanted to do, and am getting paid to do something I've chosen since I was five. I have the best of both worlds."

Like Eggleton, Preston has spent six months at a time in Japan, just about as far away from home as both could get. She nestled into the Pacific Rim country with a certain joy. She loved testing out the food. She got a kick out of going to electronics stores and seeing products that she says probably won't be in North America for another three years. And, other than the fact that she is blonde, she blended in easily. "I was average height over there and I'm five-foot-two," she said. "If you are tall or have fair hair, the older Japanese do a double-take. The younger Japanese in their teens and their twenties are very western and they don't look much different than we do. There are the same trends."

But Preston was astonished one day, as she was waiting to cross a street in Japan, to find someone petting her hair. It was an elderly woman, awestruck at the sight of the Canadian's sunlight-coloured locks. "Her eyes were bugging out of her head," Preston says.

The hardest part of living in Japan was the language barrier, Preston says. "It was not a vacation for us. We were living there and working and just trying to function on a day-to-day basis." And there were only two translators for sixty people. "You just hope you can guess the right direction to the laundromat," she says.

By the end of their stay, Preston says she could order a meal, ask for separate cheques, and request *hoto coffee* at a McDonald's – just enough to make do if the translators were otherwise occupied.

A language mix-up also led Preston to believe an ankle injury that she incurred attempting a triple loop just three weeks before the tour's end was serious: a Japanese doctor appeared to tell her she had cartilage damage, something that would require surgery. Because of the perceived diagnosis, Preston's Toronto physician, sports-medicine specialist Dr. Michael Clarfield, told her to come home at once. But when he saw her, he found that her injury was actually torn ligaments.

As soon as Preston stepped into the Los Angeles airport, she was taken aback by the height of North Americans. "All of a sudden I was a midget again," she says. "Everybody was five-foot-nine." When she turned to browse through one of the airport shops, she stopped and stared in disbelief. "I must have looked like a kid in a candy store, gawking at all the English-speaking magazines," she recalls.

In Japan, the troupe heard very little of the English language. Almost none of the television channels ran English-speaking programs. Only three cities in Japan delivered CNN. That meant that, during only three weeks out of a six-month stay, the troupe heard English news on television. Because there were no English magazines to be found, Preston subscribed to several that were delivered to her hotel, wherever she was, through company mail. "They circulated like crazy," she says. Even finding a paperback to read was a problem. Few stores in Japan stocked books written in English. When Preston was able to find some, the cost was prohibitive: $15 to $16 for a paperback.

Members of the troupe got their world news other ways. Several had brought their computers with them and cruised the English-language websites, keeping abreast of issues. In the suitcase of the Disney traveller, anything is possible. It's almost magic, the way they carry their homes around the world with them.

"We don't have small suitcases," Preston says. "Last year, in the United States, I carried a VCR and an answering machine. That's your life and that's your home. When we're boarding an aircraft, we have more baggage than I've ever seen in my life. When you're going for seven months straight, and taking clothes for three different seasons, you want to be comfortable."

Some of the travellers take tablecloths to throw over a desk or a room table, and set up candles in their lodges to conjure up homespun images of a cosy coop. It takes a special kind of person to throw a hat on any peg in the world and call it home.

When he is in North America, the resourceful Eggleton carves out his own kind of abode on the road. For the week that he was at SkyDome, he camped his twenty-five-foot Winnebago near the baseball diamond, right at centre field, behind the storage trunks and the tent curtain. It's his palace, not as gilt-edged as a Disney prop, but impressive in its own way. It's fully loaded, Eggleton says proudly.

The wandering Winnebago has two television sets, a VCR, a sound system, a kitchen with four burners, a can opener, a toaster, a gourmet coffee maker ("That's an experiment," he adds), a home-size freezer, and a barbecue. Sometimes he lives out beside the rink, parked behind one of the buildings. Sometimes, when the site is large enough, like the SkyDome, Eggleton parks his home-sweet-home-on-wheels inside. He even managed to squeeze it – very carefully – into the old Boston Gardens, although the fit was tight, he says, allowing only an inch on each side. If it's close enough, and high and dry inside, Eggleton can sprint from his Winnebago, in his bathrobe and slippers, to the backstage showers. At other large sites, he resorts to riding a golf cart, a latter-day knight on a modern charger, to do his errands.

Life has been good enough to Eggleton that he owns three cars. In Toronto, he had one of his favourites, a 1980 Toyota Celica Supra with 225,000 miles on it. "It's a fun car," he says. "It looks like crap, runs like a top." With great amusement, Eggleton overheard one young fan, mouth open at the sight of the skater driving up in the old Toyota. "That's Aladdin," the boy said in astonishment to his mother. "And he drives *that*?"

"An old car is fine for me," Eggleton says. "I have nothing to prove."

His Winnebago and his tireless old jalopy afforded Eggleton something else important on his North American trips: privacy. "I like travelling on my own. I like to be away from people. I work with people all the time. Being older, I need that."

Eggleton has grown with his job and, with the experience, found that working on the road with Disney has helped him to find direction in life. Both Preston and Eggleton have ventured outside the Disney world to compete in professional events, and returned to its fold with mixed feelings. During a break in her schedule in December 1996, Preston decided to compete in the Canadian Professional Figure Skating Championship in Ottawa. She was earnest about her attempt. She enlisted the help of leading choreographer Sarah Kawahara to design new programs, and flew all the way to California to do it. She chose her own music. "I worked as much as I could during my spare time over in Japan," she says. "But I had been doing a lot of shows, thirty shows in eleven days. It was a lot of work for me to get prepared." She headed for Ottawa full of firepower.

Her effort was more than admirable. She landed a triple flip–double toe loop and a triple toe loop in her technical program, and tossed in a triple loop in her artistic number. Some of her competitors failed to land any triples, or fell. Yet, Preston didn't finish in the top four, and Canadian television viewers didn't even know she had attended the championship. A television taping of the event made no reference to Preston at all.

"I was a little bit upset," Preston says. "There is a political beast in skating that will never die. Politics has been going on in skating since I was nine years old, and it doesn't really bother me. It's the fact that nobody else outside of the arena knew that I was there or saw what I did." Preston says she was working at a definite disadvantage: she hadn't had a skating lesson in almost three years, and had often been skating on small ice surfaces. But she knew she had skated well. She had all the tools. "Even if they had shown ten seconds of my artistic program . . ." Preston says wistfully.

Perhaps Preston got little respect from the judges because of her life as a Disney skater. But the image of Disney skaters simply stroking around the ice is wrong these days, she points out. "Snow White" star Sergei Tartykov, a Russian who plays the part of the prince, sometimes attempts triple Axels or quadruple toe loops in the show. Four skaters in the troupe, including Preston, do triple jumps. Another does a triple-triple combination. "I didn't join the show and forget how to jump," Preston says.

Every day, Preston does a triple toe loop and a double Axel somewhere in her routine, and occasionally attempts more difficult triple Salchows, triple loops, even tricky triple flips if the ice surface is big enough and her spirit is up. "I spent too many years working on them," Preston says. "I'm not going to lose them.

"The world's biggest misconception is that, if you join these big productions like Walt Disney's World on Ice or Ice Capades, that you skate around in a costume and you don't jump any more. But the public knows what a triple jump is now. You cannot have a production like this any more and not have the skating. They like to be entertained, and they'd also like to see the triple jumps."

Once the Ottawa competition was history, Preston went back to her "normal" world with a sense of purpose and relief.

Eggleton competed in only one professional event, early in his career, and finished second in the U.S. Open in Orlando, Florida, during a Christmas break from Peter Pan. He won $6,000 (U.S.) just being himself. It seemed so easy. "I thought maybe I should pursue this instead of working so hard in the show," Eggleton says. "But I'm glad I took the show. I've become a better person because of it. If I had gone to professional competitions [only], I don't think I would have changed. I don't think I would have become the person I am now."

Thinking of his younger days as an anti-establishment rebel, Eggleton notes: "It always seems to be the most controversial skaters that do the best. Karen is very strong-minded, like me. I'm a strong-willed person. I always wanted to buck the world. To do this, you have to be strong-minded. It's not for the weak of heart."

Eggleton first arrived at Disney's door full of bitterness, frustrated at the path his amateur career had taken. But the job that took him around the world gradually stripped away the bitterness, every time he set foot on the ice. "No one loves skating more than I do," he says. "Every day I skated, it was a show, and it's taken away any bitterness I had." And the job taught him lessons he would not otherwise have learned. Even the roles he has played for Disney have been strangely ironic. But he had many demons to conquer when he started with the tour.

The bitterness that stuck in Eggleton's craw for so long was born of his own independent nature. He constantly collided with the skating establishment of his time. Once, a skating-tour organizer took the mis-behaving boy by the scruff of the neck, loaded him on a bus back to his home in St-Bruno, Quebec, and phoned his mother to tell him he was coming home. Sometimes he just partied too much, they said. Once he set off a fire alarm in a hotel.

Even in his own academically oriented family – his father is a high-school principal, his mother and sister teachers – he admits that he was "the black sheep."

Eggleton was a brilliant amateur with technical expertise and a flair for showmanship, who frequently fell from grace. The year that Vern Taylor landed the first triple Axel in competition at the 1978 world championship in Ottawa, Eggleton was a free-spirited thirteen-year-old kid in Quebec who had just decided to turn his attention to figure skating. It was late in the game for a figure skater, but Eggleton was no stranger to skate blades. In his career, he has mastered three different kinds of blades. He was the top scorer in one of the hockey leagues he played in, at the midget AAA level. Hockey was his first love. His biggest dream was to play in the NHL, but he was getting banged up too much, and he could foresee difficulties in that future. It was one of the saddest days in his life, he says, when he decided to give up hockey. But he also was a high-level speedskater, and he was the Canadian junior champion in barrel jumping, a sport that was particularly popular in

Quebec. (Just before the 1984 Canadian championship, Eggleton says he considered competing in the Canadian barrel-jumping championship, to be held the week before. But he had not competed in the event for two years, and was no longer a member of the Quebec Barrel Jumping Association.) He was a talented oddball, with an unusual skating background and a flair for dramatic storytelling.

In spite of his late start, Eggleton started to land triple Axels only three years into his new career, at a time when triple Axels were as rare as Halley's comet. Eggleton was a misfit in Quebec, which had not produced many high-level figure skaters at the time. The first barrel Eggleton had to leap in his figure-skating career was politics, he says.

Eggleton was a seventh-generation Quebecker, but he was an anglophone in a province that has historically struggled to maintain its French culture. "On top of all the politics with the Quebec federation, there was also the politics of being English in the Quebec province," he says. "If I wasn't battling with my Quebec association, I was battling with coaches. It was a non-stop battle." At one point, Eggleton says he coached himself. It's not surprising that he felt a kinship with Gary Beacom, another Canadian rebel who also felt no need for a coach.

Eggleton almost quit skating before the 1984 Olympics while training with Doug Leigh, Brian Orser's coach, in Ontario. The relationship wasn't working out well, he admits. Leigh demands dedication. Eggleton remembers feeling discouraged, riding a bicycle during a September snowfall back to the home in which he boarded. Money was tight, and the struggles seemed insurmountable. One day, he left for home in Montreal. "I told my parents I wasn't going to skate any more. There was just too much crap," he says. He had left his previous coach because his "thoughts conflicted with hers."

He sat in his room for one and a half months, did nothing, grew a beard. "I was so upset and so disappointed at the world and the way everything functioned," he recalls. His parents, who had already invested a lot of money in his skating career, let the kid's emotions swirl for a while, but one day his mother walked into his room and suggested Eggleton give skating another chance, just one more year. He took her advice.

That year was the season leading up to the 1984 Olympics. At the time, the Canadian Figure Skating Association had a policy that it would send its junior men's champion to the Games in Sarajevo to allow him to gain experience. Eggleton managed to get himself to the Olympics by winning the junior title, although he believed that the Quebec and Canadian associations were pushing another young talented skater, Marc Ferland.

Eggleton says he was awarded the spot on the Olympic team, but only after the Canadian Figure Skating Association had a long meeting with Canadian Olympic Association officials. The meeting went so long, Eggleton says, because the CFSA did not want Eggleton to go, but the COA said it must stick to its criteria.

Everything about Eggleton's career was clouded in controversy. His placement on the Olympic team had ramifications for other skaters, too. Because Eggleton was given the Olympic berth, senior skater Gordon Forbes missed out and was awarded a spot on the world-championship team instead. But there is only one Olympic Games. It was a difficult moment for Forbes – and for Eggleton. His Olympic teammates seemed less than pleased. One of them told him he had no idea what Eggleton was doing on the team, he says. Eggleton felt unwelcome from the first minute.

At the Olympics, Eggleton finished twentieth, at what was actually his first international competition. In a kind of protest at the pressures surrounding his presence on the team, he landed an illegal back flip in the long program.

Forbes went on to compete at the world championship that year and finished ninth.

The rest of Eggleton's career was a story of brilliant promise and jarring disappointments. He finished third in Canada in 1986 and made the world team again, but finished only twentieth at the world championships. He hung around for three more years, in spite of devastating injuries and the loss of government financing because of his poor placements. He bowed out of amateur skating after a dismal effort, while skating injured, against the advice of doctors, at the 1989 Canadian championship. At the closing banquet, various judges told him he should hang up his skates. He agreed. He took a job offer to play Peter Pan for Disney.

In many ways, there is a lot of Eggleton in the roles he plays as a Disney skater. They are almost symbolic of the direction his life has taken, the changes he has felt. The irony did not escape him that his first role was as Peter Pan, the boy who never grew up. "I thought about it at the time. It's as if there is someone standing over me, wanting me to become the best person I can be. I played that part for four years. Why didn't I grow up before that and apply myself? It was like a polite punishment."

Eggleton remembers his years in school when he missed one-third of his classes because of figure skating. He took difficult courses, he says, but never studied, never did homework. All this while his sister was attending McGill University, one of the most highly respected academic institutions in the country. Eggleton attended the school of living by his wits and his charm.

For years, Eggleton flew about the stages of the world, a twentysomething boy clad in green tights. Did he feel silly wearing the childish outfits? "I did," he admits. "But you know, it was my job. That's what I do. I did it very well. There's no one that could do that job like I did. It was great flying around the building. I've accumulated so much frequent flyer miles with Peter Pan, they gave me a carpet [as Aladdin]. Now I can sit down and fly."

Still, Eggleton seemed at first to be reluctant to take the job as Peter Pan. When Feld's group asked him to come to Toronto to audition for the part, the Montreal skater told Disney to come to him, if they wanted him. "If you want me, you send somebody to videotape me," he told them. (Eggleton has always acted as his own agent.) They did, and hired him from a videotape. But when the job as Aladdin opened up, Eggleton figured he'd paid his dues as a green sprite. He actively sought the part just about the time he was completing a European tour of Peter Pan. "I wanted the job," he says. "I knew this would be more of a progression, so much better. I knew I could fit it so much better, because there is so much Aladdin in me."

Eggleton faxed a letter to Feld, the weekend that the firm was making up its mind about who to cast as Aladdin. "They wanted somebody new, somebody fresh," Eggleton lamented. "But a lot of people in the company knew I could do it." Two days later, the company told Eggleton he had the job. "I was ecstatic. It was the biggest day of my life."

Jokingly, Eggleton says that, as Aladdin, he has discovered what hormones are, what girls are. He got to grow his hair long. He graduated from green tights to baggy white pants. The vernal Pan was gone for good.

Like his role as Peter Pan, it was an apt move to cast Eggleton as a mythical boy with charisma. In many ways, Eggleton is Aladdin, an engaging, rollicking rebel of the skating world who had a habit of stumbling rambunctiously into trouble as easily as mudpuddles. Eggleton even looks like Aladdin, with thick dark hair that blows in a mutinous wave at every wild stroke, and a set of dimples that would lure any Jasmine to his side. Most of all, Aladdin learns important values during the production. And, by playing Aladdin, Eggleton has, too, he says. In the story, Aladdin is given three wishes when he discovers the genie. For his first two, Aladdin wishes to become a prince and shed his meagre existence as a poor, thieving street vagabond. He wants to look good. He wants material things. Then he realizes that people's feelings and values are more important, and he grants the genie his freedom through his third wish, rather than remaining a prince. "He grows up through it," Eggleton says. "It was a progression for me, going from Peter Pan, the boy who never grew up, to Aladdin, who realizes values."

Eggleton learned about people, too, in a way that competitive skating had not taught him. "I had to grow up very fast," he says, remembering the battles of his amateur career. "You learn how to deal with politics and with people. So you're beyond your years that way, but you're very immature in others.

"Like a lot of athletes, you haven't had the worldwide street smarts. They go out of their training environment and all of a sudden they're in the real world and bang. It's hard for them. It's hard for them to fit in with everyday, normal people."

Eggleton has learned about people from his magic-carpet ride as Aladdin, touring the cities of the world. He has spent an extended period in every city in the United States. "I know how people are. People in Los Angeles, Texas, Long Island. The road really does change you. When you live on the road, you become a citizen of the world.

"You realize that everywhere you go, people are the same. All they want is to be happy and have friends. It doesn't matter where they are. You learn things at the very deepest level."

For Karen Preston, working as a Disney cartoon, skating in a voluminous yellow skirt and a black wig, has given her life and freedom. She left the amateur world in tears after the 1994 Canadian championship in Edmonton, when she finished third, and just missed a berth on the Olympic team.

"I enjoy it, way more, I can't even express how much more, than amateur competitions," she says. "No longer is eleven months of my life riding on six and a half total minutes of performance time at nationals or at worlds. Now, I get twelve shows a week in each city. And it's easier to entertain a family, or a grandma and a grandpa or two young adults, than it is a panel of nine judges. It's way more rewarding to see happy, smiling faces than it is to see long, stern judges' faces."

In front of friendlier eyes, Preston came of age and graduated as a skater. She was always seen as an amateur skater with a moonlight coolness about her, concentrating on the task at hand, not reaching her audience emotionally. But these days not only does Preston skate, but she acts. Snow White shows innocence, fear, joy, warmth, light-heartedness, love. Preston was convincing enough, that, in Seoul, her fans began to yell 'No!' in their language, just as the wicked queen talked her into taking a bite of the poisoned apple.

"I'm really proud of myself for doing that," Preston says, "because for so long people were always saying, 'She's so athletic, there's no creativity. She's not artistic.' Well, you cannot not be artistic and perform in a show like this. I'm proud of the work that I do and I think that I should be."

Preston never fails to keep the doors open to her past. She is an uncommon wanderer, sending bits of her thoughts and her travels to old friends at home through letters and postcards. "I do write a lot of letters, particularly to people that I went to high school with, that had nothing to do with skating, that were just my friends, that were always there for me regardless of whether I was on the top or on the bottom of the heap. Some of them have even come to visit me on tour. They say they can totally understand how I get drawn into this. One of them came to visit me in Miami in early November and we were lying out on the beach when he said, 'No wonder you like this.'"

She still writes Elvis Stojko and Marcus Christensen, a Canadian skater with whom she used to train. She frequently writes former coaches Osborne Colson and Ellen Burka. "You hear of so many people that just go away and are never heard from again," Preston says. "People aren't sure whether they're dead or alive. I didn't want to be like that."

Preston, a make-believe princess, and Eggleton, a prince-of-thieves-cum-hero, have found permanence and meaning in their nomadic, fantasy-laden lives. To them, Disney is not a playground, but a way of life with a variety of rich rewards. "I can't go back to where I used to be," Aladdin sings in the show. Eggleton and Preston never will.

The Inner Life: A Psychologist's View

S usan Humphreys knew she was her own worst enemy. At eighteen, she had lit fires of hope with her lyrical movement and her ninth-place finish at the 1994 world championship in her first attempt. By eighteen and a half, she had put all the fires out as she struggled with a back injury. She slid from being Canada's top-ranked female skater during the early part of the 1994-95 season into a being an also-ran. But cutting deepest of all was her scorched will, her lack of belief in herself, in her dreams. One day, she blurted to her coach: "How can I be so good and so bad at the same time?" What made Humphreys excel as a figure skater – her passion and emotion – also shook the delicate balance between body and mind and sent her whirling out of control. "I felt like I was looking in a mirror and the person I saw was telling me you can't do it," she says. All it took to come apart was a flash of doubt.

Skaters need more than a locker-room pep talk to erase such doubts. "It's a very complex game," said sport psychologist Peter Jensen, who has worked with skaters, such as Brian Orser, and with athletes from other sports. "Not many people appreciate the complexities of it, and know anything about how people grow and evolve and develop. It's a challenge."

Because coaches aren't always equipped to seal up the chinks in a skater's confidence, sports psychologists have become an increasingly important part of the team. Some coaches swear by their influence. Others aren't so convinced. "We are constantly using psychology," said Christy Ness, coach of Kristi Yamaguchi. "If you can't get through to a skater, then you might seek outside help. But that's the only time you would use a third party. There isn't a need for a third person there. It's the same as agents [for Olympic-eligible competitors]. I think it would have been hard for Kristi to win an Olympic medal if she'd had an agent. It would have been one more person giving an opinion. It's hard enough to keep the skater, the coach, and the parent all working on the same wave together."

Some skaters just can't afford professional help to find their way to success. Ukrainian skater Elena Liashenko, accustomed to skating in front of spare audiences in Europe, was completely overwhelmed when she faced the boisterous, gigantic crowds at the world championship in Edmonton in 1996. She froze, lost her focus, and finished twelfth, hopelessly intimidated in a high-tension act. Yet she had once finished sixth at a world championship, and won a bronze medal at the 1995 European championship. These days, the Ukrainian federation has little money for "frills," such as psychologists. Yet for some skaters, they are not frills. They are necessities.

"As the game changes, people are going to need assistance, even with coaches becoming better educated about what skaters need," says Jensen, who teaches courses on mental preparation for both coaches and skaters as part of Canada's coaching certification program. Jensen has watched figure skating explode in popularity, pushing young skaters into a glaring spotlight, under pressure of an all-or-nothing performance. All eyes are watching. Television ratings are high. Fans fill rinks, and mine for every nugget of information. And skaters are all alone on a cold patch of ice, surrounded by critics. Susan Humphreys knows it all too well. "The world is watching and they don't miss much," she says. "You're only as good as your last skate."

In Jensen's mind, the skaters of today face pressure from all directions, although he will tell them sometimes that stress is really something they place on their own shoulders, like an unwieldy yoke. "But I think the pressure is increasing dramatically," he says. "There is a ton of pressure on the kids." There is pressure from the skating environment itself – criticism from judges, and the audience, and the embarrassment of making mistakes in front of all of them – as well as all the stresses that teens face as they grow up. There is pressure on skaters from parents, searching for vicarious success, from a myopic environment that focuses only on skating at the expense of life outside the sport, from the sport's artistic demands on both males and females, from the uncertainties of injury. "It's a real quagmire," Jensen says.

Inside the rink, the skaters wade through unexpected situations that tug at their resolve. "There are the things that happen in a competition, when you find yourself in second place and you didn't expect to be there," he says. "Changing their expectations is a tremendous way for athletes to put pressures on themselves."

If one poor skate sets a skater onto an uncertain path, then Susan Humphreys has been on a roller-coaster ride, with the back injuries and doubts that have plagued her for several years. Because of her injury, she showed up at competitions over two seasons with a less-difficult arsenal of jumps than others. It helped her stay in a safe cocoon, however. "Last year [1995-96], I had a little bit less pressure, because I wasn't trying the hard things," she says. "So even with my best skate, I couldn't have finished in the top three in a competition [like Skate Canada]."

But at Skate Canada during the 1996-97 season, Humphreys had the tough tricks back, and with them came more stress. "I knew that, with two good skates, I could be in the top three," she says. "And with that comes more expectations from everybody – your coach, the association, your family. There are a lot of people involved. I want this for myself, but I also want it for them."

Humphreys did not finish in the top three at that event. After a disastrous short program, she sank to ninth and last place. She was disconsolate, in tears. The night before the long program, she hardly slept. "I went in with more pressure on myself to do it, and not to fall apart," she recalls. "One of the hardest things to do is to come off a poor performance." Practice the next morning was a thorny exercise. Humphreys even pondered what she was doing there. "I wondered, 'Is it ever going to get any better than this?'"

It did. When Humphreys decided she had nothing to lose and everything to gain, her fortunes changed. She skated well enough to finish fourth in the long program, ahead of Canadian champion Jennifer Robinson. Three of nine judges placed her third. For Humphreys, it was a victory, a delayed comeback. And finally, three months later, she won her first Canadian championship. But it was a slow ride, and one fraught with roadblocks and tensions, many of them building up off the ice.

Skaters are under such pressure that it takes a special person to be able to cope with it, Jensen says. And it takes a very special person – coach or parent – to ensure that, when their skating days are over, "they have done a service to the human being."

It is a worry, Jensen says, because it is very difficult to truly develop character in an athlete within a competitive framework. Skating has its characters, such as Toller Cranston and Christopher Bowman and Tonya Harding and Oksana Baiul, but the competitive environment often works against the development of character, of the whole person. "The implication is that your child would be better off in figure skating than hanging around street corners," he says. "Yet there's not one single piece of research that would prove that. It's true in all sports."

Often, a skater's success boils down to the kind of home life and background they have, and to their relationships with parents and coaches, Jensen says. Sometimes they don't have a home life at all. In the old Soviet and Eastern bloc, and even in Canada, some skaters move away from home at an early age, flocking to top training centres and coaches. "You are entrusting the development and values and all those things to someone else," Jensen says. "That's not unique to figure skating."

Home life or not, skaters, coaches, and parents sometimes live in a bubblelike existence. "They are like rink rats," says Jensen, who used to teach at elementary and high schools. "There are more than a few of them who are like schoolteachers, who can't talk about anything but teaching. . . . As soon as you're with skating people, that's all you end up talking about. The topic never seems to shift from skating.

"So everything is under a phenomenal microscope in that world. The people who have dedicated themselves to figure skating, their sense of meaning and purpose in life comes from it. They're very myopic. Phenomenally myopic."

The skater is at the centre of this inward-looking world. There is little time and opportunity for an outer life. A helpful parent picks up all the mundane chores, so the child can make best use of his or her time to learn skating skills. Often parents just don't understand the world. It is as if their child lives on another planet, and they have been left out of the journey.

The parents of Canadian men's silver medallist Jeffrey Langdon were ordinary folk who had to come to terms with the circles in which their young son moved. "He just lived in his own egocentric world that he had," says Al Langdon. "He lives in a kind of world where you have lunch at [a French restaurant], stay in five-star hotels, where you are catered to. He lives in a world that is different from Karen and I. You have to ride with the punches and understand that's who he is."

Al is amused when he sees information sheets or profiles of skaters handed to the media with questions about hobbies, or what skaters do when they are not training. The responses go something like this: all manner of sports, chess, reading, keeping fit, dancing, theatre, music, eating out, telephone calls. Many of the choices listed could be seen as activities that help in skating, or off ice activities that increase their knowledge of artistry. Konrad Schaub, a former Canadian skater who left to skate for Austria, once wrote, jokingly, that his hobbies were yodelling and accordion. "It's all hogwash," Al Langdon says. Most of it isn't true, because they have to say something. These kids don't have a life outside the rink. They think it's normal, because they're always together. You look at them and know they have sacrificed everything. They really don't have a life away from the arena."

His son's own life is centred around activities at the rink. All of his friends are other skaters. His father wouldn't think of asking him to go out and play catch; Jeff never learned to throw a baseball. It's not something he cared to learn, or had time to learn. Does his son's narrow focus worry his father? "It's a little bit scary, because all the eggs are in one basket," he says.

And it's a lonely life for a skating child. When coach Louis Stong was growing up as a young boy near Toronto, he was the only male in his class who competed in figure skating. Long and lanky, he was immediately conscripted to the school basketball team, but he returned one time from a Canadian skating championship to find he was no longer on the school team. "That kind of stuff happens because we're away so much," he says. "And you even begin to be excluded socially."

Skaters tend to find friends who are other skaters. Nobody understands what a skater endures more than another skater. Friends in school melt away. "Their perception is that you don't have time for them, so they begin not to have time for you," Stong says. "It's a lonely life for a kid." The door gradually swings shut on a skater's narrow world. The end result can be an unhappy one.

"Skaters are certainly isolated from reality," says Stong, who coached world champions Kurt Browning and Barbara Underhill and Paul Martini, as well as Olympic bronze pairs medallists Jill Watson and Peter Oppegard of the United States. "Suddenly, when it's over, there's a big hole, because there isn't anything else in their lives. It occupies so much of their time and thinking and, all of a sudden, there's nothing there."

Some skaters stay in the sport longer than they should, finding themselves at loose ends when their best competitive days are in the past, Stong says. If they leave the sport, they also leave behind their social lives. "If they give up skating, they give up all that goes with it, including the friends. They don't have any others. It's very scary."

So closed is this wispy world of early-morning haze and late-night spotlight that some skaters have not learned how to look outward, how to relate to others. They have become the centre of their universe over many years. "There's no question," Stong says. "It's not good for relationships. Pairs and dance couples are a little different, because they have each other to think about. It's a huge generalization, but I've seen it many times. First marriages may not be a success."

The lifeline of hope comes from a thoughtful parent, vigilant about the psychological development of a young skater. Neva Browning was always able to pull her son Kurt back to earth at every step, to keep him from getting "arena head." Oksana Baiul had no parent at all to fasten her values firmly in her heart when she needed them most in a world full of false glitter. Parents are key players, in many ways.

As mentioned earlier, there are parents who are careful about the well-being of their children and there are parents who are swept into a maelstrom of competitive desire, almost imperceptibly, in spite of all their good intentions. As a sports psychologist, Peter Jensen is an outsider who looks on with objective eyes and tries to sort the motives and the pitfalls. "I don't see any more evil people in skating than anywhere else – people who are manipulative and trying to mislead others. It all happens with the best of intentions," Jensen says. But, he adds, there are not many people within the sport who appreciate its complexities and how people grow and develop."

Skating parents make many sacrifices, but at times Jensen is concerned about some of their motives. "The parents' message should be: 'Just skate well. I don't really care where you finish.'" he says. "Some parents know the right things to say, but then they beat the kids to the results board. The kids have got to fight their way through the parents to see how they did. The parents' behaviour doesn't match what they say. And who's to blame? That's the way we all are."

The competitive environment brings out the worst in people sometimes, Jensen says. It comes with hopes and wants and overweening visions, fully charged, and difficult to wrestle back into the real world. It's a challenge to remain a fair, open-minded, kind, and judicious parent or a coach who is truly interested in the development of a whole person, he adds.

With the backing of the Canadian Figure Skating Association, Jensen stages workshops for parents, in which he tells them that their skaters already have a coach; what they need is a parent. And for skating, they require a new set of parenting skills.

In the fantastical world that is figure skating, some skaters spend more time with coaches than with their own parents. Their influence on a skater is significant. The ideal coach is one who coaches the whole person. The really successful coach is one who can turn out good people, not just good skaters, Jensen says. "You need very thoughtful people. Coaches are phenomenally concerned about this. Sometimes, they don't know what to do."

But Jensen says that in many cases it is not the coach who teaches skaters to transcend the skating life and move on when it is over. He thinks of former Olympic bronze ice-dancing medallist Tracy Wilson as a success story. Her skating career ended with her partner's death of AIDS, but Wilson eventually became a sought-after sports analyst who is currently working for CBS. "When you look at some of the people who have been able to transcend [skating], in no way was it a coach who influenced them to move out to other pastures, and do other things," Jensen says. "It was the person themselves or their parents. It's what they came into the game with."

Jensen remembers working with university basketball players, discussing with them issues that went far beyond their sport. "We would talk about a whole pile of things. But the skating world is a very closed shop," he says, thinking of skaters' reluctance to look and think beyond a narrow focus.

Canadian champion Karen Preston lost her title one year when she decided to set aside her university courses and concentrate only on skating. For one season, Preston entered the closed shop completely. But she found it was a mistake; she focused too intently on one experience to the ultimate detriment of it. The following year, she picked up her university courses and friends, and skated so well that she landed a spot on the Olympic team.

"It's the ones that drop everything and put all their eggs in this basket that suffer," Jensen says. He sees it happening in other sports, too, and laments the loss of bright young people who direct all their energy and resources towards excelling at a sport such as junior hockey – and then never make it. Meanwhile, promising careers have been scuttled in the race for an unobtainable goal. "We lose them as teachers or doctors or lawyers," Jensen says. "And they are still sitting around talking about what might have been."

For every sad coaching story, Jensen says he can think of an equal number of inspiring stories about coaches who understand what a young person needs to grow up with a healthy outlook on life. He has seen coaches who have been good for skaters, have been with them when they suffer disappointments, and who look out for their general well-being. Doug Leigh, coach of Elvis Stojko, is one of them, a "straight-shooter," Jensen says.

In the training centre he founded north of Toronto, Leigh toils diligently, forging his own way. He plays no political games. And he gets results. During the 1995-96 season, skaters from his Mariposa Skating School won three of the four senior titles in Canada. Jensen, who teaches coaches to explain tasks with clarity, to recognize good work, to instill positive attitudes, has watched Leigh at work with quiet surprise.

"When you stand beside Doug Leigh, you wonder where the hell he is coming from," Jensen says. "He uses metaphor upon metaphor upon metaphor: backchecking, level playing field. But people who have been around him for a couple of months, they know his lingo. He talks with precision and clarity. The whole message is, 'You can do this.' He does so many things right, and he does it all quite naturally. You can't move in that rink without getting the message: 'We expect you to have a positive attitude around here.'"

It's as if Leigh has taken instruction on how to teach effectively, with a few courses on sport psychology, particularly with motivation. He hasn't. Only a year before the Olympic Games in Nagano, Japan, Leigh still hadn't achieved his level-four coaching certification, the minimum necessary under Canadian sport rules to accompany an athlete to the Olympics. Leigh seems to teach by instinct and life experience. Not all coaches have the knack or knowledge, Jensen says.

Although many amateur coaches in other sports are affiliated with universities in Canada, most skating coaches in the country are not highly educated people, Jensen points out. (In the United States, the situation appears to be reversed. Carole Shulman, executive director of the Professional Skaters Association, says 80 per cent of member coaches have university degrees.) Many skating coaches in Canada have been former skaters who have moved on in their lives to teach. In Canada, figure-skating coaches lag behind coaches from other sports, such as rowing, cycling and hockey, in getting certification. "Particularly among the older coaches, they've always done it their way, and they're not so anxious to take the training," Jensen says. A couple of years ago, thirty coaches attended Jensen's mental-preparation courses in the coaching-certification programs, but only three handed in assignments.

Yet the complexities of the sport and the needs of its skaters grow even greater. The real quagmire is a potentially ominous triangle that includes skater, coach, and parent. "Working within that triangle is very difficult," Jensen says. "And the kid is the one in the middle. Sometimes, if the parents side with the coach, the kid's got three people telling him he's not doing it right. It's awkward."

To come out of the skating experience with inner life intact, skaters need thoughtful people surrounding them. They need parents or coaches who constantly check their actions and their words and ask themselves if they are handling situations correctly, Jensen says. Skaters aren't the only ones who need a helping hand from a psychologist. "You don't get that many people who are that aware," Jensen says.

Among the ills that can escape the notice of coaches and parents are eating disorders, common mostly among young woman, but also known in small numbers of men. Although people with the problem often end up in hospitals under the care of medical doctors, it is pri-marily a psychological ill, brought on by low self-esteem, a desire for perfection, a searching for unconditional love. Eating disorders are accidents waiting to happen in the skating world, with its emphasis on body image and appearance clouding the minds of young women who are wrestling with physical changes at the same time they are learning triple jumps. Shannon Allison, a Canadian skater who seemed pointed for stardom, is an example of the skating-world pressures that concern Jensen and that frustrate medical doctors such as Dr. Robert Lee (who delivers his point of view in the next chapter).

Allison is a survivor. When she showed up at the Canadian champi-onship in Ottawa in 1996 at age twenty-three, her goals were not to win medals, like her peers. It was a miracle that she even made the roster. For that, her heart soared because she had conquered a troubled past.

By the time Allison had turned twenty, she had fumbled through most of skating's ills, its dark side. A promising skater who won a bronze medal at the 1987 world junior figure-skating championship, Allison hit bottom soon afterwards. A growth spurt derailed her jumps. A constant spate of injuries plagued her. She was unsettled by a round of coaching changes and changes in training venues. And, between the time she was fourteen and seventeen, she suddenly became a young woman. "They had to be the worst years I ever went through," she says. "They are the hardest years of a teen's life, and I had skating to deal with as well." She found herself trying to stifle a growth spurt and struggling to maintain the weight of her girlish days, when she was several inches shorter. Allison developed an eating disorder.

Allison was a prime candidate for the disorder. She had no self-esteem or confidence. And she was a perfectionist. "When I couldn't do what people expected of me, I felt as if I was letting everyone down," she says. "They continued to want more and I couldn't give it, so it got worse."

And she took part in a sport in which appearance is a factor in success. She does not believe she is the only one. "With all the young kids trying to be number one, and training to be the best, and with weight such an issue in skating, there is no way that it can't be a factor with a lot of kids," she says.

Allison was considered by many to be the successor to 1988 Olympic silver medallist Elizabeth Manley. But as Manley's career was ending, Allison's troubles were beginning. She was a victim of the strident quest for success. Allison was barely seventeen when she finished fifth at the 1989 Canadian championship, hobbled by injury, and she eventually quit skating for two years.

"They always say that quitting skating is a hard thing to do," she says. "They say it is hard to let go. But I went to go on the ice and I couldn't make myself do it. I didn't want to go out there. I had no desire. I extremely hated this sport. With all the frustration and anger, I just thought I don't need this any more. . . . It was easy to let go."

What hurt her the most in her turbulent years was that the people around her seemed to forget about her needs, Allison says. Because of her early success, people began to focus on her skating. If she failed to live up to expectations, doubting questions dogged her every step: "Something is not working. What are we going to do about it? How are we going to fix it? How can we make it better, fast and now?" But all the time Allison felt that nobody stopped to wonder what was happening to her in all the striving for perfection. Nobody asked her if she was handling the pressures and the changes well, or how they affected her. "Nobody really cared about me," Allison says. "They just cared about the results that I was putting on the ice."

Allison now works as a coach in British Columbia. Because of her experiences, she is mindful of the inner workings of her young students. She said she would ensure that she would take the time to find out what was happening to a student internally, and take that into consideration in her plans. "I wouldn't make choices for that person that maybe weren't the right ones psychologically or emotionally," she says.

As she grew into a young woman, Allison seemed to live with a rain cloud hanging above her head. Her injuries staggered her resolve. She developed a chronic back problem after colliding with another skater during a practice at the 1988 Canadian championship. Sometimes the problem would flare up so severely, Allison would have to lie on the floor for a week. Now she does exercises to strengthen her back. At best, she experiences "only" aches and pains. Then she sprained an ankle so badly that she had to wear a cast partway up her leg for six weeks. She also damaged a ligament that put her out of training for three months – just before the 1989 championship that she might have won. None of these accidents served to boost her morale.

Her eating disorder was only one source of her frustrations, but it was a significant one. One of her trainers, she says, had a tendency towards disordered eating. In the end, however, Allison took full responsibility for developing her own case. It was as if she looked at herself through a fun-house mirror, all distorted. Even though she burned calories with a rigour in her sport, she ate little: a piece of bread in the morning, a tiny muffin for lunch, a salad for dinner. Twice a day, she took aerobics classes. Her weight dropped to 112 pounds on her willowy

5-foot-6 frame, and Allison worried that she could not lose more. "My metabolism had slowed down so much I couldn't lose more," she says. "I would feel irritable, hungry all the time."

Allison often felt as if she were going to pass out. In practice, she couldn't get through the first thirty seconds of her program without being out of breath. She had no energy. She felt cold all the time. "When I really got skinny, nobody said anything but my parents and my friends," she says. Her coach said nothing.

Allison conquered her problem by working with a nutritionist, but unwillingly at first. In the beginning, she admitted, she manipulated the people around her who were trying to help. She lied about how little she ate. It had been a medical solution to a psychological problem. Eventually, Allison says, she grew tired of fighting her illness and dealing with food all the time. That spurred her on to solve her problems – that along with a growing sense of confidence.

In the two years that Allison did not compete, she got married and attended Simon Fraser University in British Columbia with her sights set on becoming an elementary-school teacher. Finally, she began to grow, both inside and out. "I started to find out a lot of things about myself," she says. But it took its toll on her marriage. Her husband was happy with life as it was. Allison found that she was changing, but her husband wasn't changing with her. They divorced.

"I started to like myself," she says. "I began to think, no, I'm not a bad person. I was finding out what I wanted to do in life."

Allison decided to turn professional at a time when there was no possibility of turning back into an amateur. It was as if she wanted to put a definite period to the end of her skating sentence. She did it because of her distaste of the sport. She wished to harbour no lingering wishes about her skating future.

But, as she began to heal, the International Skating Union offered reinstatement. Allison took it. A month before the qualifying events for the national championship, Allison suddenly remastered all her triple jumps. When she finally landed a triple Lutz, the most difficult triple that women usually do, she was ecstatic. "I never ever thought I'd ever land them again," she says. She hadn't landed one in about ten years.

By the time Allison made it to the Canadian championship in 1996, she weighed 125 pounds, a tall, statuesque skater who owned her own home, was close to getting her university degree, who had another life outside skating. She had finally won on her own terms, without winning a medal of any colour.

Eating disorders feed off the ideals of image and line and appearance, the very stuff of figure skating indeed. The artistic side of skating brings an unusual set of psychological stresses for both males and females. Females battle a stringent ideal of beauty, of weight and body type, that can lead to eating disorders. Sometimes the ideal is an unspoken one, born of glossy pages in fashion magazines.

At times, the ideal is part of a rule: some professional skating tours demand that female skaters weigh in once a week. If they gain weight beyond set limits, they are subject to penalties, perhaps a $10 fine the first week, a day's pay the next. Or they could lose their jobs. According to one former performer on a skating tour, the rules have had an adverse effect on females, who resort to binging and purging, to starvation diets, or to living on water for two or three days before the weigh-in – this despite performing in two or three shows a day.

After having talked to skaters on tours, Peter Jensen fears that many of the female partners in the top pairs teams in the world fail to eat properly. He knows of one young woman on a tour, who had one of the largest body builds among her touring peers, and "she's always had a bit of an eating disorder," he says. "She looks huge next to the others. And she's saying, 'I'm going on this ice with them and look how they look.'"

World pairs champion Lloyd Eisler, who has toured both as an eligible and an ineligible skater, says there is no question that eating disorders are a part of skating, but he does not think they are "as prevalent as everybody would like to believe." And it's not a problem only in pairs skating, in which it is advantageous to have a tiny female partner. Female singles skater suffer, as well as female ice-dancing partners. "In ice dancing, they want women who are six feet tall and only one hundred pounds," Eisler says. "Where those people come from, I'm not really sure."

And it's not only a problem that females stumble into: Eisler knows of a very small number of male skaters who have eating disorders. They, too, have concerns about appearance in a sport that stresses perfect body line.

A strapping athlete at 5-foot-11 and 180 pounds, Eisler admits that he watches his weight. "I have no eating disorder," he says. "When I competed, I knew what weight I competed best at, how I felt, how I looked on video, how my coaches said I look best. That maybe wasn't a weight my body could hold. I could weigh 200 pounds, and still my body could hold it. But for pairs skating, and for the look in skating with [partner Isabelle Brasseur], I knew what I had to weigh. For me, that didn't mean not eating. It just meant watching what I was eating, properly looking after my nutrition, not having five meals a day and thirty beers a week. Anything in excess is bad for you."

But many females in the sport diet to excess. Eisler says he has seen young women on tour eating a couple of pieces of lettuce, a couple of carrots, two fusilli noodles, and a huge piece of dessert for dinner. "The rationale is that you're living on sugar, and that's what's getting you from point A to point B," he explains. "They feel that dessert gives them the sugar, and, if that's all they have, they won't gain as much weight as if they had a big dinner. In their eyes, all they're having is one dessert."

They also live on caffeine. Eisler says he has seen female skaters down ten to twelve cups of caffeine a day, hoping that its diuretic properties give them an edge in losing weight, as well as living on its energy buzz.

Both Eisler and Jensen point to coaches who focus on weight and appearance in their athletes as part of the problem. "Part of the problem is the coaches who push, push, push to weigh every day. I think that gives a complex to a lot of people," Eisler says.

Jensen says he knows of coaches who insist that a pairs girl should weigh 102 pounds. "But that 102 pounds doesn't change whether you're 6-foot-2 or 5 feet tall," he said. "You have people dabbling in things, and they just have no idea what they're creating."

As a part-time coach at the rink in Boucherville, Quebec, where he trained, Eisler says he is vigilant in asking students about their health, if he suspects an eating disorder. "We're partially all to blame for putting the expectations on these people," he adds. He asks them if they are healthy. "I don't care if you miss jumps . . . down the road it's going to pay off, if you're not going to have any psychological problems. I'd rather see the people healthy than win a medal. The medals will fade, they go away. No one remembers you. You have to live with yourself."

But with his peers, it is not so easy to step into someone else's private life and urge a change, Eisler finds. People with an eating disorder may deny the existence of the problem to themselves, or they may be caught on a roller-coaster ride of fears they cannot stop. "They like to convince people that nothing is wrong," he says. "But the worst thing is, everybody knows. If you're not healthy, you don't need to be a genius to figure it out. Everybody has a good set of eyes. . . . They think that if no one knows and if we keep it quiet, maybe it will go away."

Jensen says the complex, stress-filled environment of skating requires support services to help skaters find their way through it all, yet society has a stigma about "working in a mental dimension. No one ever talks about eating disorders. Everybody just hides it away."

For the first couple of seasons, Jensen wanted to stage seminars on eating disorders for Canadian national training camps, but he found the Canadian Figure Skating Association was not at all keen about running them. Finally, officials agreed. "We got some of the skaters who admittedly had eating disorders who were still skating on the national team to talk to the other skaters about it," Jensen says. "Those were probably the most effective seminars we did."

By its very nature and because of its popularity, skating puts a magnifying glass on the problems its youth faces: growing up in a complex world and a complex sport, doubts, parental pushing, coaches who ignore the inner life of a skater. "We won't see the results of a lot of this until the kid is in his thirties or forties," Jensen says.

"There's an old adage: you have to do it alone, but you can't do it by yourself," Jensen says. "I think that's true in figure skating. The game is just too complicated. A lot of coaches like to think they can handle it all or the association thinks it can handle it all, but the truth is, they can't."

Some succeed, however. "I don't get mad," Susan Humphreys says after finishing fourth in the long program at Skate Canada. "That's my problem. I give in. But it's one thing I didn't allow to happen today. I was everything that people said I haven't been."

A triumph of will and self-esteem.

Of Bunions and Sore Knees

Dr. Robert Lee was off duty, but there he was, making the rounds at a post-competition party. This time, there were no bags of ice to settle on knees – only an ice sculpture of a skate rising majestically out of a bed of fruit – no slashed brows to stitch, and no bandages to bind around knotty feet. Instead of a stethoscope against his chest, he had his tiny daughter, snoozing without care, yawning as she passed through the arms of a German skater to a Canadian judge to an international skating official. Young, soft-spoken, and thoughtful, Lee was the picture of a family man, wrapped up in the arms of sport.

Lee, thirty-three, was the official sports-medicine doctor at the Skate Canada international competition in Kitchener, Ontario, during the fall of 1996, and he had plenty to do. Chen Lu of China came knocking at his door in the concourse under the seats, looking for help to dull the pain of a stress fracture in her foot that had never been allowed to heal. She pulled out of the competition. German pairs skater Mirko Mueller was also hustled into Lee's room, bleeding from a cut over one eye, inflicted by the flailing elbow of his partner, Peggy Schwarz, during a twist move. Four stitches and a black eye later, Mueller was on his way.

But Lee's interest in his work goes far beyond patching up the odd unlucky skater that crosses his path. Half of the athletes in the clinic that he started with a partner in Waterloo, Ontario, in September 1995 are less than eighteen years old, and many of the others university age. (His clinic is situated near two university campuses in the small city.) About 20 per cent of his patients are over the age of forty, the weekend runners with throbbing knees and ankles and shins. He knows the woes of athletes from almost every sport: rowing, badminton, kayaking, running, hockey, motocross, and he is most interested in preventing them. Well read, he puts out feelers for information in every direction, gleaning interesting tidbits from radio interviews, from study, from peers, keen to know anything about sports trends and how they fit into his work. He is concerned, determined to put it all right.

Lee is like many other sports-medicine doctors who have treated athletes in the figure-skating world: they work in specialized clinics, not skating clubs, and treat a wide variety of patients from all sports. When they are dealing with the skating world, their work is focused mainly on preventative measures, because traumatic injuries in skating are rare. Because skaters train for hours every week, for at least a decade, their most common problems are overuse injuries, when a muscle or a knee or a foot or a back has just taken too many beatings for too long. One early American study found knee injuries were the most common problem among skaters.

"Skaters bring more knee problems than any other injuries to a physician's attention," wrote U.S. team doctor Angela Smith, in the book *Sports Injuries: Mechanisms, Prevention and Treatment*. Most are caused by overuse; for example, a skater may attempt a jump twenty to a hundred times in a single day, according to Smith. And wonky knees can severely impair a skater's performance; knee action is important in jumping, and in ice dancing the knee is the primary tool.

Foot or ankle and lower-back injuries are also the bugbears of many skaters. Foot or ankle woes stem from ill-fitting boots and jarring jump landings; back injuries occur from landing jumps, as well, or from lifting partners in pairs or ice dancing. Fitness is also the domain of sports-medicine doctors: a skater has to be very fit, in various ways, in order to land a series of difficult jumps and other elements during a four- or four-and-a half-minute program.

Dr. Norman Gledhill, a physiologist who works out of a clinic at York University in Toronto, is a doctor skaters seldom see at a competition. He does most of his work during the season. As chairman of the medical and scientific committee of the Canadian Figure Skating Association for the past fifteen years, he tests the fitness levels of all athletes on the Canadian national team, twice a year. All skaters on the national team are very fit, he says, even ice dancers Shae-Lynn Bourne and Victor Kraatz. People have a misconception that dancers – who do not do the athletic jumps and spins and throws of other disciplines – are not fit, Gledhill says. But Canada's world ice-dancing bronze medallists have passed his tests with flying colours. Skating a senior competitive program is comparable to running a four-minute mile, according to Angela Smith.

The association's committee is responsible for giving all of the medical and scientific support to national team athletes. "We tell them what areas they can make improvements in," Gledhill says. "And when they get closer to their performance time, we tell them where they have made their improvements and how close they are getting to the levels they should be at."

The committee also arranges medical examinations for the athletes, to ensure they don't have a condition that will impair their performance. And, with financing from the CFSA, the committee arranges to send a doctor and a physiotherapist with national team members whenever they attend international competitions. "Year-round we're looking at optimal health," Gledhill says. "But at events, we're dealing with minor up to major injuries."

When doctors operate as medical officers at competitions, they work strictly as volunteers, giving up a week or two of work at their own clinics. Sometimes they may forfeit $2,000 or more in pay, says Lee. And when the doctor is sent out of the country, the job becomes more complex: a doctor also tends to become a chaperone, checking to see if the food the athletes are served is adequate, if they have enough water, if they are getting enough sleep.

The Canadian association sends medical support with athletes to competitions because there is no guarantee that an organizing committee of an event in another country has access to good care. The International Skating Union says organizing committees are obligated to provide medical care at events, but the international body issues only guidelines on the subject, not rules. "What we consider to be nominal coverage in Canada might be optimal in some other countries," says Gledhill. "In certain countries, the coverage is less than adequate."

With this in mind, the Canadian doctors take with them full medical kits with sterile sutures and needles so they don't have to worry about getting supplies in a country where they may be hard to find.

At an event, it is difficult for doctors to stop a skater from performing with an injury. Unless the skater is a minor, they cannot order a skater to stay off the ice; they can only strongly recommend that he or she do so. There are many examples of skaters who have taken responsibility for their own serious injuries, and competed despite them. At the 1994 world championship in Japan, Isabelle Brasseur skated with a painful cracked rib that impaired her breathing. Elvis Stojko attempted to skate at the 1995 Canadian championship only days after he severely injured his ankle, but, suffering from excruciating pain, he withdrew from the short program after skating less than half the routine. At the 1991 Canadian championship, pairs skater Christine Hough struck her head and was carried off the ice after her partner, Doug Ladret, fell on top of her during a twist move that went wrong. However, a few minutes later, even though Hough spoke of feeling disoriented, she returned to the ice and, with the help of her solicitous partner, won the silver medal.

Still, Gledhill says doctors have succeeded in stopping skaters from competing, particularly with something like a concussion. He remembers doctors grounding one skater who had struck his head; they withstood pressure from both the skater and his parents, who wanted to continue. "You have to take the best interests of the athlete to heart, and that may mean not skating," he says. "The best interests is the health of the athlete." It's not a decision that doctors have to make very often, he adds.

Dr. Andrew Pipe, the chairman of the Canadian Centre for Ethics in Sport, says sports physicians may have little power in the legal or regulatory sense to stop athletes from competing – particularly in non-combative sports – but they are developing a growing awareness that the athletes are patients first, athletes second.

However, doctors often deal with "incredible cultural pressures" in some sports, such as gymnastics, where athletes are expected to play while hurt. "I've heard certain physicians involved in gymnastics agonize publicly about what they should be doing when they see what they think is tantamount to child abuse," he says.

On a couple of occasions, Pipe says he has had to deal with downhill skiers who insisted on competing even though they had hurt themselves. When this happens, Pipe says he asks the athlete to sign a document that states he has advised the athlete not to race while hurt and that he may discuss the issue with the coach. At this point, the athlete tends to reconsider his or her decision, Pipe says.

"You get into kind of hazy medical, legal issues here," he says. In the United States, the debate tends to get very sticky. South of the border, there have been several successful suits for the right to play against medical advice, Pipe says.

Even in a non-competitive situation, when a skater suffers an injury that may force him or her to miss a practice or two, a sports-medicine doctor has to weigh the options. It's never wrong for a doctor to urge a skater to stay off the ice, advises Angela Smith, but a determined athlete may not react well. "A dedicated figure skater either follows the advice and becomes depressed, follows it only partially and continues hurting and feeling guilty, or neglects the advice entirely," Smith wrote.

Research on figure-skating injuries lags far behind that of other sports, Smith says, but, in recent years, doctors have been zeroing in on skaters' health concerns, particularly after a Canadian study by team doctor Robert Brock, who found over a one-year period that 47 per cent of national-level skaters suffered from overuse injuries. Smith's study on American skaters at the same level showed 78 per cent were hobbled by the same type of injuries, which can be prevented by paying special attention to appropriate stretching and strengthening exercises.

At the 1997 world figure-skating championship in Lausanne, Switzerland, Gledhill attended an international congress on medicine and science in figure skating, where leading doctors traded ideas and findings. A major focus of the congress was boot-related injuries. "Shoemakers torture our skaters with their skating boots," said Dr. Wolf-Dieter Montag, an orthopedic surgeon from Germany who is also a member of the medical commission of the International Olympic Committee. The answer, he said, was to find boots that fit a skater well. If they don't, the leather of the boot creases, the creases cause a pressure point against skin, which in turn causes an abrasion that can lead to infection. This is precisely what happened to Canadian champion Susan Humphreys, who had to withdraw before the free skate at the Lausanne event. Her withdrawal initially cost Canada a spot at the 1998 Olympics.

The congress also discussed the injuries that occur when boots were unable to support the constant jump landings of skaters in a sport where triple and even quadruple jumps have become all-important. The advice that came from the congress was that skaters should work on strengthening the muscles of their ankles and make sure that they warm up properly before they compete or practise. "The manufacturers of figure-skating boots should think of better ways to get an isolated additional stability for the ankles to prevent forced supination [turning] during the landing," advised another study that examined boot-related injuries at the Olympic Training Centre in Dortmund, Germany. The study noted that skaters shuck their boots when the leather around the ankles breaks down, causing a loss of support. But it also pointed out that the more often skaters depended on the boots to support them, the less support their own weak ankles were apt to provide.

The findings ring true with coaches and boot retailers, who hear tales of skaters whose boots are constantly breaking down or giving them angst. The sport is demanding more of the boot, they say, because of the increased emphasis on doing triple jumps, even at a young age. Skaters are seeking stiffer, thicker, tougher boots to give them support when they land, but with the increased inflexibility comes injury. To avoid problems, coaches will now have to rein in their skaters, keeping them from doing too many free-skating practices, coaches and doctors say.

The other answer, says retailer Audi Racz, is to return to the days when skaters developed good skating technique, which doesn't require stiff boots, but high ankle strength. Since compulsory figures were dropped from competitive skating in 1990, skaters have abandoned the fine technical aspects of skating, which the tedious tracings taught, he says.

"Now we see some skaters that are using such horrible techniques," he says. Racz fears coaches will spend too much time concentrating on teaching triple jumps at the cost of good skating techniques. "We are always trying to talk skaters into skating in softer boots. But that would mean they would have to skate the hard way, because you have to be more technically correct in them."

And wearing softer boots would help develop the ankle strength, according to medical research. "If we could genetically grow people with really thick ankles, and muscles and tendons down there that were double the size, it would be a piece of cake," Racz says.

Some skaters have naturally stout ankles. One of them is four-time world champion Kurt Browning, who is known for his technically difficult footwork. "The circumference of his ankles is remarkably large," says Racz, who has handled Browning's boots since the time he was a junior champion. "He doesn't have to rely so heavily on his boots to hold him up."

Apart from his stint as official doctor at Skate Canada, Dr. Robert Lee is unlike the national team doctors who are paid to probe the ills of Canada's élite. Although Lee sees some top-level skaters from a nearby skating club, most of his clients are not national team members. But to him, they are just as important. His mission, he says, is to focus on the young, maturing athletes who can hopefully develop healthy attitudes towards sport. Perhaps, if he educates them well, he will keep in check the overuse injuries that hobble skaters, and find a way to keep young girls from developing eating disorders, a psychological problem (discussed in the previous chapter) that manifests itself in the physical realm first and confounds sports-medicine officials as much as psychologists. Sports medicine for Lee is not just a job; it is a calling.

Lee first bumped into the concept of sports medicine when he was a young recreational runner with a wonky knee. Off he trundled to a sports-medicine clinic in Toronto, at a time when the idea of a specialized sports clinic was still fairly new. Through medical school, he was exposed to sports-medicine work again, and young Lee began to think. Throughout medical school, he had always been an advocate of preventative medicine, like healthy eating and exercise, but doctors received little exposure to this aspect of health during medical training. "Most doctors don't," he says. "You see sick people. You tend to get most of your training in hospitals, emergency rooms."

Lee at first wanted to become an orthopedic surgeon, but he "chickened out," because he said orthopedic surgeons tend to be very busy, with little time to spend with patients. "They see a lot of trauma, like broken hips, broken backs, and broken knees," he says. "They have good intentions on teaching their patients to exercise, and stretch, and warm up, but they just don't have the time."

Lee was lucky enough to learn from some of Canada's best-known sports physicians. After working with noted sports specialist Dr. Michael Clarfield in Toronto, he was intrigued. "This is kind of a neat thing that you're doing, Mike," he told him. "The fact that you spend most of your time looking after athletes who are well motivated and want to get better. Unlike a lot of people out there who have no motivation to get better from their illness."

Lee was only twenty-three when he graduated from medical school, and headed straight for the University of Western Ontario's sports-medicine clinic for more experience. A couple of decades ago, there were only a handful of people involved in sports medicine in Ontario. The real inventors of sports medicine in Canada, Lee says, were a handful of orthopedic surgeons who had been asked to cover professional sports competitions or Olympic Games in case of emergencies. Typically, doctors ended up drumming their fingers at most events, showing up with their bags at competitions and trying to kill time. "It's very rare to have anything catastrophic happen," Lee says. "And if it is catastrophic, there's very little a doctor can do but stabilize the patient and call the ambulance."

So, about twenty years ago, these doctors decided to develop a preventative type of medicine for sports: nutrition, weight training, stretching, consulting with a physiotherapist, fitness trainers. If there was a dangerous trend in sports, such as backchecking in hockey, the group of doctors decided to lobby for rule changes. Lee watched the medical wave, fascinated by the newness of the territory.

Lee not only learned the techniques of his trade, but was able to watch those techniques being put into practice. When he was a medical student, he worked with orthopedic specialist Dr. Robert Brock, who was then the national team doctor for the Canadian Figure Skating Association. He was able to observe a handful of high-calibre figure skaters come for treatment and advice. He had no idea who any of them were. The skating world did. Their names were Brian Orser, Elizabeth Manley, Christine Hough. Because he did not know them, it never occurred to Lee that he should be starry-eyed. Lee treated them like any other person off the street. Later, he understood that this sort of ignorance was bliss.

"Doctors have to be objective," Lee says, pondering a rising issue about the quandary of a sports physicians: should they be fans or doctors seeking what's best for a person's well-being?

"But if you're a fan and somebody like Matt Dunnigan goes and gets a couple of dozen concussions, and you're the team doctor, you want the team to do well, so are you not going to be objective about letting him go back to play?" Lee muses. "If you're not a fan, why else would you spend all those days freezing your butt off on the sidelines? If you are not a fan, are you an employee, hired by the team to be the doctor – and if they don't like what you do, can they fire you? They might not like what you have to say. They may say, 'We're paying to see Eric Lindros skate, and so are sixteen thousand other people, and we don't care what you say, we're going to make him play.'"

Lee prefers to remain objective about his patients. A skating groupie he is not. At Skate Canada, he watched with surprise as some volunteers working in the medical area hustled after skaters to get their auto-graphs. "It was really hard for me to work with people who were really in awe of these skaters," he says. "They were fans. A lot of them broke protocol, asking skaters when they were in the medical room to sign autographs. Personally, I'm not into that. I have to work for the skaters behalf, first. . . . That's how you gain their trust." Some other doctors and physiotherapists are fans first, however, all striving to become the official physicians of a professional basketball or hockey team. Some of their peers call it the Groupie Syndrome.

Lee's sports clinic is an hour's drive from Toronto. There he turns his focus on young, developing athletes, rather than a professional team or élite athlete, trying to instil in them a sense of balance, and of common sense in the face of a sport that has turned to glitter and dollar signs. He tries to lead them to believe they must remain realistic. He will remind competitive junior or senior skaters on their way to the national championships that they are not earning a million dollars yet. "Skating is not the most important thing in the world if you have a stress fracture," he emphasizes to them. "I don't care if your parents have just spent $12,000 on you this year to get you this far."

It is necessary to remind skaters of these points, says Lee, who sees a lot of pressure in families that focus on the amount of money they have spent on the skater. Once, he treated an eleven-year-old pre-novice skater who had developed a stress fracture in her foot from trying double jumps. The injury was serious enough that it threatened to keep her out of the divisional championship, the qualifiers for the national event. The girl's mother broke down in tears in Lee's office, telling him: "She has to go. This is her first year, and already we have spent $11,000 on her."

"There is a lot of this going on," Lee says in amazement.

But then, the whole nature of sport for children has changed – and changed in ways that affect Lee's work. On the one hand, research has found that young children are spending increasing amounts of time parked in front of television sets and computers, inactive and sedentary. On the other hand, Lee says, others are exercising – and overdoing it. Then they show up in Lee's office with overuse injuries.

The latter may be victims of an overstructured organization of sport, Lee suggests. A decade or two ago, young children tended to just head for the street and play baseball and street hockey with all the neighbourhood kids. It was unstructured play, with no adult supervision. "Child psychologists will tell us that if you take a bunch of ten-year-olds, put them out in a field . . . really fascinating things develop," Lee says. The natural team leaders become team captains. For the most part, kids play pretty fairly, and make up their own rules. They play for fun. "The most interesting thing is, kids stop when they get tired," Lee says.

Social trends have changed that idyllic scene, however. Now, with both parents working and a fear of sending nine-year-old children out on the street to play or to walk to the park, children are often sent to a structured sports program, led by an adult coach. But with these programs, children no longer have free play. Parents tend to send their children to swimming lessons or tennis camp, or to the basketball league or to figure-skating lessons. And when adult coaches become part of the mix, the playing habits of the children change. They no longer play for fun. They play to please the parents and the adults. They don't stop when they're tired. They keep going. "And not enough adult coaches realize this," Lee says. "They're not trained in pediatric psychology."

Because these trends have intensified over the past five or six years, Lee fears there will be a mini-epidemic of sports injuries among children. Many of today's yuppies act as volunteer coaches, and they fail to understand that eleven-year-old Johnny's knees are sore because he has just come home from his second practice today, and he has practised every day for the past two weeks.

In certain ways, some children are taking the problem into their own hands. According to the Coaching Association of Canada, some 70 per cent of youngsters who have been introduced to organized sport drop out of it by age thirteen. Figure skaters, however, seem to be some of the most highly driven.

One question Lee always asks those children he sees who often seem to have chronic injuries: "When was the last time you took a week off and did nothing?" Some are baffled by the question. Some cannot remember their last vacation. Lee was astonished to find a ten-year-old girl who had taken time off from skating only at Christmas during the past year. One hadn't taken more than a weekend off from her sport in the past year and a half.

Given the intense years of training necessary to produce a top-level skater – and the very structured nature of training – skaters would appear to court injury and burnout. But Lee says basic skating is actually a low-impact sport. "The basic strokes of skating are very easy to do, and very easy on your body," he adds. But the threat to a skater's health comes with the changes in the sport in recent years: the rush to do more difficult triple jumps, the dropping of compulsory figures, putting more emphasis on training for free skating; the increase in competitions and shows available for élite skaters.

Many suspect the changes have created more opportunities for injuries, but no research has proven that injuries are on the rise. "Sports medicine research is so difficult," Lee says. To prove it, a researcher would have to take a group of skaters from ten years ago, determine their injury rate, then compare them to a similar group that is matched according to body type, age, height, weight, level of skating, number of training hours, and other variables. A daunting task.

Figure skating is a difficult sport to study because it does not tend to produce the kind of traumatic injuries seen in hockey. Pairs skaters compete with the highest amount of risk of head injuries and other calamities. "But most skaters have these difficult-to-judge-and-to-quantify overuse injuries," Lee says. "Their knees hurt. They have back pain. They need physiotherapy. They need to rest for a bit. They have ankle pain. They have a stress fracture. Because the injuries aren't life-threatening, or easy to categorize, it's really difficult to assess how badly skaters are injured."

Therein lies the rub for sports physicians who treat figure skaters: how do they define an injury? Many figure skaters have competed while hurt. Irina Slutskaia of Russia slammed with great force into the rink boards during a practice at the 1997 world championship in Lausanne, Switzerland, and left the ice clutching her back in pain, leading many to believe she would withdraw. But Slutskaia appeared, landed difficult triples with her teeth clenched, and won the bronze medal. As soon as she finished, she clutched her back again. Some skaters have chronic back problems or knee problems, such as Russian ice dancer Evgeny Platov, who competed in Lausanne in spite of great pain. Immediately afterwards, he underwent surgery to repair it.

"If everybody stopped for every little ache or pain, nobody would play sports," Lee says. "The question is, When is an ache or pain or muscle pull bad enough to be called an injury?"

Is it an injury when a skater misses a competition? A week of practice? A day of practice? Football or hockey players would find it hard to play full games with an injury, but a severely injured skater often finds it possible to tough out the pain for the four or four and a half minutes of a long program. It's usually only after a skater tries a skill repetitively while in pain that he or she develops a stress fracture, and then realizes that he or she really shouldn't have done this, Lee says.

The nature of skating leaves coaches, doctors, and parents with a confusing problem, Lee says: How do they teach eight-year-old athletes the difference between something that is sore and something that is an injury? And how do parents and coaches discern the difference between a skater who is rather lazy or "wimpish" and one who is really hurt?

At the élite level, skating, by its very nature, selects very determined, highly motivated athletes. "So determined that they'll do anything at any cost," Lee says. "And that's why they're good, because they can handle the pressure, and therefore they can handle the pain. That makes it doubly difficult to objectively measure the pain or injury, because psychologically they're very, very strong people."

Lee says he tries to deal with the conundrum by giving talks and staging slide shows for skaters, even at the pre-novice level, to teach them about anatomy and the need for stretching to avoid injury. He tries to coax parents and coaches into the sessions, too, at a local club in Kitchener–Waterloo, and even goes further afield to clubs in smaller skating centres in Ontario that have no access to sports-medicine clinics. He worries most about the worldwide problem of young females who fail to reach their potential in skating, bogged down perhaps by growth and a developing body that becomes less conducive to rotation, conflicts about the body image they are expected to maintain, or uncertainties that plague many females when they reach their teens. While the men's event is the most competitive of all skating disciplines, the women's event in recent years has been thin at the top. And there are far more girls who take to figure skating than boys.

With this in mind, Lee strives to prevent the really good pre-novice or novice girls from burning out. "Burnout" is a condition an athlete reaches when he or she becomes physically and emotionally spent after focusing so much time competing in a sport. It is an affliction waiting to happen, particularly if athletes spend all of their time playing a single sport, and even more likely if the youngster is constantly being tested, as in figure skating, with all of its skills tests and competitions. Lee sees other dangers for young female skaters, too. He is concerned that young girls are being pushed to do more triple jumps as judges are urged to reward skaters for taking risks. But Lee is uneasy about the trend. "What if you really can't do that jump, you don't have the strength or you're injured?" He sees many foot, ankle, and knee problems among young girls trying even double jumps too soon. He knows of girls trying triple jumps before they have even mastered double jumps, all in the rush to stay abreast of a tiny Tara Lipinski, winner of a world championship at age fourteen, with her daunting array of triple-jump combinations.

"The saddest part is all the people we don't hear about," says Lee, referring to promising novice skaters who flash early brilliance, then fade into obscurity as they grow older. In the past thirty years, since novice championships were first held as part of the Canadian championship, only one women's novice champion, Tracey Wainman, went on to win the senior title. And Wainman is always held as a prime example of a skater who burned out early, weighed down by high expectations.

In the United States, a total of eight novice women's champions have gone on to win senior titles in the more than sixty years since the national novice event was established in 1932. But in the past thirty years, there have been only two: Dorothy Hamill and Rosalyn Sumners. Most of the fabled U.S. women's champions who went on to win world titles did not win a novice championship.

They were more likely to have been junior champions. But still, in the past thirty years, only three U.S. junior women's champions have gone on to become senior champions: Jill Trenary, Elaine Zayak, and

Janet Lynn. The trend is clear: the odds are clearly stacked against very young female prodigies becoming senior champions. Lee fears that somewhere along the way in their physical and emotional development, the novices have burned out, much like little-league pitchers who fail to find their way to the major-league mound. Male figure skaters don't tend to burn out, Lee says.

And female skaters face other roadblocks, too. As they learn their difficult tricks, they are growing into womanhood, but the pressure to maintain a reed-thin body is an unwritten rule that sways their menu planning. Generally, the incidence of eating disorders such as anorexia and bulimia (gorging oneself with food, then inducing vomiting) occurs among 3 per cent of the population in North America. A study published in the *Journal of the American Dietetic Association* in 1989 said that the typical female skater was "well below the calorie levels recommended for moderately active females." Yet, the study looked at only twenty-three female skaters. Other studies show conflicting results: at a meeting of the American Association for the Advancement of Science in 1995, a number of studies showed that women athletes have fewer eating problems than the general population. John Albinson, associate professor of sport and exercise psychology at Queen's University in Kingston, Ontario, said that only two athletes reported evidence of clinical eating disorders among questionnaires distributed to three hundred élite Canadian women athletes. Other international studies in 1995 indicated that anorexia and bulimia occur up to twice as frequently in female athletes as reported in earlier studies.

Still, Lee said the lay press makes far too much of the syndromes of anorexia and bulimia and not nearly enough about the tendency for skaters to diet and be concerned about their weight. "They eat a little bit," Lee says, of the ones with less-dramatic behavioural patterns. "They don't starve themselves to death. But they don't eat what they should eat. They're not obsessed with their weight and their size, but they think about it."

He says that, although the incidence of true anorexia in skaters and gymnasts is very low, the tendency towards diet preoccupation is very high. "I think we tend to underestimate the prevalence of the problem if we look only at people with the actual defined term of eating disorders," Lee says.

Studies have shown that 20 to 50 per cent of college-age women – not necessarily those involved in sport – show tendencies towards diet preoccupation. Recently, sports-medicine doctors have begun to shy away from labels like eating disorders, which are specific psychological conditions. Lee said they now prefer to refer to eating problems as "disordered eating," which includes the people with anorexia and bulimia as well as people who show tendencies towards weight concern. "Not everybody is bulimic and throws up several times a day," he says. "Not every coach weighs their athletes, naked, on a scale. But it's that lesser group we worry about."

The lesser group, he says, is influenced by the unwritten rules in skating, the judges who openly comment about skaters, suggesting they be ten pounds lighter. "I struggle with that because I have very good junior-level skaters who do the doubles and triples because they have the strength in their legs to do it," Lee says. "But they are heavier. I have a couple of junior girls who are 5-foot-7 or 5-foot-8 and they weigh 145 pounds. They look like soccer players, but they can do the jumps. And they know they get judged down because they don't look thin. What can you do? They come into my office wanting some magic solution to lose twenty pounds quickly, because the coaches and the parents and the judges and other people tell them to."

The nutritionist at Lee's clinic does an analysis of the skaters' physical makeup and tells them their bodies are not meant to be thinner. Lee, who constantly gleans information from other sports, hastens to tell his clients and their parents about tennis player Chris Evert, who lost fifteen pounds on the advice of various trainers while she was playing against pencil-thin Martina Navratilova. Her playing ability melted away with the pounds. When she went back to her former playing weight, Evert began to win tournaments again, according to her autobiography. "Her advice to girls is, 'That was the weight my body wanted to be,'" Lee says. "It's a constant struggle with this weight thing."

Female athletes in many sports tangle with society's ideals of body image. Although marathon champion Grete Waitz of Norway said she had never dieted with the aim of becoming thin for thin's sake, she admitted in her book, *World Class*, that, at the age of fourteen, with all of life's stresses, she had a tendency to undereat to the point that her coach had to "almost force-feed me.

"Like many teenage girls, my body was changing, but not to my liking," she wrote. "This was the era of Twiggy, when everybody's goal was to be as rail-thin as she was. Fortunately, my eating problem was temporary and not very severe, but there were other girls on the team for whom it was much more serious. Back then, none of us realized what their problem was. There wasn't a word for it."

Figure skating is not alone in harbouring athletes obsessed with dieting. Lee has treated athletes with disordered eating in many different sports: cross-country running, triathlon, and rowing, as well as figure skating. But all of the problem's manifestations and causes are similar among athletes. One of the first signposts of a disorder is denial of the problem, Lee says. While athletes may recognize an eating problem in others, they won't admit they have a problem themselves.

Hunting for clues of disordered eating is not always simple. Now doctors are turning more attention to athletes who worry about their weight, but who don't necessarily restrict their diets. They are the athletes who will exercise more, thinking that physical activity will burn up the calories they want to shed. Their weight, too, eventually plunges with the excessive exercise; these athletes just accomplish the weight loss in a different way.

"You can see how that complicates things," Lee says. "You can look at someone who has a problem, but they're not really eating that little. They are not eating nothing. They are eating. But they are the ones that are exercising three to four hours a day."

Now doctors look for signs of weight obsessions in athletes who participate in a normal high-intensity two-hour practice, but then who will stay at the gym, use the Stairmaster another forty minutes, go running for an additional hour. Still, it's difficult to sift the motivated athletes from the disordered ones. "A lot of motivated athletes will do that extra workout, because they think that's what they need to get a competitive edge," Lee says. "How do you differentiate athletes who are really motivated to exercise three or four hours a day because they are so competitive and so focused . . . from athletes who can't help but put in an extra one or two hours of exercise a day because they think that it will burn more calories?"

For a time, all the extra work, effort, and attention to weight appears to work. That makes it doubly difficult for a doctor to suspect problems. "The biggest problem is that all of these athletes do very well," Lee says. "They're the ones that do win things. And most of them, until they start getting sick and ill, there's nothing physically wrong to find about them. They're in the best shape of their lives. You can test their blood, and they're very fit people. Doctors catch these people when it's too late."

It's too late when the athletes have exercised so much that there is no fat left, and the body uses muscle for fuel. The overwork and under-nourishment can damage muscle. "And when you damage muscle, it can lead to problems with your kidneys, because it's hard to excrete all that burnt-out muscle protein," Lee says. "That's usually when medical physicians will intervene."

Hindsight is always easy. When doctors are alerted to a disordered-eating problem, and look back into an athlete's history, they find insidious but almost imperceptible trends: a gradual increase in exercise, for one.

Sometimes sports physicians are alerted to a problem and can pick up these people when they've come in with an injury. They've hurt their ankle, or their knee perhaps. Yet, when the doctor advises them they cannot run for another three or four weeks to give the injury time to heal, they have a difficult time accepting it. "It is almost like they are going through withdrawal, the fact that they can't exercise every day," Lee says. "Then they exercise through their injuries and make them even worse, against doctors' orders, against coaches' order, against parents' orders."

Doctors need to be especially vigilant for the clues, paying careful attention to their clients, following up what happens to an athlete after a visit in order to pick up the signals. They really must delve into the reasons why it is difficult for them to stop. Some psychologists call athletes who show such symptoms "exercise dependent," Lee says. "They don't know if it is an addiction or not."

Disordered eating is difficult to sort out. "Can you call these people ill or sick? On the outside, you can't," Lee says. "They're very good-looking, very athletic-looking people. That's why for a sport like skating, it takes a lot of patience and time and attention to detail to really sort out the issue of disordered eating and exercise dependence."

The best treatment, all sports physicians say, is prevention, because once an athlete develops disordered eating, it is very difficult to treat. It's one of the reasons Lee is on a quiet crusade to educate young athletes in his city, to prevent them from taking uneasy sidesteps into a life crisis, in directions that sport-for-sports' sake should never head. How change will come, he is not sure. Perhaps it may come from teaching coaches to teach with care, he suggests. Perhaps the unwritten rules of the sport and of society should be changed, so that judges are not affected by appearance, he proposes. "The whole problem with the sport is that it's an aesthetic sport."

The most pleasing sight to Lee is a healthy child with a glow and a glint. There are thousands of them, toiling in cold rinks across the continent, all needing his attention. The future of sport and the children who play it are what matter to a young doctor who cradles his daughter to his chest, off duty.

Fanfare

S kating fans are a loyal lot. They stream through the turnstiles, brandishing tickets and skating tidbits. They have opinions. They breathe life into skating. They are responsible for having made figure skating one of the most popular sports in the world. They *are* the figure-skating boom.

Fans come in all shapes and sizes, ages and races, with likes and dislikes, and they are an impressive lot. According to a survey taken at the Canadian championship in Ottawa in February 1996, three-quarters of the rink spectators were women; almost half had an annual income greater than $60,000; about half had university, college, or postgraduate education; and more than two-thirds watched figure skating on television "very often." About one third of the 3,513 people who responded to the Canadian survey were employed full time. Another third were students.

Fans are a major economic force, particularly when a skating event comes to a city. Even though Vancouver had not been considered skating-mad, the organizers of the 1997 national championship there rang up a record $1.85 million in ticket sales, 38 per cent higher than the previous amount achieved at a Canadian championship. They pump millions of dollars into the local economy, renting hotel rooms, eating meals, taking taxis. That's not even considering what they spend on souvenirs of their visit. The 1996 Canadian association survey showed that 60 per cent of the ticket buyers visited the merchandise booth in the rink, one-quarter of them buying one item, another quarter buying two or three. A fair number went home with lighter wallets; the survey showed that 12 per cent spent more than $75 each at the booth.

With this kind of fuel to drive the sport, there are fan clubs galore for any skater of any country that sparks a response in the heart of fans: skaters from the United States, Canada, Russia, Ukraine, Germany. There is even one for American skater Michael Chack, once a bronze medallist in his country, who created the difficult "Chack-toe," a triple toe-loop jump done with arms held straight down at both sides of the body. Because of injury, Chack has not been a prominent face at U.S. championships for a couple of years. But his fans haven't forgotten.

"I didn't even know I had one," said Chack in the winter of 1997. "Somebody contacted me last year. They keep in touch and send me articles about me."

In Canada, where skating is a national sport, fandom has reached a fever pitch. At the 1996 world championship in Edmonton, it was common for throngs of fans to watch midnight practices, cheering and applauding in bleary-eyed bliss. And the vision of young girls running down the aisles to toss flowers to their skating favourites has reached the pandemonium stage in Canada – so much so that officials at the 1997 national championship in Vancouver, B.C., had to ask skaters to refrain from stopping by the rinkboards to greet them after a performance. They feared it would delay television production, as well as adversely affect subsequent skaters who had to wait nervously until their competitors got off the ice. "I am really not happy with this," says David Dore, director-general of the Canadian Figure Skating Association. "We've got to get a grip on this. It's getting completely out of control."

While young fans also stampede the aisles at American events, the numbers are far fewer and the atmosphere less frenzied. Even at practice sessions in Canada, young fans line the rink boards and the exits in hopes of an autograph, loudly yelling the names of their heroes and heroines even before the end of the session.

At the 1991 world championship in Munich, older Canadian fans enlivened the atmosphere with their scarlet-red garb and their noisy enthusiasm for any skater of any nationality. They were hard to miss, sitting like a large, bold red block at centre stage in the Olympiahalle, or in a bright corner of the sun-filled practice rink, a swan's pond away. Every day, during a lull in the proceedings, the Canadian contingent initiated the wave motion, the crowd craze that was most popular before the advent of the macarena. Finally, by week's end, even some of the sombre, fur-capped Soviets joined in, letting their arms fly to the heavens as the wave passed. That week, a reporter from Greece said that if judges were to give a gold medal to an audience, they should give one to the Canadians at Munich.

The Munich group included about fifty Canadians from the nearby Lahr airbase, where Canadian Armed Forces were stationed in Germany. But these transplanted Canadians had grown up with the skating furore at home and they had carried it overseas in their hearts. "We've been following figure skating for years," says Shirley Nunn, of Nanticoke, Ontario. "We've been to other world championships, like the one in Ottawa [1984] and the world juniors [1987 in Kitchener, Ontario]. My niece teaches at the base. I didn't know anybody [in the group] before. But I do now. It's wonderful."

Their cheers were particularly loud for Canadian skaters, who never forgot to acknowledge the people in maple-leaf red after they finished skating. Members of the group said they didn't expect it, but they met Kurt Browning – who won his third world title at the event – and even transplanted Canadian Paul Duchesnay. The group adopted the Duchesnays at the event, even though they had left Canada to skate for France six years before. The Duchesnays won their world title in Munich.

In total, about 135 Canadians went to Munich as part of a tour group, and most of them sported red sweaters that one of their team-spirited peers procured at wholesale prices. A loyal group of travellers from Canada have been wearing the sweaters since 1988. "It's really kind of a happening," says another member of the group, speaking of the woolly revelry that infected the rink.

In 1994, Canadian fans proved they were prepared to go to the ends of the earth to see figure skating firsthand. A group went to Chiba, Japan, for the world championship. One skater noticed them. Surya Bonaly of France said all she could see were "Japanese flags and Canadians."

A fan group doesn't have to be as large as the one in Munich to get noticed. At the first sniff of an upcoming figure-skating event, the Canadian SpecSkaters of Thornhill, Ontario, drop all pretensions of maturity and start to plan. They operate under only one rule: the group of eight, sometimes ten, fun-loving Canadians must never doff their home-designed fluorescent-pink sweatshirts during a competition. They are a package deal of teachers, school vice-principals, systems analysts, technical writers, company general managers, and executive placement consultants, who can outshine a flock of flamingos. They are not wealthy. Trips to far-off destinations are out.

They wear pink for a very scientific reason: Celia Louthood, one of the group members, objected to the colour of Canadian-flag red because it would clash with her red hair. Bright pink does, too, but reason is not a necessary attribute of a skating fan.

The group was not always clad in vivid pink, or any particular colour for that matter. At first, it was merely a couple of figure-skating fans in sneakers and jeans getting together for a lark. "I've always been a fan," says Cheryl Rosenthal, schoolteacher by day, mirthmaker by weekend. She had been watching figure skating on ABC's "Wide World of Sports" since the early 1960s, when Soviets Ludmila and Oleg Protopopov won their first of two Olympic gold medals. She and Celia have been fans since they were thirteen years old.

The trips to skating events began on a small scale at the 1976 Canadian championship in Kitchener, Ontario, with two couples, the Rosenthals and the Louthoods. Then luck struck: the world championship came to Ottawa in 1978. "It was our first worlds, and we didn't know enough about all-event tickets," Cheryl recalls. They discovered later that they could have purchased all-event tickets as a convenient package, without having to search day by day for enough seats together. "We sat in one place, then another, and we wondered why certain people kept sitting in the same place every night."

The next time the world championship returned to Ottawa, six years later, the group had grown to eight, quite by accident. Cheryl met Dianne (they call her Lady Di) Levstein while both were in a Toronto hospital having their second children. The talk turned to figure skating. One day, when they bumped into each other on the street, they discovered that they were all going to the world championship in Ottawa. Dianne and her husband, Malcolm, were going with two other friends, Gilda and Peter Spitz.

By chance, the Levstein–Spitz group ended up sitting directly in front of the Rosenthals, even though they had not bought tickets together. The Canadian SpecSkaters group was assembled.

"We had so much fun," Dianne says. "We had the best time."

The team shirts came six years later, in 1990, the inspiration arising from a high time at the Skate America international competition in Buffalo, a two-hour drive from Toronto. When a young, promising Elvis Stojko stepped onto centre ice to skate, the group, as one, yelled, "Richmond Hill!" ("We are not shy," Cheryl Rosenthal says.) Most of the group's members live close to Richmond Hill, Stojko's home town. Stojko turned and grinned.

At that event, Victor Petrenko, who was to become the 1992 Olympic champion, planted a big kiss on the cheek of Alise, Celia's daughter, during his well-known rock 'n' roll exhibition number. Not only did Alise carry the memory in her heart for a long time; so did her parents.

And there, during equally serious moments, Cheryl's husband, Hersh, came up with a name for the group. And the group, of course, had to have its own team uniform, a signature of their personalities.

The group designed its own coat of arms. They drew the lenses for a pair of glasses by tracing around inverted teacups. Inside the left lens, they stuck the image of a skate boot, in the other, a mutated logo of pairs skaters. A noisy but energetic dot-matrix printer chuffed out letters "Canadian SpecSkaters," one by one. Warmed up, the Rosenthals pasted the pieces together and photocopied it for posterity – and for the sweatshirt factory. For good measure, they added a black maple leaf to one arm. They sported their new pink sweatshirts for the first time at the World Cup, a professional event, in Kitchener in 1990. "We've never looked back," Dianne says.

Occasionally, the women wear matching pink-and-black earrings. Cheryl dons shocking-pink shoelaces.

"Are you here again?" Donald Jackson, the 1962 world champion, once asked them when he spotted them at an event. Eventually, he went for coffee with them.

"You Pink-Shirts are everywhere!" exclaimed CTV broadcaster Rod Black when he bumped into the group at a hotel coffee shop at Skate Canada in Kitchener in 1996.

Because of their very pinkness, they have met CBC Olympic television host Brian Williams – who once recognized them at a Blue Jays game in Florida – skating announcer Wilf Langevin, and French-Canadian skating broadcaster Alain Goldberg. Even the competitors seem pleased to see them. Some of them accost the Pink Shirts. "We see you all the time," pairs skater Kris Wirtz said to them at Skate Canada in Kitchener. "What does it say on your shirt?"

They even have an autographed photo of themselves with Canadian Brian Orser, at the 1987 world championship in Cincinnati, where Orser won gold. When Orser strolled into the audience to watch other skating events, Rosenthal simply tapped him on the shoulder. With eyes sharp as an eagle, she can spot a skater at a hundred paces. They did the same when they saw 1948 Olympic champion Barbara Ann Scott, bedecked in her sparkling finery, in a hotel lobby for a professional skating event at which she was a judge. Suddenly, Scott was surrounded by people in pink. Tucked neatly into a bulging photo album, there is a photo of two of the group members, swathed in pink, arm in arm with the Canadian icon.

Their photo album is full of other shots, too. There is Rosenthal, sitting cheerily beside a weary-looking Isabelle and Paul Duchesnay at the 1990 world championship in Halifax. And there is also a less-dignified photo of some of the group members, sitting, sucking their thumbs in unison. "We've had people who wanted to join this group,"

Cheryl says. "We've had people who asked if they could buy the sweat-shirt. They ask us if we skated. They think we must be from a preci-sion team."

Can they skate? "We push Celia around the ice on a chair," says Cheryl, with laughing eyes. They have invented a move they call the triple klutz.

Are other people allowed to join? Only Celia's daughter, Alise Frohlinger, has been allowed membership in the dubiously élite group. And Dianne's sister, Yvonne Bennett, who lives in England, has been accepted as an "honourary member," the group's tenth.

The original eight members perhaps produced their ultimate per-formance at Skate Canada in Kirchener: to the macarena. In the warm arena, Malcolm Levstein had just started to take off his shirt when the music started. It beckoned, like a siren. The SpecSkaters couldn't resist. Like a rising blush at one end of the rink, the pink shirts moved into action, with Malcolm still trying to remove his shirt.

Suddenly spectators surrounding the very visible group began to cheer and scream and clap, urging Malcolm on. Somewhat like a stripper, he started to swing his shirt over his head in spirited fashion.

The rest of the rink crew went into high gear. Marks for their per-formance flashed up on the board. Announcer Wilf Langevin read them off, marks for presentation: a row of perfect 6.0s. When the last mark popped up as a 5.9, the crowd booed noisily in protest.

"There's always one judge," said Langevin, already aware of the group's reputation for hi-jinks from meetings at various skating events. Invariably, the SpecSkaters get prime seats, often right behind Langevin. As far as judging goes, the SpecSkaters have a lot of confi-dence in their own abilities to determine the best from pinkside. "We only have problems with ice dancing," Cheryl says. "We just can't seem to figure it out."

Never having been a skater, Cheryl has drawn on the knowledge of others sitting near her, other fans who have obviously taken a turn or two around a rink. "The first [jump] I learned was the Lutz, because it is so obvious," she says. "And the Axel was the next one."

"I never got past those two," says Freddie (at work, he's Fred) Louthood, a recreational hockey player who is married to Celia.

After twelve years of pressing their noses to the rink boards, the SpecSkaters are walking encyclopedias of skating sights. Cheryl remembers seeing a tiny, girlish Katarina Witt at the 1981 world championship in Hartford, Connecticut. There, they also saw legendary British ice dancers Jayne Torvill and Christopher Dean, who won their first world title in Hartford. They marvelled at a childlike Ekaterina Gordeeva and Sergei Grinkov, whom they first saw at a Skate Canada in London, Ontario, before they won their first senior world title. And they saw Denise Biellmann, the 1981 world champion, noted for the difficult spin she invented.

They remember American ice dancers Colleen O'Connor and Jim Millns winning a bronze medal at the 1976 Olympics in Innsbruck, Austria. And twenty years later, when Rosenthal spotted Millns at a judges' ice-dancing seminar at Skate Canada in Kitchener, she still recognized him, from having seen him on television. Without pause, she approached him. "Aren't you Jim Millns?" she asked.

Millns's chest puffed out as if he had gained forty pounds, pleased that he had been remembered, she recalls.

The best of all skating events, in the SpecSkaters' eyes, was the 1984 world championship in Ottawa. It marked Torvill and Dean's last amateur performance – before they reinstated for the 1994 Olympics. They also saw Japanese sprite Midori Ito when she was only fourteen, smiling and jumping higher than she was tall. (She finished seventh, behind Witt.) "It was so wonderful to see her potential," Dianne says. "But the best thing was when Barbara Underhill and Paul Martini won, especially because they had been seventh at the Olympics. That was the most exciting. The floor was pounding. People were standing up a minute before the program ended. It was the most thrilling."

"Each time we say, we'll never top this one," Cheryl says. But somehow they do.

The SpecSkaters, alas, do not attend every event. The 1992 world championship in Oakland, California, proved to be too expensive, particularly with the unfavourable Canadian exchange rate and the cost of flights. They also missed the world championship in Edmonton.

Instead, they watched it – together – at home in Thornhill, seeking out the largest television sets the group has. And they wear their pink sweaters when they do it.

For twelve years, the SpecSkaters have been plotting skating excursions, with fun first and foremost, but, as the sport has become more popular, their task as fans is getting more difficult. "It used to be so much easier as a group to get tickets," Cheryl says. "But since the sport has become so popular, it's big business, and there's not much time for the little guy."

The SpecSkaters decided not to buy tickets to the world event in Edmonton in 1996 because "they wanted the money without knowing where we'd be sitting," she says.

"For people who have supported the sport for twelve years, we've sort of been left out in the cold," Dianne adds.

They still manage, they say, by planning on their own – and very early. But it's also more difficult to manoeuvre and meet skaters. Alise has scores of autographs of top skaters, but it's now more difficult to get them. Before Tonya Harding's friends bopped Nancy Kerrigan on the knee at the 1994 U.S. championship, skaters commonly stepped up into the audience to watch their peers perform. Now it's less likely, Dianne says.

At Skate Canada in Kitchener, the SpecSkaters sat directly above the kiss-and-cry area, the spot where skaters recline after performances and watch in anguish or joy as the judges display their marks. Suddenly, the SpecSkaters were seized by an idea: after the event for the day was over, they'd get their photos taken together in the kiss-and-cry area.

But they quickly found out they could not do that, even after-hours. A volunteer security guard told them that even he could not get down into the kiss-and-cry perch. Everything had changed since 1994.

Even so, the pink merrymakers are still at it. As soon as they heard that tickets were on sale for the Champions Series final in Hamilton, Ontario, they were on the phone, nailing down the person in charge after a cruise through a website.

When they were told they could buy tickets only at Ticketmaster agents, Freddie took on the job of going to an outlet inside a nearby Sunrise Records store. For two consecutive mornings, at 10 A.M. sharp,

Freddie lined up. As the line grew behind him, and the young clerk's fingers flew, they finally, with great difficulty, got eight tickets near the front row of the rink. In spite of everything, Canadian SpecSkaters were front and centre at one of the world's premier events for eligible skaters.

As the experience of the SpecSkaters has shown, the booming fan interest in figure skating has had a paradoxical effect on fans themselves. It has made it more difficult, complicated, and expensive for the long-term fans to follow their passion. Some feel, pessimistically, that the best years of figure skating, from a spectator's point of view, are behind them. It's more difficult to get close to skaters. Everything is more difficult, even for the tour operators.

Cathie Leak will never forget it. Every year, the Toronto travel consultant organizes a tour to the world figure-skating championship, wherever it may be. The event in Edmonton was her unlucky thirteenth, and "it was an absolute zoo," she says.

Never had the tour attracted so many people. While her world-championship tours in Europe typically attracted 100 to 125 clients, about 430 signed up for Edmonton. And they were not just Canadian fans. They came from Paris, France, and San Francisco. There were ten people, too, from Japan, all eager to get in on hard-to-find seats for an event that reportedly sold out within forty-eight hours.

Leak was so busy that she had six helpers, acting as troubleshooters for the fans, who were spread out over four different hotels in Edmonton. But Edmonton, one of the most successful of world championships financially, turned into a problem for tour organizers such as Leak.

As the Canadian SpecSkaters discovered, the event organizers demanded ticket payment up front – without giving any idea of where the seats were to be. Some of the members of Leak's group were seated in the upper bowl in a large rink that holds 17,500 people. The rest sat in the lower bowl, but all paid the same price. Understandably, some of those in the upper bowl were not happy. Leak acted as referee and punching bag.

By sharp contrast, Leak says that only about ninety people signed up for her fourteenth world-championship tour to Lausanne, Switzerland, a small city with scarce and outrageously expensive hotel beds. She doesn't expect a huge crowd will sign up for the fifteenth tour to Minneapolis, Minnesota, in 1998 either.

"I think figure skating is pricing itself out of everybody's pocket," she says, thinking of the price of all-event tickets for Minneapolis – a very chilly $500 U.S., or almost $700 Canadian. "That's a lot of money for an event in North America. In Switzerland, you expect everything to be expensive, but Minneapolis is just – there. There's nowhere to take anybody after. The hotels [in Minneapolis] are more expensive than Edmonton, and they're in U.S. dollars, too."

Leak's trips always offer an option for people to stay on another week and see the sights of Europe or Japan, or even the Rocky Mountains west of Edmonton. About one-third to one-half of her clients take up the option, but she doesn't foresee being able to offer such an option in Minneapolis. All-event tickets in Minneapolis will also be harder to sell, she fears, because it is a world championship that follows an Olympic Games, and retirements could dilute the Minneapolis field.

"There are so many events in figure skating right now, and people only can do so much," she says. "With the [Champions Series] final in Hamilton [in 1997], why should anybody spend $4,000 to go to Lausanne, too?" Nevertheless, Leak's figure-skating clients have been a faithful bunch, ever since she started by organizing a tour to the 1984 world championship in Ottawa. She was a skater herself, a member of the posh Granite Club in Toronto, and when a friend suggested she set up a tour, Leak was able to organize a trip for 125 people right off the bat. The following year, the world championship was in Tokyo. Only ten made the long trip. The next year, when the event was in Geneva, Switzerland, the numbers grew to forty. At the 1987 world championship in Cincinnati, 400 people followed Leak to the United States. Yet she does not advertise her tours. She relies mostly on repeat business, from a group of people who have become friends over the years.

In general, the people who follow Leak around the world are not parents of skaters. "They are basically people who have grown to love skating," she says. "They are not from skating backgrounds. A lot have watched skating on television and have become so enamoured of it that they make it part of their holidays."

Some fans are beloved. Their needs are simple and their love is innocent and generous. But there are a few skating fans with dark, confused hearts. One kind of fan serves to buoy a skater and push him or her to greater heights with a boisterous show of support. The other kind of fan can scare a skater to death.

Skaters such as Shae-Lynn Bourne, a world bronze ice-dancing medallist with partner Victor Kraatz, appreciate their fan support, which is particularly clamorous in Canada. Unlike most skaters, Bourne has been known to wave at her fans from the ice – even before a competitive performance, when most skaters are trying to focus on the job ahead. Other skaters, such as American Michael Chack, have been encouraged by fans, even when they have not been part of the skating scene for a time. These are fans who have helped him on his comeback, he says. "I kind of felt I was washed up, but people sent me letters, encouraging me to go on." Some skaters from countries with little fan interest feel intimidated by the intense fan following in Canada. Their knees stiffen and their performances falter. Russians like Alexei Urmanov have been accepted by North American fans; he has said he particularly loves to skate in Canada because Canadian fans are so knowledgeable – and noisy.

But, sadly, there are some fans that make skaters feel uncomfortable and anxious. Michelle Kwan was dogged by threats from a disturbed fan from Paris, France, during the 1995-96 season. Aside from some very concrete messages from Tonya Harding's friends, Nancy Kerrigan sometimes received questionable letters. One high-level skater was astonished to find that one of his Japanese fans had announced to his family that she was going to move to the United States and marry him, although he had never expressed any romantic intentions to her. Carefully, he told her it was not possible. Even one attractive figure-skating mother had to change her phone number when an extremely fervent fan from overseas hounded her after catching a glimpse of her on television. At the 1997 Champions Series final in Hamilton, Russian Alexei Urmanov told police about one overzealous fan. Police were heard advising Urmanov to call them again if the fan bothered him further. And two-time Olympic champion Katarina Witt long endured the attentions of a stalker who was eventually sent to a psychiatric centre.

The FBI arrested Witt's stalker, Harry Veltman III, forty-eight, on December 26, 1991. He was found guilty of two counts of sending threatening mail and four counts of sending obscene mail to Witt. The court said that Veltman did take some responsibility for his actions, but never admitted that the letters were obscene or threatening. He called them erotic. The court was told that Veltman harassed Witt at her house in Germany and threw obscene letters onto the ice during a skating competition in Denver.

For a couple of seasons, an overenthusiastic skating fan has trailed Russian skater Ilia Kulik. It started just before the 1995 Skate America international competition in Detroit, when she simply took a photo of him, then gave it to him. But the attentions escalated. At Skate Canada in Kitchener, Ontario, in 1996, she followed him to the opening draw for starting orders, then to the banquet that followed. She was so persistent in her pursuit of the young Russian that security officers hustled her out. She was undaunted. Eventually, she found her way to Kulik's hotel room. Kulik, who does not like to talk about the incidents, says they do not bother him.

"I have a lot of fans who write me letters," Kulik says. He has another one from Japan who writes him every week, and he smiles when he speaks of her. "Every week, I open up the post box and she has written me a letter. She writes about her life, and how she lives. It's two pages long, on pink paper.

"If they like figure skating, I am glad to do something for them. But if I write back to everybody, I have no time for skating."

Others are obsessive, too, even if they have never met their skating heroes. They focus on skaters, whose dramatic stories and achievements fill up some empty part of their own lives, say some skating observers who have met them, and have traced their comments on the booming skating information highway. The Internet is alive with constant fan chatter, some extremely knowledgeable and concerned, others angry and judgemental.

Some fans speak about skaters as if they are members of their own family. "So and so would never do that," say some fans, who have rarely, if ever, spoken to the skaters of whom they speak. Bitter arguments break out on the World Wide Web, with its capacity for instant communication, where emotion doesn't get a chance to cool. Some on-line watchers say the communication sometimes descends into "rants and hissy fits."

"They'll go on and on about some comment that one person has made about another," says one web reader. "It's obvious they've spent hours reading what everybody has said. Rumours spread like wildfire. People just talk about what they hear and expand on it twenty times."

But the Internet seems to have given them voice and a certain status. "I'm not just any fan," said one fiftyish woman to a clerk at a souvenir booth. "I have a web site."

One Brian Boitano fan was disconsolate for hours after she found herself unable to spend "any quality time" with the 1988 Olympic champion at an event. Yet, she had never met him. Boitano, who has been known to carefully attend to many of his fans, has attracted some who seem so manic that he has to find new, creative, and unexpected ways of getting to his hotel room during skating tours.

"Some of his fans say that Landover [where the world professional championship is held] is not a real competition unless Boitano is in it," says competition producer Jirina Ribbens. "Everything starts and stops with Boitano. It's as if nobody existed before Boitano. Some of his fans are 'very scary.'"

Some fans are merely intrepid, beyond the point of reason. They take to sitting in lobbies until the wee hours of the morning, hoping to catch a glimpse of a skater, and to rub shoulders with fame. Once, Kurt Browning emerged from an arena to find two female fans who follow him everywhere sitting on his Jeep. One fan boldly took over an informal fan meeting with a world-champion skater, telling her peers what they could ask him and what they could not. One group of fans decided to chip in and buy a twelve-place setting of fine china as a wedding present for a skater and his wife-to-be; they had discovered the preferred pattern through a shop registry. The setting came complete with various sizes of wine glasses, as well. It was an overwhelming, expensive gesture.

"I don't know how some of these people afford it," says one fan, who works at a well-paying job. "Some of them don't seem to work at all. You see them everywhere."

One mysterious spectator seen at some Canadian competitions fit all the descriptions of the fearsome fan: he seemed to be at every competition; he looked very scary; he was a loner; he hardly moved from his seat; he even watched the practices.

Police were so uneasy about his presence that they questioned the quiet spectator at the Champions Series final in Hamilton. From early morning until the last medal was awarded, Reid Bruce sat, almost motionless, alone, a heavy mane of black hair cascading to his elbows, brown eyes drinking in the action, features covered by a beard and moustache. He seemed an ominous sight. But on closer inspection, he proved a gentle soul. He, like most fans, was not scary or zealous at all. He was not what he seemed.

Bruce politely rises to let a spectator pass, then apologizes for speaking too quickly. He is a poet from Sarnia, who also draws in pencil, who became enamoured with skating after watching the 1984 Olympics in Sarajevo. "I never skated, but I wish I did," he says, almost inaudibly. "I wish my parents had enrolled me."

Bruce doesn't travel far, limited by scant funds. He takes the train to events, and stays in hostels. He admires Elvis Stojko for his "awesome" talent, Shae-Lynn Bourne and Victor Kraatz for their "dynamic, sensitive style," world champion Todd Eldredge of the United States, 1996 Canadian champion Jennifer Robinson, and two-time Olympic champion Katarina Witt, whose youth, expression, and beauty in 1984 left a lasting impression.

It has not occurred to the fortysomething man to ask for autographs or to write fan letters. "It does interest me," he says, thinking carefully about writing letters. "But I guess I'm always reluctant to write something, because I don't know how it will be received. I'm very shy."

And would he actually approach a skater? Not likely. "I like to main-tain a sense of respect for them, that extends to their personal lives," he says carefully. "I try to keep a sense of proportion."

So there they sit, the very pink, bubbling Canadian SpecSkaters and the silent, dark-haired artist, on opposite sides of the rink, buoyed by the same sights, tickled by the same dramas. Between them, the chil-dren scream for autographs. In the midst of all the furore and the frenzy, two-time Olympic champion Dick Button reminds his friends: skaters should always feel lucky to have fans.

Gary Beacom: Read at Your Own Risk

Gary Beacom is skating's best-loved oddball, a mad scientist on blades. He is a rubber-ankled, deep-thinking, mesmerizing ice artist, whose novel ideas stand the skating world on its head. He pushes the sport forward in new directions, yet he looks backwards into forgotten times with fresh eyes. He glides around his own solitary patch and sees the sport like no other. When Beacom takes to the ice, nobody knows what to expect. In short, he's just different.

If everything in the skating world operated in a clockwise direction, Beacom would be part of the counterclockwise sweep. He is a one-man counterpoint to the way life works in the skating world, with his views on boots and blades, music and choreography, edges and jumps, coaches and judges, nutrition and doctors. And nobody could ever imagine him skating to a Disney animated movie. Yet the worth of Gary Beacom to the sport is immense, and his notions have worked for him, somehow. To understand the sport of figure skating is to understand all of its forms and angles, including the Beacom one. His peers bow to his quirky magnificence.

These days, Beacom dishes up his thought-provoking pieces in Sun Valley, Idaho, a Canadian who never won a world title – or even a Canadian one. Twice he was second to Brian Orser in his own country.

He competed once at an Olympics, in Sarajevo in 1984, where he was best remembered for kicking the rink boards in disgust over poor marks he received for a compulsory figure.

"The only thing better than fame is infamy," he said years later, in his laconic, comic way.

Nevertheless, Beacom has carved out a long-lasting professional career for himself with all sorts of unusual tools. He uses wonky music that nobody else would consider. He uses skates the way nobody else does. He glides on silvery blades that nobody else has ever seen (and sharpens them himself). Sometimes he pads around the house in bladeless skating boots. He drinks diluted hydrogen peroxide to cleanse his system. He skates edges the way nobody else would dream. He has avant-garde ideas about nutrition. The contents of his fridge are unusual, to say the least. He walks his own way on the subject of coaches and judges. He has never used a sport psychologist, although some would say he needs one. His choreography, spilling from his own pate, is beyond the pale. In fact, he is famous for his on-the-spot creations: ad libbed, interpretative choreography. Non-choreography, in a sense.

"I like to fly in the face of tradition," Beacom says. "That is part of what it is to be creative."

Who else but Beacom would begin a professional career playing the devil? His first paying job was at the top of the skating galaxy: he was one of the seven original members of the first Jayne Torvill and Christopher Dean World Tour. Beacom was unforgettable in a long number called "Heaven and Hell," adapted from a full-length ballet called *Deadly Sins*. Garbed in horns, blood-red hose, cropped black leather-look bustier, and little else but black lips, Beacom was positively frightening as a devil.

It wasn't the last time he played the role. He was also cast as a devil – and a magnificently likeable one – in Kurt Browning's "Tall in the Saddle" television special. On the screen, Beacom threw back his fur-capped, bearded head and laughed maniacally, shaking tails of furs, and legs wrapped in pelts. "For some reason, people cast me in that role," Beacom says. "I guess it's because I go against the grain. They think I'm irreverent. I don't think I'm irreverent at all."

Perhaps he has been misunderstood all this time.

Beacom's signature piece is a strangely comical routine, quietly compelling and completely fitting. He is best known for his "I'm Your Man" program, with music written and sung by premier Canadian poet Leonard Cohen, who has since shaved his head and lives in a California monastery. Somehow, the poet fits the *patineur*.

"He is very profound, but with a sense of humour," says Beacom, who has a degree in philosophy and physics from the University of Toronto. "He speaks a real truth, but not with great intensity always. 'I'm Your Man' has a certain truth to it, but it's done with a lot of wit. His voice is very compelling, a really neat voice that draws you in."

On the ice, Beacom has a way of drawing his viewers in, too. In "I'm Your Man," he appears in crisp shirt and tie, stroking in a very undignified, unbusinesslike fashion, even standing on his head, until he hits the chorus. Then Beacom suddenly straightens, crooks his arms into the air, and parades his biceps.

Beacom originally created the choreography for a competition in Sun Valley in 1993. "I'm Your Man" proved to be such a hit that he started getting fan mail again, from all over Canada and the United States.

His early numbers were not nearly so well received. After Beacom's two-year stint ended with the Torvill and Dean tour, he created a tour of his own that went to a handful of cities in Canada, then to New York. At least it was a step up from "some dinky stuff" that he did, including skating on plastic ice and wearing antlers on his head at an Ottawa venue. But in Montreal, only a hundred people showed up for Beacom's show, called "Hard Edge." "It was definitely experimental," Beacom says.

The show included three unusual routines, a twenty-two-minute solo to synthesized music, a seven-and-a-half-minute number to bird calls, and a twelve-minute jazz solo. The twenty-two-minute solo was pure Gary Beacom. He videotaped many of his skating and footwork innovations, then turned it over to Darcy Guddat, brother of Gia Guddat, his partner. Darcy composed the music on a synthesizer to exactly match the tempo and the character of the steps. "It was a long demo piece," Beacom says.

The program was meant to display Beacom's innovations, different ways of stroking. "You think of stroking as being backwards or forwards crossovers," he says. "But I developed all different styles of stroking that were unique."

And unusually difficult to carry out. Always, Beacom challenged the surety of his blade. In the solo, Beacom would bend forward so that his head hung upside down – while he was stroking backwards. Or he would reverse the customary arm positions skaters use while stroking. That had the effect of making him rudderless as he glided over the ice, testing his balance and his hold on the blade to the utmost. Or he would stroke with his arms swinging horizontally back and forth, almost like a helicopter. "There were some simple footwork patterns," Beacom says. "Most of the moves were repetitions, kind of almost like going into a trance."

Did Beacom worry about taxing the attention spans of his viewers as he went into a trance for twenty-two minutes? "That crossed my mind," he admits. "It was for a very particular type of audience. The best audience was in New York, because people that are used to going to ballet are used to sitting there for that length of time, becoming absorbed in a piece."

Beacom drew some good reviews from the *New York Times* for the show he did in the Big Apple. But after he moved to Sun Valley, Idaho, to work as an artistic director at the famous outdoor rink, he pulled the number out of mothballs and performed it again. "I don't think Idaho was quite ready for it," he says, with a smile in his voice. "The reaction seemed adequate, but my boss, who produces the show, thought it was a little self-indulgent."

Beacom did get praise from the purists for his novelties, but mostly when he practised the number. Strangely enough, as soon as people plunked down their money to see him skate, they seemed to expect a little more intensity. When he practised in a casual atmosphere, observers had no expectations. "They were sitting around bored. . . . People got a kick out of it," he says.

Beacom also enchanted viewers, in a manner, with his bird-call number, entitled "Alberta Biography," choreographed by Frank Nowosad, who was, like Beacom, born in Calgary. "It was a real artsy piece," Beacom says. "It definitely got people's attention."

Nowosad, a gentle, soft-spoken intellectual, took his cues from an album of western bird calls recorded by birder Roger Tory Peterson, the man who is widely known as the author of field guides for bird watchers. Nowosad spliced together the calls from birds native to Alberta. The whole thing was Nowosad's brilliant idea, just barmy enough for Beacom. Indeed, Beacom's music matches him to the tip of his toes. His choices are wonderfully quirky. Always, he keeps an open mind. "There's a lot of good music out there that's untapped," Beacom says. "Skaters tend to see somebody skate to something and they think, 'Oh great, I've got to skate to that, too.' But you get a lot of repetition. I try to listen to as much music as possible and keep my ears open."

Often, people will just hand Beacom a tape. That was the way he got hold of "Malevolent Landscape," by Patrick O'Hearn. When he skated to the music, a mysterious veil of bleak, cold sounds, like hammers tapping icicles, Beacom performed in a simple, black body stocking that covered even his face.

"Somebody just handed that to me and said there's some great stuff in here," Beacom says. "Sometimes people hand you things and there's no chance. You just wonder what they were thinking."

For one, Beacom rejects Spike Jones ("That's a little too wacky for me," he said). Once somebody handed him a soundtrack from Walt Disney themes. Beacom is hardly the vision of Snow White or Cinderella or Mary Poppins. "I don't know where they were coming from," he says.

In sharp contrast, one piece of music that Beacom accepted with some excitement was "I Think I'm Losing My Marbles." A rinkman who played the music, flooded the ice, and mopped up with the Zamboni at the Toronto Cricket Curling and Skating Club had handed Beacom a tape with songs by Mendelssohn Joe, just for his listening pleasure.

But the music was perfect. And when Beacom and partner Gia Guddat began to develop the concept of hand-skating, Beacom thought immediately and understandably of lost marbles. Who wouldn't?

Hand-skating was a Beacom accident, born of inspiration from an unusual move. He was working on choreography for another number, and attempting to do a version of a spiral often performed by 1978 world champion Charlie Tickner. Tickner used to plant one hand on the ice, and spin around it, with his body low to the ground – a sort of less-dramatic version of the so-called hydroblading moves done by Shae-Lynn Bourne and Victor Kraatz. (Beacom is intrigued by those moves, too.)

"I got to thinking, if I had a skate on my hand, it would be easier," Beacom recalls. At first, he planned to do hand-skate moves only as a thirty-second gimmick. He pictured him and Guddat emerging from behind a curtain with skates on all fours. But the marbles music was five minutes long, and too enticing and goofy to ignore. They ended up spending several months choreographing the final piece, searching, experimenting, and finding different ways of moving and interacting. Since then, thousands of people have seen the hand-skate routine wherever Guddat and Beacom perform on the Tom Collins tour of world figure-skating champions that wends its way through more than seventy U.S. cities every spring, as well as on other professional tours and shows.

"The first time people saw it, it wasn't that controlled," Beacom says. "But people got a kick out of it." He and Guddat have been doing the routine for about five years now, although they started to work on another version to different music. When last seen, they performed with lips and skates and lensless glasses painted in two neon colours. When they do the number under low lighting, the positions evolve into a merry wave of neon hues weaving patterns over the ice.

The hand-skate concept was made possible with a little help from the hardware store. Guddat places her palms flat on the bottom of the skate boot, but Beacom's hands are a little wider, so he has adapted his skates. Charged with inspiration, he ran out to the hardware store in Sun Valley, bought some gate handles, and screwed them into the boot for hand-holds. Beacom has done other things to his boots, too. To accommodate the extreme angles at which he often skates, he performs what seems like sacrilege to a new pair of boots. He grabs a file and scrapes off part of the sides, to reduce the chance of them rubbing against the ice.

But Beacom, by all accounts, has plenty of boots to play with. It's not uncommon to see ten pairs in his line-up, although last fall he said he had only three pairs on the go. At the Canadian Professional Championship in December 1996 in Ottawa, Beacom wore a pair of brown – not customary black – skates with unusual blade posts (double posts under the heel), and mounted perfectly flat to give better balance. He also showed up with an unusual pair of blue suede skates.

In his collection, he has skates for all purposes: flexible skates, skates made of layers of heavy leather, suede skates, neon skates. Skates cannot be made both flexible and strong, he notes.

"Stiff skates are definitely better for jumping," says Beacom, who went through a period when he did no jumps at all in his routines. "But I do like my skates more flexible than most. When you're doing footwork, you are more agile if you're standing perfectly upright. If your skates are too strong, you can't bend the ankles, so you bend the knees and the waist.

"If you are bent at the hips and tilted, you may be a little more stable for jumping, but you can't manoeuvre as well in footwork. If you are flexible in your boots, you can bend your knees and ankles and stand more upright. That's the technique I've developed."

Most of Beacom's skates relax, just like him. He doesn't quickly chuck them after they lose their hold. "I tend to keep them around for a few years," he says. "Sometimes for three or four years. I always have more than one pair of boots on the go."

Beacom's strength comes not from his boots, but from his own flexible ankles. "I can bend my instep forward quite a ways," he says, almost proudly. He says the strength comes from all the hiking trips his parents took him on when he was a youngster, living near the Rocky Mountains in Alberta.

"He does stuff that I don't know how his body can take," says fellow Canadian Isabelle Duchesnay, perhaps thinking of a jazz number where Beacom's ankles are bent at extreme angles while his feet are pointed in opposite directions. "He is made in a very special way. It's just mind-boggling to watch him. He uses such interesting and difficult moves. They are challenging to somebody else, but he knows exactly what to do.

"He's a contortionist. He should be in Cirque du Soleil. He has balance to die for."

Beacom has been seen gliding down the length of the ice in a handstand, walking a balance beam, in a way, on his skates, making them work to his will, testing the power of his convictions on the blade. His views on skating grow from his strengths and are fed by them. To Beacom, skating is not just about mighty triple Axels and quadruple jumps. Rather, it's all about the use of the edges of his blades. He pays far more attention to edges than most singles skaters.

"The thing you can do on the ice that you can't do on the floor are those edges," he says. "Because you can glide the edges, I try to use them to the maximum. I work a lot on subtle things like keeping the edges pure and continuous and smooth. I work a lot on what part of the blade I'm on. I spend a lot of time, actually, just stroking and working on different edges. That's the basis. I think if you get that down pat, your jumps will improve."

If anybody could appreciate Beacom's skills, it would be an ice dancer, whose work revolves around the quality of edges and footwork. Beacom leaves Isabelle Duchesnay in awe. "I wish I could do half of what he does," she says. "He can do footwork on one foot from one end of the ice to another. He can do off-balance footwork. He'll be leaning to the left, while he is on an edge he shouldn't be on. He'll be at a ninety-degree angle, on an edge that is impossible to reach for most.

"And the complexity of the footwork. It's not just for five seconds. He will do one and a half minutes of intense, complicated, tricky footwork. That's the most amazing thing about Gary. Every number, every time, he's the one I'm going to prefer watching."

It's hardly surprising that Beacom has become the champion of antique figures, sometimes called special figures, a true test of being able to work edges. He's one of the few left to bear the old torch. Most skaters today don't even know what special figures are. Between 1870 and 1890, when special figures were most popular, the practice was called "continuous skating," because a skater would perform a series of designs on the ice while on one foot – without allowing the free foot to touch down. It is basically a lost art, the tracing of intricate shapes, such as rattlesnakes, fish, leaves, letters of the alphabet, numbers, double shamrocks, Maltese crosses, oxhorns, even a pair of spectacles. A Canadian skater, George Meagher, invented a large repertoire of them, and an American, Dr. Barrin, used to cut one of his initials with one foot, and, at the same time, the other initial with the other foot. Special figures were the ultimate test of skill on blades.

Who else could pull off such clever things these days, but Beacom? "They're very difficult, compared to the compulsory figures that we did," he says. "Sometimes you really have to study the picture [of an antique figure] to find out how it's actually executed."

Beacom has been known to trace his name on the ice, admitting that it is unfortunate he has a "y" in his name. He has scribed flower patterns, lopsided propeller patterns, linear patterns that swirl in loops down the rink. Beacom was lucky enough to learn the figures from the late Tim Brown, four times a U.S. silver medallist during the late 1950s. Nowosad had invited Brown, a close friend, to Sun Valley.

"He was one of the few people that knew a lot of them," says Beacom of Brown. "He was an intellectual type, a musician."

Nowosad, who died in 1993 of AIDS, was also intrigued by the special figures. He knew about special figures done in olden times by a duet or a group of four, who would converge in a centre circle, diverge to do various figures and loops, and come back together. With this history in mind, Nowosad created an entire routine with a group of people at the National Ice Theatre of Canada, where he worked.

"That was the essence of figure skating a hundred years ago," says Beacom. To do the antique figures, a skater has to bend his knees. To do that, he needs flexible boots, just like Beacom wears.

The antique figures have served as inspiration for Beacom. He has even used them in his choreography. "I don't know whether anybody would recognize them as antique figures, but they'd certainly recognize them as something different. It's sad that we've lost the art."

Perhaps skaters these days don't look back often enough. "I think the sport is becoming jump-oriented," Beacom says. Perhaps that will change, too, with the proliferation of professional events, where skaters can sometimes take a flyer on a new idea. Beacom has learned much by looking back in history, even to 1976, when Dorothy Hamill became the last female to win Olympic gold without any triple jumps and John Curry presented a well-rounded performance.

"[John Curry] didn't just go out there and hurl himself into seven or eight triple jumps," Beacom says. "He did a really musical, really well-choreographed, well-presented performance, with good form, good lines. He did a number of technically difficult things, too. But everything was in there."

John Curry was the master of edges, like Beacom. And Beacom uses every edge to the utmost when he launches into his interpretative phase, too. "I like to show people that there's more than one way of doing things," he says.

He showed them at a professional competition in Pensacola, Florida, in late 1996, when he started a program while moving, rather than from a normal standing start. "That somehow popped into my mind a few minutes before the performance," he says. "For that particular performance, I was sort of flying in the face of another idea, namely choreography itself. That performance was all improvised. There was no set choreography.

"By doing that, you're sort of free to keep an open mind. If an idea pops into your head, you can go with it."

Beacom has been in a phase of improvising over the past couple of years. He says he's had good luck with ideas gushing up at the right time from his mind's wellspring. "Occasionally, I have a performance where I'm not in the groove and it doesn't work as well as others," he says. "But I've met with some fairly good success."

At the Florida event, Beacom continued to surprise. Wearing a goatee, jeans, and suspenders, he skated to country music, weaving his way rhythmically around the rink. After what seemed like his final flourish, the audience erupted into applause, and Beacom took his bows. But suddenly, his music started up again, and he launched into a dizzying display of hair-trigger footwork. In Beacom's books, why should a performance not continue after a final bow?

Improvisation brings something to a performance that carefully laid-out steps do not, Beacom says. "The quality of the performance is different. I think you gain something and you lose something by improvising. The music is fresh in your mind. In the process of choreographing, you have to listen to that music over and over again, to the point where you get sick of it.

"I pick a piece of music I like, and I don't listen to it very much before the performance, just to get an idea roughly how long it is and how it's structured," he explains. "When I hear it in the performance, it's still fresh, and I feel it's more inspiring. I rehearse just as much as the next person, only I don't spend the time choreographing and setting steps. I spend the time practising improvising to different pieces of music. And I spend the time on technique."

Few other skaters dare to improvise, but Beacom said he knows of some who do vary their performances, like French skater Surya Bonaly. Perhaps it's only to the extent of doing a triple Salchow instead of a triple toe loop, but Beacom says Bonaly is "just very light about how she approaches this kind of stuff."

Beacom is both light and serious about things. And daring. At age thirty-six, Beacom took a careful look at the boom in professional competitions and decided to get himself back into the game. It was a major surprise when Beacom landed triple Lutzes and triple flips at the Canadian Professional Championship in December 1996 – after more than a half-dozen years of setting triples aside. The last time he performed a triple Lutz was during the late 1980s at a Dick Button professional competition in Landover, Maryland.

"I can count on one hand the number of times I performed a triple Lutz in my professional career," Beacom says. "After I turned professional [in 1984], I kind of let them slip, and it's tough to get them back again." Beacom hadn't even tried a triple Lutz in about a year before the Florida competition, where he squeaked one out. "I just felt like going out and doing one," he says. "It was a big challenge for me. I was lucky to get it to happen. I was doing them in practice, struggling with them a little bit, but doing a few. The adrenalin of the competition just sort of helped me through."

Only about two days before the event, he had started landing the difficult jump again. He also started landing triple Salchows again, a jump he had let slip totally for about eight years. In all, he had about four back in his repertoire.

In recent years, Beacom has also suffered from injuries, which may explain, in part, why he left out jumps altogether in some events and concentrated only on displays of unusual edges. In 1992, he broke a bone in his foot. It took a year to heal. In mid-1995, he tore some cartilage in a knee. "The knee is better now, so I started doing them [triples] again," he says. "I've worked really hard on my triples the last six years, but I've had a few injuries that slowed me down. I'm getting a little older. I'm starting to get more injuries. I'm getting up there with Scott Hamilton, and he's still doing all his jumps."

Nobody knows any more how long a skater's career will last. In the past, there were few professional opportunities, but with so many options these days, skaters have more of an incentive to stay in shape, Beacom says. "We might see skaters retiring at sixty-five, I don't know."

If all of his parts hold together in spite of his idiosyncratic manoeuvres, Beacom may be a skater who endures. He certainly works at being healthy. His views on nutrition are diligently distinctive.

It's hereditary, obviously. His great-grandmother started vegetarianism in the Beacom family. "I've been a vegetarian all my life," Beacom says.

Call it alternative health. Beacom eats only when he's hungry, maybe only twice a day. And he's allergic to wheat, because, he says, he ate too many bread products when he was younger. "If you overdo it, you eventually become addicted and allergic to it."

He gets this theory from a book called *Brain Allergies*, written by a doctor who urged people to eat as wide a variety of foods as possible. His theory was that any food eaten every day could eventually produce an allergic reaction. Beacom also reacts slightly to rye and oats. Instead, he feasts on other kinds of exotic grains, like quinoa, amaranth, millet, and teff.

Many of his food choices seem reasonable enough, but think again. Beacom's not big on vitamin supplements, but recently he has started taking liquid minerals, which he admits is a recent fad. The source of his interest is a tape strangely entitled, "Dead Doctors Don't Lie." It was a title that beckoned to a guy like Beacom.

"They sort of run down the medical profession," he says of the tape's contents. "They say that because of the way the soils have been depleted, a lot of us are deficient in certain minerals. [The author] thinks that many, many diseases are linked to mineral deficiencies."

In many ways, Beacom is a pollution-preventer's dream. And he's fit as a fiddle. He cycles. He cruises over the roads in rolling Sun Valley on his in-line skates, or he'll hike instead. He runs. He golfs. He plays tennis. Several years ago, he took up skate-skiing, a version of cross-country skiing. He even entered the Boulder Mountain Tour, a famous midwinter cross-country skiing competition over thirty kilometres (eighteen miles) of trails in the U.S. Rockies. Beacom finished about two hundredth out of a thousand entrants, which included some Olympic competitors.

Beacom's accomplishment was remarkable. The longer the race, the better Beacom likes it. "Three- or four- or five-minute [skating] programs are not my ideal," he says, remembering his twenty-two-minute solo.

Beacom has missed the Boulder Mountain race the past three years because he has been busy improvising on the Tom Collins winter tour of skaters. "The thing I like about [cross-country ski races] is that there are no judges," Beacom says.

Beacom and his judges have not always been on the same wavelength. His best-known dustup with judges occurred in 1984 at the Sarajevo Olympics during the compulsory figures.

"I remember it crystal clear," Beacom says. He traced his first figure "really great, I was proud," but the judges placed him eleventh. The second figure, same thing. "I didn't know. I couldn't look at the figures to see if they were clean," Beacom says. "I always give the judges the benefit of the doubt."

But when he traced his third figure, a backward change loop, he felt it was the best of the men's competition. "I feel to this day every other skater in that competition should have been disqualified," Beacom says. "I was the only person who skated the loop to specification. You're supposed to fit three loops in a circle. My middle circle was round. It was the right size. And my loop size was also the right size, according to specifications. I was the only person in that competition that even came close to the specifications.

"In addition to that, I skated the figure very well. It was traced [a skater must make two exact tracings over the original imprint, without wobbling away from the lines], it was lined up. I knew it was a good figure. In my mind, there was no way they could take that away from me. I expected to win the figure. I knew deep down I wouldn't."

The judges placed him eleventh.

"It was the same old stuff. I just had a little fit of rage and kicked the boards. It was the thing closest to me at the time."

The incident has nettled Beacom, off and on, since. Since then, others have told him: "Get over it Gary, move on."

"I have gotten over it," Beacom says. "It hasn't left a huge scar on my life. I've managed to make a career out of skating. But on the other hand, I think I do have a right to be irritated by it."

After the incident, the Canadian *chef de mission* and the judge's referee scolded Beacom for his behaviour. "The referee sat me down and had to tell me what a bad boy I was," he says.

"Looking back, I think I should have challenged them and filed a formal complaint. What recourse does a skater have? Could I have filed a lawsuit against them? It's a difficult job judges have, but it's a huge responsibility and politics is just very unfortunate. It's fraud, is what it is."

Beacom was the first to congratulate German skater Norbert Schramm, who had a similar experience, and dropped out of the world championship a month later in Ottawa after he had skated the second of three compulsory figures. Schramm was so annoyed at what he thought were poor marks for his figures that he retired from amateur competition altogether. "Nobody can see a figure and [judges] can put up whatever marks they want," Beacom says. (It is difficult for spectators to see the figures from their perches in the stands; to tell how well one was skated, it was necessary to walk out on the ice, like the judges, and look directly downward at the tracing.)

Compulsory figures were abolished from world championships after the 1990 event, but Beacom still gets irritated at the way skating events are judged. "I think the approach is all wrong. I think a 6.0 is something you should see once in a decade. And a 5.9 is something you should see once a year."

Beacom thinks judges tend to get boxed in at the top when they give out inflated marks, that they do too much planning of where they will place skaters, that they try too hard to predict the outcome of an event. "I think the judges should have a general standard of performance in their mind and not worry about who's going to beat who," he says. "I just think a judge should be knowledgeable enough to sit down and watch a performance and compare it to all the performances they've ever seen in their life and assess it."

He thinks part of the problem is that the judges are not full-time skaters. "They kind of get out of touch with what their skating is, and what's difficult and what's easy," he says.

In professional competitions, this happens frequently, Beacom says. "I think judging seems to have become somewhat shallow in that they count triple jumps. Winning an Olympics is a great asset and really quite an achievement. But I don't think you should wear this crown for the rest of your life and rely strictly on that. Reputation plays too big a role in judging. Sometimes an Olympic champion will go out and skate badly, but because they're Olympic champion, they get propped up."

Beacom says he already knows he will automatically finish fourth, no matter what he does, if he competes against three world champions in a pro event. "Perhaps that's all I'm worthy of, I don't know. But I know this for sure, that I'm not going to place any better than fourth." Still, he says he doesn't find it discouraging. "I look at it as a chance of performing. I like the opportunity to perform. So be it. It's not something I have no control over. I'm not going to get uptight about it."

And he didn't really, at one competition several years ago in Sun Valley where U.S. coach Kathy Casey was acting as a professional judge. At a professional competition, which comes with less pressure than an Olympic-eligible event, the atmosphere is looser. Beacom took advantage of it. "She ripped me off unbelievably in my first number," Beacom says. About ten minutes before Beacom was to skate his second routine, an observer said, with an incredulous tone in his voice, "Did you see the mark Kathy Casey gave you?"

"It got me all fired up," Beacom says. "So I thought, 'I'm going to get her.'" Once on ice, Beacom skated over to Casey in the judges' row and handed her a dollar bill. Beacom thinks it actually worked: she gave him higher marks for the second routine.

"It does seem to be possible to bribe the judges, even in bright daylight," he says jokingly.

The audience seemed to be behind him, too. It gave him confidence.

Nobody else had ever tried such a thing with a judge. But then, few skaters do without a coach, either – at least willingly. Beacom decided to skate without a coach for the last two years of his amateur career, when he was also busy working on his university degree.

"I think I learned a lot from coaches over the years," Beacom says. "I was told everything I was ever going to be told and I just needed to apply it. Part of the reason for that was that I was going to university and I didn't have time to skate eight hours a day. I only skated a few hours a day. I just wanted to go out and skate. I didn't want to be standing around, taking instruction. I just wanted to go out and apply what I thought I already knew.

"I think guidance is important. Coaching is important. But I think it's overemphasized in many cases. Training is important and discipline is important, too. Many skaters perform better with a coach who disciplines them and encourages them to train. It's somebody they can feed off. Some of us are just a little more independent. We just prefer to go out and do our own thing and use our own time and take responsibility for our own training habits. That was the case with me."

Beacom says he was never directly criticized by the Canadian Figure Skating Association for giving up on coaches, but "I definitely think I was a little ostracized because of my different ideas.

"I just felt that politically I was sort of a threat to the system. I quit skating because I was kicked off a team. I don't know if that was directly because of coaching, but I think I just got a little bit too . . . *iconoclastic.*" Beacom said he was kicked off a Canadian team sent to the NHK Trophy in Japan in the fall of 1984 after he had skated poorly at Skate Canada two weeks before that in Victoria, B.C.

"I admit, I wasn't at my best for that competition," he says. "Skating without a coach, I had my best performances. It worked for me. I skated consistently. That Olympic year, I skated in five international competitions and skated five clean short programs.

"But then I had one bad competition, Skate Canada. . . . I had a new program which was a little bit too overambitious. I didn't have it well-enough rehearsed and didn't skate it that well."

Beacom says he also had bad luck at the event. The ice was poor. One day, Beacom's event was postponed until after midnight because paint was coming up through the ice. Beacom had skated over the paint in his warm-up, slipped, and crashed into the boards. "It ruined my blades. I had to get somebody different to sharpen them for me. It was just a bad event for me."

A short time after the event, Beacom was dropped from the NHK team. "They used some excuse, and I didn't get to go to Japan," he says. "I took it personally at the time. I had this invitation sitting on my desk from Jayne and Chris [Torvill and Dean], and I had told them, no, I'm going to stay amateur. But then when I was kicked off the team, why, I bolted. I got out of there."

That was when Beacom retired from amateur skating, and accepted the invitation to join Torvill and Dean on their world tour. Off he went to Australia for rehearsals. He had also just graduated from university, so he had nothing to tie him to one spot.

Beacom found it difficult to juggle university and élite-level skating at the same time, but, looking back, he says he would not have done anything differently. "Having an athletic and a scholastic pursuit, I think they balance each other nicely." Education was highly valued in his family. He never questioned the assumption that as soon as he finished high school, he would go on to university.

Still, both pursuits affected each other negatively. "I didn't do as well as I could in either," Beacom says. "I was not a great student in university, and I don't know if I was as consistent a skater as I could have been. It was a full-time schedule. I had to become really efficient with my scheduling.

"It was difficult. You go to a competition in the middle of a semester, and you miss a week, then there's this gap in your knowledge."

He even suggested that he would have done well to have dropped his professors as well as his coaches. "It maybe would have been better if I had just read my own books and done my own education," he says. "I think that an education is important, but not necessarily a public education."

Since then, Beacom has been educating himself – privately, of course. He is trying to learn to speak Russian. He reads a lot and rarely watches television – he doesn't own one. Television, he says, tends to provide programs that are "kind of propaganda-like." It's a waste of time and addictive as well.

Instead, Beacom pores over large and weighty tomes, the kind of stuff that Isabelle Duchesnay says "would put me to sleep.

"He's a very cerebral person," she adds.

Lately, Beacom says, he's been reading a lot of political theory and law, because he has a cause: individual rights, very small, manageable governments. He considers himself a libertarian, not surprisingly. These ideals landed Beacom in no small amount of trouble with the U.S. Internal Revenue Service for failing to file federal income-tax returns. Beacom says he has a philosophical and legal objection to the existence of the IRS. He also wants to challenge the sixteenth amendment to the U.S. constitution, which authorizes a tax on incomes. He paid his taxes up until three years ago.

With these thoughts weighing heavily on his mind, he turns back to a simpler world – Beacom must go over to a friend's house to watch an amateur competition. He said he enjoys watching a purely athletic performance with good technique, good jumps and spins. "There's nothing better," he says.

"But [amateur events] are never creative or intellectually stimulating."

What he brings to his sport comes from outside the sport. "I like doing a lot of stuff beside skating," he says. "I read a lot. I have a good education. That's why I've been able to contribute something that's creative in the sport."

That is why, when Beacom takes to the ice, he does not skate to the beat of *The Sleeping Beauty* or *Carmen* or even *The Phantom of the Opera*, the fodder of his peers. Instead, his audiences will hear little-known tunes like "Soul of a Man" or "Lullaby of the Leaves," lilting, haunting melodies that are rarely used. Beacom turns them into visual channels of thought, and with a touch of caprice, he adroitly teases any who stop to watch.

And many of them do stop to watch. He is a rare antidote for blinkered thought. He's just different, that's all.